WATER

Water

Abundance, Scarcity, and Security in the Age of Humanity

Jeremy J. Schmidt

NEW YORK UNIVERSITY PRESS

New York

NEW YORK UNIVERSITY PRESS
New York
www.nyupress.org

© 2017 by New York University

References to Internet websites (URLs) were accurate at the time of writing. Neither the author nor New York University Press is responsible for URLs that may have expired or changed since the manuscript was prepared.

ISBN: 978-1-4798-4642-9

For Library of Congress Cataloging-in-Publication data, please contact the Library of Congress.

New York University Press books are printed on acid-free paper, and their binding materials are chosen for strength and durability. We strive to use environmentally responsible suppliers and materials to the greatest extent possible in publishing our books.

Manufactured in the United States of America

10 9 8 7 6 5 4 3 2 1

Also available as an ebook

To my parents, Al and Betty

The mythology may change back into a state of flux, the river-bed of thoughts may shift. But I distinguish between the movement of the waters on the river-bed and the shift of the bed itself; though there is not a sharp division of the one from the other.
—Ludwig Wittgenstein, *On Certainty*

CONTENTS

ACKNOWLEDGMENTS

Adorning the foyer of William James Hall, where most of this book was written, is a quote from an essay William James wrote on the environment. It reads: "The community stagnates without the impulse of the individual. The impulse dies away without the sympathy of the community." I deeply appreciate the intellectual communities, at Harvard and elsewhere, that gave the ideas in this book a sympathetic hearing. I hope, in kind, that it may provide impulse for others.

Steve Caton generously supported this project from beginning to end. The discerning voice that he brought to our many conversations significantly enhanced my scholarship. Dan Shrubsole provided the initial impetus for the book. My attempt to answer his questions about the relationship of international "water decades" to water management structures the text. As I revised the book, Brian Noble organized helpful opportunities to share it with colleagues. Finally, a decade ago I came from a small farm (where I hand pumped water to our animals) to McGill University. There, and since, Peter Brown has prompted me to take a much wider view of our shared planet. I thank these supervisors for their unflagging support.

Helen Ingram's work, encouragement, and example have sharpened my thinking regarding how issues of justice and equity intersect with what we are doing with, and to, water. Christiana Peppard offered thoughtful comments on the full manuscript. Comments on draft essays were offered by James Wescoat, Sarah Whatmore, Nathaniel Matthews, Elizabeth Fitting, Lindsay Dubois, Susan Flader, Caterina Scaramelli, Ramyar Rossoukh, Emrah Yildiz, and participants in Harvard's 2013 Water Workshop, especially Toby Jones.

Several librarians, archivists, historians, and editors made contributions of crucial difference to this book: Cynthia Hinds and Linda Carter in the Tozzer Library were very helpful in alerting me to materials and collections, and George Clark's impeccable cataloging of Harvard's Environmental Science and Public Policy Archives made research a joy. Staff at the National Anthropological Archives in Washington, DC, provided excellent insights and tirelessly searched for boxes of materials. Cris Paul and Susan Farley provided office support, kind encouragement, and often tea. Victor Baker helpfully pointed out historical connections. Jennifer Hammer and Constance Grady were immensely helpful editors and efficiently coordinated the anonymous workhorses of academia: the reviewers who read and critiqued the manuscript. I acknowledge the permissions granted by Harvard and the Smithsonian to use archival materials from the collections cited herein. Parts of Chapter 3 were previously published, and I acknowledge the Creative Commons license to my article "Historicising the Hydrosocial Cycle" *Water Alternatives* 7, no. 1 (2014): 220–234. Indexing was provided by Clive Pyne, Book Indexing Services. All errors and omissions are my own. The Social Sciences and Humanities Research Council of Canada provided funding.

I would also like to thank Sohini Kar, who brings a singular joy to my life and work, often across large expanses of salt water and through considerable hoopla.

I dedicate this book to my parents, Al and Betty, who may very well never read beyond these acknowledgments and instead return to their concern for those less fortunate, whose lives they care for deeply and to whom they open their home and hearts. You are blessed examples.

Introduction

Entering a New Era of Water Management

In 1977, California was facing a drought. By then, California water politics already bordered on legend. The Oscar-winning movie *Chinatown* (1974) had dramatized the politics, treachery, and straight-up lies used to appropriate this life-giving, profitable liquid. Jerry Brown, California's youngest governor in a century, was no stranger to the drama. His father, Pat Brown, had helped to create this corrupt water dynamic in California when he was governor. The elder Brown had pulled off political sleights of hand few had had the gall to try, including misrepresenting the costs of water projects on the order of billions of dollars.[1] This sort of subterfuge is an option when there is water to be had (or taken), but backroom deals don't count for much when there isn't. Such was the case in 1977. That year, the younger Brown convened the Governor's Conference on the California Drought. He invited Luna Leopold, the first chief hydrologist of the U.S. Geological Survey and then a professor at the University of California, Berkeley, to deliver the keynote address.

Luna took the stage not only as a leading American hydrologist but also as the son of Aldo Leopold—the ecologist whose work on soil conservation was cited when President Franklin D. Roosevelt was looking for ways to keep America's land from blowing away during the Dust Bowl of the 1930s.[2] Luna's speech began by arguing that the overlapping of economics, geography, and culture meant that "none of us knows how to put into operation a philosophy of water management, but there may be some merit in examining some of the elements that might be included in such a philosophy."[3] For Luna, the first step was to scale our expectations, and our water use, way back—a task that required cultivating a reverence for rivers. Luna repeated this message often, emphasizing the idea that there is an "unwritten gut feeling that the resources of the planet, and of the nation, are worthy of husbandry—indeed are es-

1

sential to our long-term well being."[4] Although Luna repeated his message time and again, he didn't hold out a lot of hope that things wouldn't get worse before getting better.

In 2015, drought returned with a vengeance to California. Jerry Brown was governor once again, this time as the oldest governor ever elected in the state. The 2015 drought, however, was different. Experts argued that it was an outcome of human actions that had changed Earth's climate.[5] So not only were the politics of water management once more unavoidable, it was also likely that the lessons learned historically might not be applicable in the future. In this context, Luna's idea of a "reverence for rivers" appears almost quaint, and his belief that a philosophy of water management is too complex to be developed seems obvious. The reasons abound: There are too many political, economic, and cultural values layered on top of too many water demands, often too little supply, and too many gaps in policy and knowledge. Plus, water flows. It won't sit still. It won't even stay a liquid. Water's shape-shifting ways make it too hard to ferret out what it is doing in the cavities it occupies among humans, non-humans, and the environment—let alone to manage all of those weird spaces. At best, water management is a bricolage of ideas, norms, strategies, and techniques. In sum, as Luna argued, a philosophy of water management sounds nice, but it is just too ambitious.

The global numbers seem to support Luna's take, especially as human water uses accelerate in ever more complex and profligate ways. By the mid-1990s, humans collectively appropriated half of the Earth's annual supply of accessible freshwater, largely as the result of water use increasing at several times the rate of population growth in the twentieth century.[6] In some places consumption rates have leveled off, and even declined, but often because water demands shifted spatially as industrial processes moved locations. Complicating matters is the highly variable impact of human activities. On a summer day in the United Kingdom, anywhere from 50 to 80 percent of water in some rivers is treated wastewater, released from daily detours through urban and industrial toilets.[7] On a similar day on Canada's prairies, up to 50 percent of stream flow comes from water imprisoned in a millennia-long sentence in glaciers that, like many worldwide, are shrinking rapidly from global warming.[8] Evidence of human interference with global water systems is striking, including water shortages in Rio de Janeiro, the empty Aral Sea, and the cavalcade of fifty thousand large dams built and untold multitudes of people displaced by them over the last century to usher in modernity, to name only a few.

Against this backdrop, in 2008, leading hydrologists openly questioned whether water is manageable at all.[9] From a hydrological perspective, water had been manageable because the water cycle was assumed to be stable, with variability from year to year fluctuating within natural limits. But on a planet where humans were changing the climate, the assumption of hydrological stability couldn't be maintained. Climate change, the hydrologists argued, did not simply change the patterns of water's natural variability. Rather, changing the climate altered the Earth system itself. The knock-on effect was that the very idea of a stable water cycle was thrown into a tailspin because, if the Earth itself is not operating within natural limits, then neither is the global hydrological cycle. Unfortunately, water is not entirely unique in this regard. Scientists now caution that we must seek a "safe operating space" in which humans live within the planetary boundaries of the Earth system and the interconnected dynamics of climate, freshwater, and global biogeochemical cycles.[10] All told, scientists argue that we are now part of an "unfolding water drama" that requires new ways of managing water in the Anthropocene—a term used to describe how humans now rival the great forces of nature and are themselves a geological force.[11] The evidence seems to bear out Leopold's claim that there is no overarching logic to humanity's audacious water grab. In 2015, a study in the journal *Science* found that human water impacts had been underestimated by 20 percent—the equivalent of two-thirds of Earth's largest river, the Amazon—every year.[12] Given these facts, rather than marshaling a comprehensive water management philosophy, the prevailing wisdom is that the best we can do is to work piecemeal toward something better.

This book takes the opposite view. Its aim is to show that many water problems are, in important ways, the outcome of a philosophy of water management that already exists. Indeed, there is already a philosophical basis connecting culture, geography, and economics to a view of water management that began in the United States and has now gained global reach. Though it has not been recognized as such, this philosophy has enrolled various academic disciplines in its service, including, but not limited to, anthropology, economics, geography, and geology.

To illuminate this philosophy, I follow anthropologists who approach water as a "total social fact" that ricochets throughout multiple aspects of social life, albeit often in unseen and underappreciated ways.[13] As it happened, when the philosophy of water management was in its formative stages, early American anthropologists had a similar idea. They, too, thought water was critical to all aspects of life, yet they also thought that not enough had been done to secure social and political institutions to Earth's geological processes. For them, the way to secure U.S. society and its institutions to the absolute necessity of water was to treat it as a kind of total geological fact: Water was the agent that connected Earth's geological processes to social life. To manage water, then, was to manage the conditions that made social life possible.

This philosophy of water management was initially articulated at the intersection of geology and early American anthropology: To manage water was to manage the bridge between life and non-life and, thereby, to shape the course of planetary evolution and social development. Furthermore, societies that knew this fact held an institutional advantage that proponents of the new philosophy claimed was an evolutionary step forward. The upshot was that these societies and their forms of life—their laws, institutions, practices, and customary habits of thought—were deemed the template for developing and managing water, not only for themselves, but also for the weal of evolution itself. Ultimately, this philosophy formed the basis for what is today called "global water governance." The contention that there already exists a philosophy of water management and that it wields global influence is a bold claim. To support it, this book shows how a common way of thinking about water gained consensus. I term the project of assembling this common thinking "normal water": a program for bringing water's social and evolutionary possibilities into the service of liberal forms of life. By "liberal forms of life" I am talking about the spectrum that orders agreements and disagreements within liberalism, such as contests over how to balance individual freedom with collective security. As this book shows, these kinds of contests and their resolution were, and remain, central to how a particular approach to water management gained consensus.

Initially, crafting a common way to think about water was accomplished by categorizing it as a resource. This classification is now so common that it appears natural, but in the United States water was not a "resource" until 1909. This relatively recent idea has had significant repercussions for other ways of understanding water that do not share with liberal forms of life ideas or practices regarding the secular basis for the rule of law, the priority assigned to individual autonomy, or the notions of rights, personhood, and property used to establish and maintain distinctions between private versus public spheres. Of course, there are many other aspects to how shared forms of life are practiced, yet because water is central to so many features of our individual and shared lives, universal claims about how to manage it have severe consequences. This fact is not lost on water managers. As this book details, the philosophy of water management was often developed with an appreciation—not always very nuanced—for how water interacts with alternate notions of subjectivity, social relationships, and the symbolic goods held as intrinsic ends by different groups. Although the consequences of directing water toward projects that supported their own cultural ideas were not lost on water managers, they still frequently rejected alternatives as either too metaphysical or, sometimes, just less developed. Yet despite their own pretenses to objectivity, water managers crafted their own myth around the belief that liberal societies are uniquely equipped to manage the vast array of social and evolutionary possibilities made available by water.

The myth of normal water—the aim of bringing water's social and evolutionary possibilities into service of liberal forms of life—has led to several contradictions in the attempt to forge a global common sense regarding water. Here is one example: In 2010, the United Nations declared a human right to water and sanitation. At that time, there was much rejoicing by those who counted this right a victory over privatized, market-driven forms of managing and governing water. But the jubilance was short-lived. Shortly thereafter, the UN Secretary-General, Ban Ki-moon, stated that the human right to water was not counter to free-market rationality. In fact, he claimed, some of the best ways to deliver on this new right may actually be through markets. Experts explained this contradiction by identifying a common liberal heritage that defines public, human rights and the private property rights required for market transactions.[14] So, what looked like a contradiction was in fact a debate over two ways of achieving broadly liberal goals of human dignity and social progress. Yet if this explanation is correct, we should wonder not just how a common language of rights came to be used on both sides of a global debate but also how both sides came to have a common understanding of water.

We could explain this conundrum as an instance of liberalism's long history of contradictions, such as its early arguments that because slaves were private property the state could not simply make them free through guarantees of public rights.[15] To do so, however, would miss how practices direct water toward certain goals and, thereby, enhance the prospects of meeting certain ends rather than others. Instead of theoretical answers to contradictions over water rights, we should consider how diverse and heterogeneous cultures settled on a particular understanding of water in these debates. We might follow Ludwig Wittgenstein, who argued that investigating the civil status of a contradiction is the task of philosophy.[16] This book asks: How do contradictions over water, such as those over the right to water, gain civil status? Or, put another way, Why do we have these water management challenges and not others?

Normal Water

In his book, *The Taming of Chance*, Ian Hacking argued that gathering an avalanche of numbers about populations, their activities, and body sizes was part of moving away from ideas of "human nature" toward accounts of a "normal person."[17] Hacking was interested in how contingent social and natural phenomena were understood, accounted for, and subsequently governed. Along similar lines, this book examines how different types of contingency were, and still are, woven together through a philosophy of water management that crisscrosses over four senses of the word "normal": (1) a sense that what is normal is a matter of social convention; (2) a technical sense of normal that comes from its use in describing a linear line that intersects some other line or surface; (3) a geologic sense in which normal denotes a relative downward movement by the tectonic plate on the high side of a fault line; and (4) an antiquated, medicinal sense of normal that referred to the ratio of solutes in water or blood.

In this book, "normal water" refers to the program of bringing water's social and evolutionary possibilities into the service of liberal forms of life. It is by gathering different kinds of social, technical, and geological contingency into a common way of imagining the health of societies and the Earth that a particular philosophy of water management became normal. These crisscrossing claims are all buried within, and maintained by, the idea that water is a resource. In considering how claims from anthropology, economics, geography, geology, hydrology, and philosophy (to name a few) came together in an account of water's contingent relationships, it becomes evident that water management is not the haphazard bricolage Luna Leopold thought it was. There is, rather, an underlying philosophy that has been enormously successful precisely because it has not been seen as doing all of this coordinating work.

Exploring different senses of normal water reveals how culture, geography, and economics are linked in a philosophy of water management. For instance, "normal" can refer to social conventions: for example, turn the tap off when you are brushing your teeth. These conventions can run deeper, reflecting collective judgments regarding rights, politics, economics, or ritual. In some cases, judgments regarding water cannot easily be dissociated from particular ways of living without altering, or in some cases abandoning, those ways of living themselves. Normal water is also technical and concerns the choice and deployment of technological know-how, such as that used in the engineering of dams or irrigation works. In this sense, normal water orients a messy and complex world in a particular way. In its geological sense, normal water links biological and social life to accounts of planetary evolution. Finally, normal water relates social, technical, and geological considerations to concerns about health, both in the sense that ecohydrologists mean when they speak of water as "the bloodstream of the biosphere" and in the sense that all individuals and societies require water for healthy lives and livelihoods.[18]

Normal water, then, employs social, technical, and geological claims to link social and evolutionary possibilities to the health of liberal forms of life. But forms of life are neither static nor homogeneous, and so normal water has had to evolve alongside different iterations of liberalism within which American water managers have operated. In many ways, exchanges between water managers and state officials gave both academics and the state a common set of tools with which to think. In fact, there is a long history of experts like Luna Leopold moving between state agencies and scholarly communities. Once these connections are identified, it becomes more apparent that many water challenges are not the result of some haphazard conglomeration. They are, rather, the outcome of a common way of thinking. As this book details, this way of thinking had its origins in the desire to manage water in purely evolutionary terms that linked the American social sciences to geology. In this way, it anticipated and is directly relevant to contemporary efforts to once again link anthropology, geography, and other social sciences (and humanities) to claims that the Earth has, or is on a trajectory to enter, a new geological moment: the Anthropocene.

Anticipating the Anthropocene

Earlier, I noted that the philosophy of water management was initially articulated at the intersection of geology and anthropology. This took place in the late nineteenth century, in the wake of Charles Lyell's identification of the geological epoch in which modern civilizations evolved. When it was announced in 1885, the Holocene—which means the entire or whole recent period—identified the planetary conditions since the last Ice Age and approximately captured human history after the agricultural revolution. Many thought that geology had profound implications for explaining how we should understand humans, the planet, and their study. There were also implications for how humans should care for the Earth and, thereby, for their own evolutionary prospects. Fast-forward to the twenty-first century, and we see similar concerns regarding a newly proposed geological classification, the Anthropocene, and its implications for the evolution of the planet and of life hereon.

In contrast to the Holocene idea of a planet that conditions human evolution, the Anthropocene is—proposed, at the time of this writing—a period meant to mark the epoch in which humans also significantly alter geological processes.[19] The atmospheric scientist Paul Crutzen and the aquatic ecologist Eugene Stoermer coined the term "Anthropocene" in 2000.[20] The Anthropocene is a time in which humans have come to rival the great forces of nature and in which humanity's total share of Earth's material and energetic throughput has accelerated at a phenomenal rate.[21] At present, there are two strong contenders for marking this change in the geologic record: radiation fallout from mid-twentieth-century nuclear testing, and the development of plastics.[22] Both are uniquely human, and both will be around for a geologically long time. But there are other potential markers, such as the increase in atmospheric carbon dioxide from human agricultural activity and fossil fuel use and the decrease in atmospheric carbon that occurred when vegetation surged in North and South America after colonial diseases swept through indigenous societies and killed millions.[23]

The concern of this book is not with what "silver spike" is chosen to identify the Anthropocene (if indeed one or a set is chosen). In the aegis of geologic time, nuclear radiation, plastics, climate change, species extinction from habitat loss, and colonial atrocities may appear synchronously with other stratigraphic scars humans may leave behind. It's difficult to predict, and none of us will be alive long enough to know, which brings up a different point: There is no scientific reason to make a decision about the Anthropocene now. We could wait a few millennia to see how things settle out geologically, which would afford all the advantages time may bring. But there is no appetite for waiting. Instead, there is a host of political, ethical, and scientific contests over the Anthropocene that are often articulated alongside calls for an enhanced sense of planetary stewardship given the urgency of Earth's ecological malaise.[24] As the historian Dipesh Chakrabarty put it, now that we have stumbled into the Anthropocene, there are all sorts of questions about how human histories intersect with geologic time.[25]

The scale of human transformations of the Earth system troubles many widely held ideas. For instance, it was once presumed that Earth's natural biomes functioned as a background to the foreground of human action, even if humans altered them over time. Human transformation of the Earth's surface is now so extensive, however, that "anthromes" (human biomes) more accurately reflect what land cover looks like.[26] Like the idea of "natural variability" rejected by hydrologists owing to climate change, there is no background "nature" for biomes any longer. Similarly, new classification systems have introduced "novel ecosystems" as a way to categorize landscapes that reflect the effects of human activity on ecological processes.[27] These have been followed up with new ideas, like "anthroecology," that seek to explain human ecology in geologic terms.[28] This attunement to the coevolution of people and planet is designed to index the Anthropocene to the human transformation of the biosphere.[29] The upshot is that there is no longer any ground, in a literal or metaphorical sense, upon which to make distinctions between humans and nature.[30]

The philosopher Clive Hamilton has argued that dividing humans from nature is an outdated conceit of the modern social sciences that, to the extent that these disciplines are premised on that divide, is unfit for understanding the Anthropocene.[31] As this book shows, Hamilton is not alone in thinking that the modern social sciences and humanities need a fundamental overhaul for use in this new geological era. The English professor Timothy Morton has also argued that in the Anthropocene there is no background place—no nature—that somehow persists "away" from anthropogenic activity and that this has significant implications for how we study the world.[32] But we should note that ecofeminist, indigenous, and post-colonial scholars have long argued that the conceptual division of humans from nature operates on the same oppressive logic that renders other classes, genders, and peoples as subordinate and likewise deems their bodies, homes, and environments as "away."[33] So it is not a novel claim to reject the society/nature dualism as unsound. Furthermore, and as this book shows, in the influential case of water, the problem is not the society/nature divide but, rather, a failed attempt to reject that dualism. This failed attempt braided unequal power relationships into ways that human-water relationships are understood in both the social and natural sciences that link water to the Earth system in the Anthropocene.

In addition to theoretical concerns over the society/nature dualism, the Anthropocene raises concerns regarding how the histories of the Earth and of human societies should be understood. There are two elements to this issue. One has to do with the conceptual history of the Anthropcene itself, and the second with how that history affects political and moral claims about what ought to be done about humanity's outsized impact on the Earth system. On the first element, Clive Hamilton and Jacques Grinevald argue that the Anthropocene is a fundamentally novel idea that was not anticipated by previous geological understandings of nature or the environment.[34] In making this claim, they reject the conceptual history that had previously been offered for where the idea of the Anthropocene came from.[35] That history began with the idea of humans as geological agents offered by the famed ecologist George Perkins Marsh in his classic nineteenth-century work, *The Earth as Modified by Human Action.*[36] According to this history, once humans were seen as geological agents, the search for a unified account of knowledge took a new form in which human knowledge was viewed as having an evolutionary history, too. The result was the concept of the "noösphere" developed by two Catholic theologians, Pierre Teilhard de Chardin and Édouard Le Roy. The latter was closely associated with the French philosopher Henri Bergson—who once adroitly claimed that the steam engine changed everything.[37] The noösphere, however, was developed most by Teilhard de Chardin, who posited that it was a realm of evolution in which some beings, like humans, become aware of their own evolutionary history in geological terms and, with that knowledge, consciously take up a specific evolutionary direction (though not necessarily a telos).[38]

The idea of the noösphere influenced the Russian geochemist Vladimir Vernadsky, who saw it as a way to link life in general, and humanity in specific, with the Earth's mineral and chemical processes. Vernadsky subsequently developed the concept of the biosphere, a key forerunner to global biogeochemistry and models of ecology that incorporated the wide array of interactions that different evolutionary actors have with one another.[39] Given this history of ideas about humans and geology, it is not too surprising to find a conceptual history of the Anthropocene that runs from Marsh through to Vernadsky. But Hamilton and Grinevald reject the claim that these earlier ideas anticipated the Anthropocene because they hold that these previous views did not treat the Earth as a system.[40] They argue that the conceptual novelty of the *Earth system* made the Anthropocene possible and that this only arose only in the latter half of the twentieth century, such as through large interdisciplinary collaborations that followed the creation of the Scientific Committee on Problems of the Environment by the International Council of Scientific Unions. These large scientific collaborations were paced by new concepts, such as James Lovelock's "Gaia Hypothesis," which posits that the Earth system is self-organizing.[41]

If we turn to the second element regarding the conceptual history of the Anthropocene, there is a contest over how to conceptualize the quantitative impacts of human activity on the Earth system in relation to the actions of the humans responsible for those impacts. The worry here is that claims about humanity writ large paper over the oppression of other cultures, other species, and the planet by those primarily responsible for the Anthropocene, and this motivates a subsequent claim that any definition of a new geological era should reflect these political, economic, and moral dynamics.[42] Of course, not every connection of humans and geology matter in the same way. If they did, the Anthropocene would be a grab bag of previous ideas, from the Harvard geologist Nathaniel Shaler's worry in 1905 that humanity's planet shaping force needed to be corralled in service to imperialism to Robert Sherlock's 1922 claim that the British landscape was shaped by humanity's unique geological agency while the rest of nature remained inanimate.[43] Part of the reason it is important to be aware of contests over the conceptual history of the Anthropocene, however, is because they can affect attitudes toward governing people, related institutions, and the planet that reflect broader value judgments about the kinds of knowledge most relevant to governing both societies and the Earth system.[44]

The contention of this book is that, when it comes to water, the argument over whether the Anthropocene is conceptually novel or the outcome of incremental conceptual development that would link it to particular, culpable groups of humans that accelerated impacts of humans on the Earth system misses a key point: namely that, if it is possible for leading scientists to link the "unfolding water drama" of *any* human society to the Earth system, then there must be some common understanding of water across the Earth system sciences and water management. Indeed, it is a central claim of this book that there is such an understanding and that this common understanding has a history that begins in the late nineteenth century and winds its way into interdisciplinary scientific networks, including the Scientific Committee on Problems of the Environment, which conceptualized water as part of the Earth system in the twentieth and twenty-first centuries. As the Anthropocene took shape in the new millennium, this history is what makes it possible to think about water management in common ways across planetary hydrology and modernity's human dramas.

Book Overview, Structure, and Caveats

This book examines a philosophy of water management that began in the United States and expanded globally, though it has not been widely recognized. This philosophy began by rejecting older ideas as too metaphysical or at least too far down the evolutionary ladder of social development to be seriously entertained. But the new philosophy has its own mythical elements; namely, the idea that liberal forms of life are uniquely equipped to manage the vast array of social and evolutionary possibilities made available by water. Of course, this water management philosophy did not emerge all at once, not least because even in its early stages it was expected that societies would evolve and that water management had to be capacious enough to develop alongside them. Since it began, however, this philosophy of water management has pivoted on crafting a story about geological, social, and technical understandings of water and the health of societies and the planet. This way of thinking, ensconced in the idea that water is a resource, is now commonplace globally.

As this common way of thinking about water took shape, it consolidated into a global narrative about water management. This narrative is often found at the beginning of policy statements or presentations from practitioners, academics, economists, hydrologists, and policy makers. Although it varies, the broad strokes of the narrative are that water was once abundant but has now become scarce. Mismanagement intensified water scarcity such that water is now a security issue that must be considered with respect to interstate conflict, human development, and planetary health. These propositions of water's abundance, scarcity, and security play a special role in the philosophy of water management, not least because they have been deployed beyond the United States in places such as Brazil and Israel and even to characterize global water problems.[45] These propositions are also important because they order water within a complex Earth system in ways amenable to, and constitutive of, a particular view of the world. To see how this is so, this book is structured to show how the philosophy of water management made claims about abundance, scarcity, and security that are now widely used and that find their ways into accounts of water in the Anthropocene.

Structure

The book has four parts that detail how a philosophy of water management that supports liberal forms of life brought water under a single, global scheme and what that implies for the Anthropocene. The genius of normal water's program of bringing social and evolutionary possibility into a single planetary story is that it does not deny that alternatives exist but simply posits that we should do without them. In short, we should manage water resources without privileging any particular cultural understanding of human subjectivity, the different social relations that take shape around different water use practices, or the different symbolic ends that others may hold as intrinsically meaningful. These three philosophical concerns—over subjects, social relations, and symbolic goods—are developed in the first three parts of the book. Part IV returns to the Anthropocene with this history and philosophy in tow and examines what it implies for thinking anew about water.

Part I begins by situating this book among others on water management and outlines its methodological approach. It is critical of accounts that rely primarily on theories about modernity and that subsequently offer little consideration of how water management shaped what counts as modern. It then dives into the topic of water abundance, using the works of John Wesley Powell and William John McGee—who insisted that, to save ink, his name be written, unpunctuated, as WJ McGee—as the central foils through which water became a resource in the United States. They extended geological agency to water and people as part of a broader project in political economy and state formation. Quickly put, the philosophy of the subject articulated by Immanuel Kant was under scrutiny in the nineteenth century because of how it viewed the relationship of mind to matter. Also of concern was the task of exorcising British colonialism from American thought. In response, Powell, McGee, and many others sought an evolutionary account of the human subject in a universe without a mind/matter divide. Their view was that there is an abundance of geological agents, of which water was critical. Through close association with the White House and the upstart discipline of American anthropology, McGee transformed this view into the fulcrum for adjusting the liberal state to the task of managing water and for moving beyond colonialism. His view united water to the social characteristics of "the People" of the United States in service to his two most enduring ideas: conservation and multipurpose river basin development.

Part II considers water scarcity. It shows how one case of water management in the United States was generalized into a model for international development. To make this move, the temporal emphasis on geological abundance was reworked into a spatial sensibility that treated the United States as the model for post-colonial development. Earlier ideas were not abandoned, but they were reformulated in a view that drew (flawed) parallels between the U.S. experience and the post-colonial moment arising after World War II. It was no longer the characteristics of Americans that mattered but democratic methods for escaping colonial rule. The philosophy of water management subsequently shifted to support a new geopolitical register aimed at coordinating international development and to promote liberalism abroad, a salient aim throughout the Cold War. Water managers and geographers, particularly David Lilienthal and Gilbert White, were particularly influential in this period. This led to a series of international water decades during which a global picture of water began to be crafted in an effort to naturalize the American experience and to avoid the charge that it was simply colonialism in a new guise. By 1977, the global acceptance of scarcity was a founding proposition for water management.

Part III focuses on security, an idea that had been key to international development since its inception but that became especially important in the late twentieth and early twenty-first centuries. After the judgment that water is scarce, water experts worked to establish a metric for scarcity that did not privilege any particular set of social standards. But no consensus was achieved. Instead, the solution was to manage water without reference to the symbolic goods held as intrinsic ends by any particular society. This brought water security to the fore. Water security combined, in a reflexive moment, resource conservation and international development under the guise of sustainable development. Initially pursued through integrated water resources management (IWRM), the philosophy of water management subsequently morphed to include what became known as a "water-energy-food-climate nexus." At the same time, water security encountered numerous challenges regarding the fit of global ideas with different cultural meanings of water. These tensions come to prominence during the UN Decade of "Water for Life" from 2005 to 2015 when, right in the middle, the human right to water and sanitation was passed in 2010.

Part IV returns to considerations of the Anthropocene, but with a closer look at how the social sciences are entangled with the "natural resources" that mediate relationships between social worlds and the Earth system. It focuses on understandings of the Anthropocene in the social sciences. In particular, it questions the widely circulating idea that by "making things public" there are opportunities to move beyond the dualism dividing society from nature and to consider non-human agency more closely.[46] I argue that "making things public" is inadequate because it fails to see that water problems are the outcome of a failed nineteenth-century solution to the problems associated with the society/nature dualism. Building this line of argument into the final chapter, I argue that in many cases the most helpful project social science can undertake is to disrupt internally the ongoing colonial project of water management, especially in educational institutions that often reproduce it. I consider an example by returning us to a different Leopold—Aldo. In Aldo Leopold's work there is an effort to disrupt the philosophical ideas of conservation and water management that carries broader lessons for the Anthropocene.

Caveats

A lot of what this book does not do, and what it expressly does not attempt to do, is tied to the methodology behind what it does. Detailed further in the next chapter, my approach follows Wittgenstein, particularly his insight that philosophical problems are bound up with practice—or, as in the example regarding rights to water above, the way a contradiction gains civil status. To understand contradictions over water we need to get a sense of the practices through which these contradictions are understood. But these practices change over time, and so do the meanings associated with them. As the epigraph to this book suggests, sometimes our mythology is put in flux, and the riverbed of thought shifts. Wittgenstein distinguished between the flux of water in a river and its underlying bed, even though there is no sharp division between them, as though the former is variable and the other stable.[47] Both are contingent, but both are necessary to have a river. Similarly, I argue, it was by finding ways to internalize the claims regarding social, technical, and geological contingencies, and their effects on human and planetary health, that water management lurched forward alongside the shifting riverbed of liberalism.

Given this orientation, this book does not adjudicate among the manifold ways that water crises or meanings of water can be understood.[48] Its argument is not premised on, or beholden to, inferences that frame water problems in one way that, by the end of the book, will reveal what a good philosophy of water management looks like. Rather, the aim is to understand how a view of water as radically contingent yet necessary for life became entangled with a set of practices deemed the most appropriate for enhancing the prospects of liberal forms of life. I take this approach because it is undeniably the case that water management practices entangle us together with others—those ambiguous combinations of (not merely) means and ends.[49] This entanglement beckons us to consider which others we are wound together with as we learn to make judgments about water in ways that shape a common world. Treating others with respect is not only, or even primarily, a theoretical task of exploring radical alterity. Nor does creating space for alternate water use practices imply that the U.S. water experience is or should be the reference point for establishing difference with respect to theories of modernity or of otherness. In the next chapter I say more about how I have reversed the onus so that, instead of thinking about water through a theory of modernity, we ask what questions arise for modernity as the result of water management practices.

The book relies significantly on historical sources. Yet I do not attempt to assemble a history of irrigation, land-cover change, or the ins and outs of different government policies or bureaucracies in the United States. There are many good resources on these topics, and I draw on them to provide further context to the work presented here. What distinguishes this book is its attempt to follow the threads of key philosophical practices that are latent in the consistent ability to link social, technical, geological, and health claims in water management. As a result, many of the individuals who feature prominently in the book may be unfamiliar even to water researchers and professionals. There are, of course, previous works that bridge from engineering and river-basin development to the social ideas that informed them.[50] This book attempts this on a larger scale. Similarly, this book is not a history of modern hydrology or of water and Earth system science. Again, however, I have worked to keep it conversant with these fields in order to show how understandings of the Earth were worked into claims about the world.

One unavoidable feature of the current global water milieu is the contentious debate about whether water is a public good or whether water, and the services that deliver it to people, should be privately owned or controlled. This book is not about that debate per se, but as already hinted at, I do seek to shed some light on why this debate has taken shape in the way it has. The line of thought I develop in this regard considers the way that understandings of what is public or private have been modified over time. Relatedly, I do not explore the implications of this work for decolonization or what political strategies may be made of human rights. This book focuses instead on a clearer diagnosis of the deep and persistent colonial roots of water management. A more contentious aspect of the book will be that it implicates ideas now widely held in water management and many academic disciplines as contributing to unequal power relations. But I have left open, and hopefully have helped to identify, spaces for place-based articulations, resentments, and resurgences appropriate to different responses to inequality. I have done this to highlight how normal water naturalizes social and evolutionary possibilities in a way that displaces and dispossesses alternate forms of life. In this way, the book links a particular way of making up the world to one of its constitutive elements—water—and the propositions of abundance, scarcity, and security that have been used to legitimate management practices.

A final caveat concerns the primacy given to the U.S. experience. This orientation is defended and qualified throughout the book, but a few comments are worth making here. The first is that the U.S. experience was influenced by many international sources. Americans traveled internationally, and many international figures and ideas came to the United States. International traffic in ideas, legal norms, technologies, and approaches to governance all influence American water management and things this book does not consider, such as the design of urban water systems.[51] A second is that it is not only U.S. ideas that are influential internationally: The British and Dutch reconfigured landscapes in India, across East and West Africa, and in Java in the service of colonialism.[52] French canal builders and German water engineers helped inaugurate forms of impersonal state rule.[53] Both Spanish and French approaches to watershed management predate certain developments in the United States.[54] China and Russia have been major players internationally, and they remain so.[55] Clearly, then, U.S. water management does not have total or universal influence. In the next chapter I clarify the methodological components to this caveat in order to draw out how this book relativizes the U.S. experience without downplaying the significant role it has had in shaping common understandings of water as a resource.

PART I

Abundance

1

First Water, Then the World

Modern water management has often been characterized as radical. Radical, that is, in the sense that states have often taken the control of water to an extreme. In the mid-twentieth century, Karl Wittfogel developed an influential thesis that this sort of radical management is frequently on display when state bureaucracies control water to achieve a kind of total power over the organization of society, institutions, and industry.[1] Since then, numerous accounts have been offered of how previous civilizations attempted to achieve social or political power through the control of water. These attempts often failed, sometimes quite spectacularly, because some key variable was overlooked, such as climate change, or because cultural biases created a distorted view of nature. Some just put too much faith in their own ingenuity. Whatever the reason, the literature on water management is awash with these sorts of cautionary tales. A few recent titles that affirm the need to learn from these failures include *Water: The Epic Struggle for Wealth, Power, and Civilization* (2010), *Elixir: A History of Water and Humankind* (2011), and *The Big Thirst: The Secret Life and Turbulent Future of Water* (2011).[2] The thesis behind such accounts is intuitively plausible. Indeed, for the most part, as water goes, so goes society.

Epic stories of water and civilization, however, are not entirely satisfying, especially if they assume that since time immemorial people have been striving to effectively manage water and social relationships to it. This chapter lays the groundwork for a different way of thinking. This alternative also holds that modern water management has been radical, but in a different way. It was radical because it made contingency its basis and, in so doing, undercut other ways of thinking about water and power, especially those that appeal to natural law or metaphysical authority. This form of radical management was not tied to anything necessary about individuals, the state, rationality, or the goods that make certain ends intrinsically worth pursuing. Instead, the contingent facts about water, and the social and evolutionary relationships that depended on it, provided the basis for water's political, economic, and moral value. Yet this contingency presented a double-edged sword: Although water was necessary for life on Earth, the fact that it actually did support individuals, institutions, or states was the outcome of evolutionary chance. Conceiving of the very idea of water management as the result of chance, and from this premise rethinking how to manage the relationships between water and society, subsequently formed the basis for water management in the United States. This was a radical idea.

Once the idea that water was necessary and contingent was struck upon, the first proponents of America's philosophy of water management developed a view that could hardly have been grander. Water management was seen as the apex of a unified theory of planetary evolution, social development, and the social sciences required for the self-direction of evolution and society. This philosophy, they claimed, was not only superior to the views of other cultural perspectives; it also corrected metaphysical tropes of western thought that had lingered since the Enlightenment. It was nothing short of a new foundation for science. In the words of WJ McGee, who we will become familiar with as one of the key players in this new take on water, this philosophy came "as no petty plaintiff. If in the wrong, it is a colossal blunder: if in the right, it is a New Organon."[3]

Putting aside whether or not this philosophy has been a colossal blunder for the moment, this chapter outlines this book's approach to the philosophy of water management and its grandiloquent self-presentation. This explanation is necessary because, while the contemporary intellectual milieu eschews master narratives and totalizing stories, the philosophy of water management presents itself as just this sort of account. Further, because I am claiming that this philosophy has resonance and influence today, I need to show how I came to this conclusion without reproducing a sort of total history. This is because I agree with critiques of master narratives: They reflect, and often reify as historical fact or canon, one perspective on phenomena—whether individuals, social relations, institutions, events, or environments—that are in fact more accurately characterized as diverse, evolving, and full of heterogeneous actors, societies, and institutions.[4] As many counternarratives have demonstrated, there are almost always subtending and subaltern stories that go untold or unheard. Since we cannot exhaust these, it is unwise to presume we will ever get a complete picture. In short: There are no total histories.

This presents a conundrum. On the one hand, the philosophy of water management presents itself as (quite possibly) a New Organon, the next step in scientific progress since Francis Bacon. On the other hand, and as we will see, this totalizing account is chock full of idiosyncratic assumptions about one nation's water experience (the United States) and, at that, one story about that experience. Yet even though this philosophy was not actually the kind of master narrative it claimed to be, it has now passed through multiple iterations in the United States and has had profound effects on twentieth- and now twenty-first-century geopolitics. Somehow the New Organon went global. The challenge, then, is to not simply discount master narratives while also gaining purchase on how this philosophy of water management worked in many non-global ways to bring vastly different individuals, social relations, and institutions into its evolving fold. As the anthropologist Catherine Lutz puts it: Empire is in the details.[5]

Remarkably, it was often the ideas on the losing side of intellectual debates that ended up having greater effect on water management. In the case of American anthropology, for instance, these losing ideas have been almost completely purged from the disciplinary canon. This makes the loss twofold: First, the ideas that informed the philosophy of water management have been lost from view in social sciences that have long been concerned with relationships between people and planet, notably anthropology and geography. Second, there has been a failure to see how these losing ideas found their way into key political institutions that have shaped common ways of thinking about water and, often, the categories academics use to study it.

Compounding our lack of understanding of how these losing ideas affected policy is that contemporary studies of water management tend to be read against broader theories of modernity. These theories make and defend assumptions about things like state power, scientific rationality, technology, and divisions of humans from nature. Some employ Wittfogel's ideas of water and total power. Others draw on James Scott's influential work *Seeing like a State* in which he argues that a period of "high modernism" used scientific rationality and certain institutional formations, like state bureaucracies, to make previously chaotic things (e.g., forests, water, and cities) legible to the state while pushing others out of view.[6] By putting these chaotic things onto state ledgers, they became the sorts of things over which states could gain high levels of control. High modernism was radical because it ordered chaotic phenomena within a relatively narrow vision and took that vision to an extreme. Applications of Scott's analysis to water management are often combined with other accounts of modernity, such as that of Bruno Latour. Getting a sense of these accounts serves to both introduce some widely held ideas about water management and to situate this book among others. After introducing other accounts of water management, I outline my approach so a clearer assessment can be made of how the American social sciences shaped a view of the planet that fit with a particular social world.

Water Meets Modernity

In the literature on water management, there is a common refrain about what we should learn from the follies of previous civilizations. With various modifications, it goes something like this:

> "From time immemorial water has been unmanageable, but through science, technology, and the grand projects enabled by human ingenuity, great feats have been achieved. But the outcomes of those accomplishments—mega-dams, irrigation systems, industrial processes, and municipal waterworks—are having unintended consequences. Mastery over nature is pushing rivers, lakes, and entire ecosystems off balance. Indeed, it has pushed hydrologic systems to the point where the very idea of "natural balance" is in question. Now we must rethink water management itself, particularly the idea that there will be grand solutions to the challenge of managing water."

Versions of this refrain abound.[7] Many begin by identifying how water started off, in pre-modern times, as entirely Other. There are many potential places to start this kind of account: Over twenty-five hundred years ago, Pherecydes of Syros thought of Chaos, the mythical Greek figure, as water. Formless and disordered, Chaos called forth Gaia to establish order. Among the pre-Socratics, Thales of Miletus famously held that in the beginning was water and the world was full of gods. In the Abrahamic religions, the spirit of god hovers over the waters (à la Chaos) before land and life are called forth (à la Gaia). Similar accounts are found in secular variations where water is "life's matrix," to use the words of Paracelsus.[8] Of course, water has long been central to many religions and beliefs, from the Vedic texts in India to New Zealand's indigenous peoples.[9] Beginning with water as Other, the triumph of the modern age was not just that it subdued water but also that it harnessed water's symbolic power such that that we no longer interpret floods or droughts through appeals to the capricious acts of gods or nature. The flip side of the story—the cautionary part—is that modern water managers were too optimistic in supposing that the rudimentary sciences that many state institutions were built upon are sufficient to handle the complex social and ecological systems that water courses through. So although water has been brought into an ordered fold, many modern management practices have, like the collapsed civilizations we must learn from, gone too far.

Counterpoints to the above refrain are often found in the verses that link each instance of water management to the context in which it is applied. These show the nuanced ways that, despite technological and scientific achievements, water never wholly succumbs to modernity. Rather, some water and some ways of relating to it always remain ungoverned in the push for rational forms of management.[10] Further, the rejoinder goes, the water that is governed is not subdued in a wholly, or even primarily, rational way. Rather, control over water is accomplished through power relationships that oppress "others" and perpetuate inequity based on gender, class, religion, or ethnicity.[11] So water management was hardly an exercise in emancipating us from the burdensome chains of metaphysics and myth. Moreover, the idea that this supposedly rational vision is now under threat due to mismanagement is more accurately viewed as a crisis for those who are benefiting from the current, unequal arrangement. In short: Water problems do not fit linear accounts about the rational control of water and the march of human progress. Rather, water management's common refrain refracts a host of social and political relationships, and relationships to water, that are all open to contest.

In this book, I do not adjudicate these debates. I wish only to note that both sides generate one picture of the world from within another. This is not a slight. It is a generic claim about the sited production of knowledge. As Nelson Goodman put it: "Worldmaking as we know it always starts from worlds already on hand; the making is a remaking."[12] As I show here, the idea of situated conceptual development is itself a key part of what has given the philosophy of water management such staying power and what distinguishes it as modern in its attempt to internalize the contingent ways in which knowledge is produced. On the one hand, it is to make up the world with no macro Other—no source of original chaos that is beyond comprehension. On the other, it is to make the ethnocentric claim that the Earth is contingent in a way that opens it to self-direction, even enhancement, once social institutions are situated within a scheme of unrepentant contingency. To begin, it is worth situating my view in contrast to the predominant water-meets-modernity story.

High Modernism

James Scott's *Seeing like a State* is a frequent point of departure for many water-meets-modernity stories. Early in that book, Scott refers to the Tennessee Valley Authority (TVA) in the United States as the "granddaddy" of state-planned regional development. Scott's actual essay on the TVA appears in a different volume where he describes both top-down and bottom-up ways that the TVA was administered.[13] In *Seeing like a State*, Scott's thesis of high modernism is that, concomitant with the rise of the modern state, there were techniques that drafted disorderly dimensions of society and nature into terms that made them legible to new forms of governance. In this transition, "pre-modern" understandings of things like water came under the calculating eye of the state through bureaucratic systems that standardized measurements and instituted new forms of accounting based on scientific rationality. In short, out went water sprites and multiple ontological kinds of water, and in came chemistry, physics, and engineering.[14] The result was a stripped down, rationally governable kind of water: H_2O. Moreover, high modernity razed all that came before it. It was not only a fresh start where rules of rationality governed what is possible. It was *the* beginning: a form of governance emancipated from traditional sources of authority altogether.

One of Scott's enduring ideas is that high modernism transformed nature into "natural resources." This has made the claim that the TVA was the "granddaddy" of high modernism quite intuitive because the TVA was created in the context of Conservation era policies of the early twentieth century United States. And, as U.S. forester Gifford Pinchot—a key figure of the Conservation movement who brought German forestry practices to the United States—was fond of saying, "There are just two things on this material earth—people and natural resources."[15] Pinchot's dualism of "people and natural resources" can be seen as a reformulation of the divide between nature and society in which humanity is no longer subject to, but a master over, a macro Other (nature) and director of the distribution of things other than humans: natural resources.

The corollary shift of nature to natural resources is one of society to population. Under high modernism, the "subject" for whom natural resources are governed exists in an abstract, idealized sense. There is no longer a subject that finds expression through traditional sources of authority, such as we might find in doctrines of natural theology that supposed that rational insights of the human subject provided a window into the mind of the Abrahamic god. Rather, the subject is known through techniques of calculating and administering programs for a population. So there is a dual move away from macro Others, whether nature or society, to a project of governing relations among others: natural resources and populations. This is a valuable insight, but it isn't sufficient for explaining the philosophy of water management. To see why, it is worth considering how high modernism has been connected to the idea that water management is a philosophical bricolage.

In her book, *Privatizing Water*, Karen Bakker argues that,

> following Scott's argument, we might assert that governments have frequently aimed to curtail, reshape, or even eradicate the local diversity found in community water-supply management systems, displacing community knowledge of water supply systems with the techne of hydraulic engineering, accounting, and water economics.[16]

Bakker's use of Scott's thesis has a twofold purpose. It is a theoretical touchstone and a particular way of narrating the story of water management. In this narrative, the scientific discourses identified with epistemic truths and technological know-how, or *techne*, are deployed by the state to replace or suppress what Scott terms the practical, or *metís*, knowledge that lies outside high modernism. For Scott, *metís* knowledge is always at work on the periphery of, or in subaltern relations to, high modernism. As such, it is *metís* knowledge that keeps a factory running on makeshift parts or explains the type of knowledge a technician uses when preparing a small water treatment system for a local flood event. *Metís* is found, not in the canons of reason, but in practice. And it is the persistence of alternative practices within the period of high modernism that confounds bureaucratic, scientific, and technological management regimes. Many of these practices are detailed in work that shows how state policies are overlaid upon, and contested by, local actors and even by networks of experts themselves.[17]

I am not suggesting that Bakker deploys high modernism as an all-encompassing account.[18] Rather, high modernism performs a narrative function insofar as it gathers contingent phenomena into a picture of the world that is recognizable as such. Thought of in this way, highly differential experiences are organized into the world picture of modern states just when the theory of "high modernism" explains the rationality of a particular set of contingent facts, such as those about water management. But assembling contingent phenomena is a different exercise from explaining the philosophy of water management. This is because the former suggests that anything left outside the purview of high modernism, which amounts to all that remains illegible to the state, either falls to *metís* knowledge or otherwise remains ungoverned. Hence the (claimed) philosophical bricolage: There are dominant forms of rationality under high-modernist periods of water management, but these do not explain the manifold of *metís* practice. Further, because water is shared across both formal and informal governance systems—across *techne* and *metís*—there is no satisfactory account of the countervailing values, discourses, and networks that provide for a coherent philosophy of water management across divergent cultural, geographic, or economic practices.

High modernism has important implications, but it presents a concealed tautology if pushed so far that it must also bear the burden of philosophical justification. This is because, if it is required to explain what early water managers thought or otherwise claimed they were

FIRST WATER, THEN THE WORLD | 31

doing, then it must also hold them to a standard of rationality commensurate with the theory of high modernism itself. This is a tautology hidden from view once we make the assumption that early water managers also held that chaotic dimensions of water, the Earth, or human experiences fit with models of state rationality. This was not the case. In subsequent chapters we will see that it is actually the case that the philosophy of water management was and remains beholden to an anthropological vision about the contingency and precariousness of existence—of human adjustment to change—not a theory of rationality.

High modernism nevertheless lends credence to claims that modern times are starkly demarcated from previous ones. Erik Swyngedouw, for instance, has extended Scott's temporal insights to the spatial shifts of state practices.[19] To do so, Swyngedouw follows Bruno Latour to suggest that states deploy multiple practices, discourses, and strategies to modernize how we sort things to either society or nature.[20] Here, the rejection of water sprites for H_2O is sought through an understanding of both state rationality (à la Scott) and the actual practices that mark modernity. So, rather than doubling back on the theory of high modernism, we look to see how water is sorted into categories that fit with, and in fact produce the evidence for, modernity: dams, conveyance structures, municipal waterworks, and so on. When we do this, we see within the spatial practices of state formation how the transition of nature to natural resources and society to population produces many of the challenges state water management seeks to address.

Appealing to Latour has a second attractive element, particularly because of his critique of modernity as a process that first translates things into social or natural categories and then sorts them between the poles of society and nature.[21] It is well known that Latour doesn't think this project has been successful; rather, it has produced innumerable hybrids, or socionatural things, that refuse the polarity between society and nature. According to Swyngedouw, even this failure should be seen for how it dispossesses water from others. For instance, water is translated into terms legible to the state and then sorted in a way that benefits state aims. Yet even if the ideal of high modernism isn't achieved, the attempt itself nevertheless crowds out the physical and social spaces where alternative practices could take place. What is left over is not just a default category that captures whatever remains illegible to the state.

Rather, it is a spatial configuration that results from certain modes of production, including a production of nature that fits with the prevailing political economy.[22]

An additional way that water management has been fit to modernity is through a focus on what kind of "thing" water is, such as in Jamie Linton's book, *What Is Water?*[23] There Linton argues that "modern water" is embroiled with scientific rationality that first renders water H_2O and then uses that form of water to construct an abstract version of the hydrological cycle. Following Latour and Swyngedouw, Linton argues that the social relations affecting how water is sorted to nature are denied in the accounts of both H_2O and in representations of the hydrologic cycle that ignore how water cycles through things like cities. In Linton's view, the "hydrological cycle" is not an objective account of water's global circulation. It is, rather, a social construction that reduces water to H_2O and uses this socially constructed "thing" to construct an abstract hydrological cycle that appears objective but that is really a product of modernity. Linton goes on to argue that water has its own relations. In this case, and as Latour suggests with respect to things more generally, to understand water as a hybrid is to understand that water itself flouts the polarity of nature and society. In so doing, water acts. It is an actant: a term designed to challenge anthropocentric notions of agency.

It is possible that these theories of water management are workable, but I have significant doubts. First, as we will see, Linton's historical claims are incorrect on several critical points.[24] Second, appeals to nonhuman agency as something new or corrective overlooks the robust, explicit role that water's agency plays in the philosophy of water management. The alternative I offer sees scientific and technical claims as part of a broader evolutionary view. Understanding how this view took hold is key to locating and understanding claims about water management and governance in the Anthropocene.

Water Meets the World

Standard water-meets-modernity stories prompt basic questions regarding common ways of thinking about water. Although I disagree with many of the standard answers, they are not socially weightless.[25] Rather, when academics publish these ideas, or use them to teach students or engage policy makers, they shape how we think. It is no secret that academics have cultural capital in the marketplace of ideas and, often, in policy. Frequently they seek more. These and other professional exchanges both produce and rely on common ways of thinking about water. But common ways are not equal ways, and they can also create blind spots. It may sound surprising, but not only are scientists still searching for answers regarding why water has certain anomalous properties, even some of our most commonsense ideas about water aren't totally settled.[26] For instance, the notion that water is H_2O is itself an incomplete picture. In fact, if all we had was pure H_2O it would not behave like water. The common characteristics of water depend on numerous other ions (OH^- and H_3O^+, among others) that affect its pH, boiling point, and so on. Chemists and philosophers continue to disagree over what water is, in part, because these questions are wrapped up in the practice of science itself.[27]

If even some fundamentals about water remain unsettled, and if understanding water through theories of modernity is unsatisfactory, what is the alternative? Clearly, we are able to talk about water in common ways even without crystalline clarity about what sort of "thing" it is and without theories of modernity. We do so all the time. And when we do, we rely on a common repertoire of practices through which water's material complexions are understood in different social and moral orders. I offer a view that does not fall back on "things" and that also is not motivated by a theoretical map within which water fits. In order to tell the story of normal water without falling back on "things" or theory, I give special place to the practices that are used to bring investigations into water's contingent physical and social dynamics to an end.

Recall the rhetoric about how the philosophy of water management may be a New Organon, a reference to Francis Bacon's *Novum Organon* and its placeholder status as the start of modern science.[28] Ignoring the fact that Bacon alone didn't get things rolling, WJ McGee argued that the view he and John Wesley Powell were articulating was a major step forward. They held that nineteenth-century sciences, including the social sciences, remained beset by debates about whether reality was mind or matter. This debate hearkened back to a time when rationalists, such as René Descartes, dueled with empiricists like David Hume. Immanuel Kant had answered both by arguing that a gap exists between our experience of things (phenomena) and things in-themselves (noumena).[29] Kant's example used water: Think of a raindrop that falls on your head. You do not experience the raindrop in-itself. You only have the experience of the raindrop hitting you, and a gap exists between what the raindrop is and your experience of it as, say, wet or cold. Using this distinction, Kant developed a philosophical notion of the "world" that was not equivalent to "nature" or even to the "sum total of given objects."[30] The world, in Kant's view, is not a "container that contains" because, if it were, we might wonder if there is a container that contains it, and so on, ad infinitum. This would lead us back into the quagmire Kant wanted out of because we could keep asking if one of those containers was ultimately mind or matter. Philosophically, Kant's "world" is a regulative ideal, the sort of thing we accept *as if* it exists.

It may seem strange to talk about Kant in a book on water management. But early water managers were very concerned with his ideas and especially the tradition of German idealism inaugurated after him by Georg W. F. Hegel. In contrast to his philosophical view, Kant's writing on politics, anthropology, and geography had a different notion of the world that aligned with the Earth (or least its surface).[31] Both Kant's practical and philosophical views of the world have been scrutinized, and, across many fields, there has been a rejection of his idea that humans come uniquely equipped to navigate a universe of mind and matter. There is an impressive diversity and creativity to these arguments, but this book is primarily interested in those that suggest that the ontological categories Kant used to secure a unique place for humans (e.g., rationality) neither exist as he thought or, if they do, are not uniquely human. These responses, sometimes loosely gathered under the idea of an "ontological turn," seek to do away with the anthropocentricism implicit in these categories and to consider how a broader set of ecological relationships affect and condition both knowledge and social worlds.[32]

Although critiques of Kant take many forms, here I highlight one that contrasts with the view of this book (later I engage others). As developed by Timothy Morton, this critique holds that Kant not only impounded what we can know behind human representations of phenomena, but he also cut off alternatives for what we can think about what exists, or about being itself. This is because Kant's account of the gap between appearance and reality is premised on a correlation of what exists and what it is possible for humans to think. So every time we try to think about what may exist beyond our phenomenal appearances (e.g., the raindrop itself), we force things into Kant's correlation between thought and being. Morton's critique aims to break this correlation, and some scholars have hastily applied similar arguments to accounts of how non-human things—like infrastructure—exert power in state water management.[33]

Morton's opening salvo is that we should do ecology without nature.[34] For Morton, the problem with nature is that it is made up of things that exist on the other side of the gap between appearance and reality.[35] Yet, rather than reject Kant, Morton generalizes the gap between appearance and reality into a condition of all objects in order to speculate about what kind of weird things ecology might reveal once we don't think on a path between only human phenomena and noumena.[36] Because everything experiences a gap between how things appear to them and how they are in reality, it's not just humans that do not experience rain in-itself. Soils, trees, and plants don't experience a raindrop in-itself either.[37] Without nature, according to Morton, everything is strange to everything else. Chairs are weird to academics. Honey is strange to bees.

Clearly, Morton's aim is not just to reject nature but also to overhaul environmental thought. One of his conclusions is that, because nature was caught up with a notion of the world wedded to Kant, we need to do philosophy and ecology after the end of that "world."[38] Yet even if we agreed with this conclusion, Morton's account is not compelling. For one, Morton is mistaken about Kant's philosophical view of the world in relation to nature. As we saw above, Kant's philosophical notion of the world does not align with what Morton renders as the basis of nature.[39] Perhaps most surprising, however, is that when Morton applies his critiques to later philosophers, such as John Stuart Mill, he ignores Mill's remarks on nature and instead treats only Mill's aesthetics.[40] Yet Mill also assailed ambiguous notions of "nature" before assigning it an amoral status that fit with his political economy and the "purely self-regarding acts" of his liberal philosophy.[41]

The problem of how we get from a weird, diverse planet to an account of the world also vexed water managers in the United States over a century ago. They, too, used new ontological categories to critique Kant and Mill. They weren't alone. Similar arguments were prevalent in the nineteenth century after Ernst Mach published his views of neutral monism, which posited the universe was neither mind nor matter.[42] Mach and others, including the American pragmatist William James, thought Kant had solved the wrong problem because mind and matter simply weren't the sort of stuff the universe was composed of.[43] It may sound odd, but these were all pressing concerns in late nineteenth-century America, especially after the geological marking of the Holocene and Frederick Turner's 1893 argument that the closing of the American frontier would have serious consequences for U.S. institutions.[44] Yet water managers devised their own response to philosophical and practical problems. After jettisoning Kant and augmenting Mill, they reconceived of the human in social terms. The world was not *my* world, but *our* world—where "our" includes all of the agents produced through geologic processes. The relations among this interwoven set of geologic agents were mediated and acted upon by water. So managing it was of utmost priority.

How did the philosophy of water management slip through the cracks? I suggest that we imagine that western metaphysics has a glitch—an ontological hiccup—right around the moment when geologic time, human history, and knowledge of that union are linked to state institutions in the New Organon. As mentioned earlier, the arguments presiding over this union do not last. Yet their effects do, with the result that water resources become a kind of luggage carrying a notional understanding of the world that is no longer held. Further, this philosophy of water management has reverberating effects as it passes unnoticed into many of the ways that we think about water today. This has led us to manage our way right into the Anthropocene as we keep finding new ways to haul this luggage—water resources—about.

An Alternate World

To make up the world without water resources requires a thoroughgoing assessment of our entanglement with them, which is why I examine normal water—the project of bringing water's social and evolutionary possibilities into service of liberal forms of life. My approach is to tell the story of a philosophy lost, not one I agree with. In fact, the existing philosophy of water management is in many respects beyond redemption. Yet it conditions the institutions of many jurisdictions that brought normal water to their constituents. Rather than try to tell a total history of these interactions, I focus on how the project of normal water was kept afloat. What concessions have been made to haul the luggage of this flawed way of thinking about?

The first thing to note is that normal water advances a monological view of the world. Examining a monological world can be likened to listening to different musicians playing the same score. The score itself provides the steps for which notes to strike, how long to hold them, and so on. Like language, however, a musical score is not everywhere bound by rules, and masters often leave their mark on a piece by exploiting the ways in which the rules are imprecise. For Wittgenstein, once we look at what people do with words, a monological view is not satisfying.[45] This is because people learn the rules of a language game through training within a particular form of life. In this view, language does not pick out facts about reality; it instead operates more like tools in a toolbox. For instance, the word "book" does not pick out an abstract concept of a book. Rather, the word "book" evokes a set of rules I have learned through practice, such as when someone asks me to pass them a book, or wonders if I have booked a flight to London, or tells me such and such a football (soccer) player deserved to be booked. For all of these uses I have learned what to do with "book." Thought of in this way, a "concept is nothing other than a word in its sites."[46] But what are those sites? How do we reach agreement if our words don't ultimately fall back on definitions but on our shared practices?

Wittgenstein's answer was that linguistic agreements are based on their being judged to fit with our forms of life. As he put it, "If language is to be a means of communication there must be agreement not only in definitions but also (queer as this may sound) in judgments."[47] For instance, we do not first learn linguistic rules and definitions and then apply them to different contexts. Rather, we learn how to judge the use of words in ways that make a host of things plausible to us and that makes others less so.[48] In this way, we don't "learn the practice of making empirical judgments by learning rules: we are taught *judgments* and their connection with other judgments."[49] It was Wittgenstein's conviction that reasons for agreement, even those agreements regarding what counts as evidence, ultimately give way to how we learn to make judgments. The upshot was that hypotheses about the "world" could not be divorced from the form of life in which such judgments make sense. As he wrote,

All testing, all confirmation and disconfirmation of a hypothesis takes place already within a system. And this system is not a more or less arbitrary and doubtful point of departure for all our arguments: no, it belongs to the essence of what we call an argument. The system is not so much the point of departure, as the element in which arguments have their life.[50]

Wittgenstein's emphasis on the practices through which judgments are taught prompted him to consider what the social sciences, especially anthropology, revealed about how language games operated in different cultures. It was an insight that dawned on him when the Italian economist Piero Sraffa thoughtfully stroked his chin and asked Wittgenstein: "What is the logical form of *that*?"[51] Sraffa's question prompted Wittgenstein to look at what people do—stroking one's chin to indicate thoughtfulness—rather than to continue the search for a logical structure linking language to reality. Initially, Wittgenstein turned to the anthropologist James Frazer and his 1890 work, *The Golden Bough*.[52] But he could not abide what he found. This is because Frazer argued that there are progressive stages of development that societies pass through from myth, to religion, to science. Wittgenstein considered this wrongheaded. Indeed, he thought Frazer to be "much more savage than most of his savages" because his explanation came via "an hypothesis of development [that] is only *one* kind of summary of the data."[53]

Frazer erred when he relied on a preconceived idea, bolstered by a "scientific" method, about the reality of social development. In this way, Frazer's picture of the world interfered with his hypotheses about the groups he studied. Wittgenstein succinctly stated that these types of mistakes arise when we "predicate of the thing what lies in the method of representing it" and become so impressed by what we think are comparable things that we think we are "perceiving a state of affairs of the highest generality."[54] On Wittgenstein's view, this isn't what is happening. Rather, what this reveals is that we are bewitched by a language game in which a picture of the world is represented in a language of facts, such as found in science or social science, believed to map onto reality. Wittgenstein thought this was a world picture that "held us captive."[55] Once we abandoned it, we would see that language does not function in a law-like way at all but is filled with fuzzy examples and riddled with loopholes.[56]

Frazer's anthropology was what Wittgenstein hoped social scientists would not do. Not only was it mistaken to judge one culture by the standards of another, for Wittgenstein this was another misguided attempt to reduce social phenomena to scientific logic.[57] Yet even though Wittgenstein found no help in Frazer, he remained steadfast in rejecting scientific reductionism. In so doing he struck upon a difficulty with monological approaches more generally: They dismiss (ex cathedra) alternative social possibilities for reaching judgments by claiming that there is a logic common to all language games. Considering all of this, it is odd that a monological approach has been counted as a strong point in recent collections touting "new materialisms" for the environmental social sciences. For instance, one recent book of essays is confidently introduced as espousing a "monological account of emergent, generative material being."[58] The impetus for a monological view of the environmental social sciences is understandable: By securing materialism to biological or planetary evolution, dualisms separating humans from nature are precluded. Yet, as we will return to later in this book, such accounts have significant shortcomings when it comes to engaging with the common ways of thinking now shaping understandings of water in the Anthropocene.

Rather than try to conform all forms of cultural life, not to mention non-human life forms, to a monological view, we might follow Wittgenstein further and hold that we should let practice speak for itself because it is practice that teaches judgment. Focusing on practice resonates with Hannah Arendt's arguments about how our public common sense emerges in relation to others.[59] Arendt's political philosophy, however, does not fully capture how practices of learning judgment are inflected by our social position, whether this position reflects the unequal terrain upon which practices are taught, the unequal terrain that reinforcing certain practices produces, or the inequalities that condition opportunities for different practices to even look like concrete options.[60] It is these inequalities that this book aims to uncover by tracing how certain practices teach judgments that render water a resource and as variously abundant, scarce, or an issue of security. Because such judgments form the basis for agreements over how to manage water—socially, technically, geologically and for healthy individuals, states, and the Earth system—they lay bare how alternatives are treated unequally, whether they are dismissed outright or when others are required to produce claims to water that conform with a particular form of life.

If we follow this a step further, it is evident that there is more at stake than Max Weber's claim that successful states are those with a monopoly on the legitimate use of force.[61] Following Wittgenstein, Pierre Bourdieu held that before a monopoly on legitimate force can be achieved, a certain amount of symbolic violence must take place in order to establish a shared basis regarding what counts as legitimate.[62] For example, individuals must start to see their entitlements to land in the language of property rights and be able and willing to follow the social customs and institutions by which a right in property is legitimately acquired and provided for.[63] All of this, however, turns on whether individuals occupy a social situation that enables them to actually make a claim, such as access to the legal system.[64] By requiring others to adopt the form of life found in constitutional states as a condition of participation, the rules surrounding how social relationships to property are articulated make a strong claim regarding whose social world disputes are convened within. Such is the case, for example, when indigenous groups are forced to articulate their claims to land or water in the language of constitutional states and their associated systems of sovereignty and rights.[65]

How might we think about water without falling into monological terms? Also influenced by Wittgenstein, Ian Hacking argues that our styles of reasoning "loop back" to affect what we consider possibilities *for us* in a particular time and space.[66] This looping happens because our practices, beliefs, customs, institutions, and classifications of things—our forms of life—not only shape our understanding but also condition what we see as concrete options. These styles of reasoning are open to many sources of influence, such when environmental changes affect outcomes and opportunities for judgment. What distinguishes the view I am advocating is that judgments sediment practices. Judgments codify ways of finding agreement when reasoning comes to an end. To once more quote Wittgenstein, "If I have exhausted the justifications I have reached bedrock, and my spade is turned. Then I am inclined to say: 'This is simply what I do.'"[67]

There are many ways of reaching bedrock. Claims regarding science, cosmology, custom, religion, class, individualism, socialism, and capitalism are all candidates. The important point is that codifying the end-point for agreement is a social practice. The collective practices through which judgments are reached form the basis of what we typically term "narratives." Narratives are collectively practiced stopping rules. The reason that some rules function as stopping rules and others do not, I submit, has precisely to do with the inequalities that beset the practices, outcomes, and uneven opportunities that condition how judgments are taught. Owing to unevenness and inequality, some rules are enforced more prominently, or held more widely, than others.

The Narrative of Normal Water

The philosophy of water management persists within its own narrative. That is, it has a set of stopping rules used to reach agreements. These stopping rules codify the end point for agreement—the bedrock provided by propositions like water scarcity—but the practices through which this takes place do not fall back on the rationality of the modern state or theories about nature or the world in Kantian philosophy. These stopping rules work because they establish common practices for thinking about water and do so in ways favorable to those pursuing the program of normal water and its aim of bringing social and evolutionary possibilities into the service of liberal forms of life. In this sense, the philosophy of water management has proved remarkably robust in its union of anthropological and geological claims. It is also monological: It installs liberal forms of life over and against others and rests on the judgments of those who use its rules to reach agreement.[68] Without understanding the practices through which these judgments came to be accepted, it is difficult to get a clear view of how we are entangled with *these* contradictions of water management, such as those over the human right to water, and not others. As Wittgenstein remarked, the "civil status of a contradiction, or its status in civil life: there is the philosophical problem."[69]

The narrative of normal water assents to three key judgments: that water was once abundant, that it has now become scarce, and, as an outcome of mismanaging scarcity, that water is now an issue of security with respect to interstate conflict, human development, and planetary health. These judgments codify practices that take advantage of differential power relations and have, over time, wed water to different iterations of liberalism and, as we will see, to a peculiar view of the United States as a model post-colonial state. Often, these judgments have been taught to students and used to engage policy makers. In what follows I make the case that normal water has "gone global" through many non-global ways of finding agreement and encouraging management practices that loop back to reinforce them. As a result, to participate in global water governance requires assent to these propositional judgments, which are constitutive for maintaining a world picture in which water is a resource.

2

Laissez-Faire Metaphysics

But as there is no royal road to knowledge, so there is no
democratic balloon path to justice.
—Major John Wesley Powell, 1887

John Wesley Powell is a fascinating figure. A veteran of the American
Civil War, he lost part of one arm in battle. He was among the first
Americans to navigate the undammed Colorado River. He studied the
cultures and languages of indigenous peoples in the American west, had
a stint as a university professor, and led the U.S. Geological Survey. He
also convinced Congress that anthropology was relevant to western settlement, which led to the creation of the Bureau of American Ethnology
in 1879, which he then directed.[1] Despite all this, Powell's philosophical
work typically does not figure into accounts of his life.[2] Perhaps for good
reason: The historian Donald Worster described Powell's main philosophical text, *Truth and Error*, as a "dead flop."[3] A recent collection of
Powell's writings dismissed it as "a long and tangled treatise."[4] In its day,
philosophers derided *Truth and Error*, and even Lester Ward, the soci-
ologist to whom it was dedicated, couldn't give it a positive spin.[5]

Powell's book is unwieldy. Yet, as the first of an unfinished trilogy, it
reveals the extent of his resistance to fundamentalist ideas of social or
natural law. Influenced by Powell, eschewing fundamentalism formed
the ethos of the philosophy of water management. As the epigraph
suggests, Powell rejected the idea of a "royal road" to knowledge or an
unwavering, democratic drift toward justice. In the unpublished letter
to the journal *Science* from which the epigraph to this chapter comes,
Powell argues there are no fundamental principles of justice, whether in
traditional sources of authority or so-called evolutionary law.[6] To think
in fundamentalist terms was to be "blinded by the fumes of *laissez-faire*
metaphysics," a phrase Powell used to dispatch the "sociological alche-
mists" who reduced social relations to a priori assumptions about the

human subject. Powell rejected fundamentalism, especially the combination of John Stuart Mill's laissez-faire individualism and the metaphysics of social Darwinism. These did not square with the lessons Powell took from geology and, with WJ McGee, applied to anthropology. Their view was that to exist is to exist socially, which echoed the French philosopher Henri Bergson's quip that "it takes centuries of culture to produce a utilitarian such as John Stuart Mill."[7]

This chapter shows how Powell and McGee combined geology and anthropology to establish a non-fundamentalist philosophy for water management. They did this in three steps. First, together with a cadre of elites in Washington, Powell and McGee conceived of agency in geologic terms through what they termed "Earth-making." Second, they rejected laissez-faire metaphysics and argued that humans were not only social beings but also one of a multitude of geological agents. Third, they developed a distinctly American way of producing geologic and anthropological knowledge. This last point was crucial. It enabled the rejection of laissez-faire metaphysics to support a political project that confronted the intellectual remnants of British colonialism. Powell and McGee then offered what is best understood as "liberal positivism."[8] In it, individuals exist socially and are known through social and natural sciences that explain how the American people were an exception to— indeed, an evolutionary move beyond—colonialism.

The Cosmos Club

If you go to 2121 Massachusetts Avenue Northwest in Washington, DC, you will be at the Cosmos Club, which was founded at Powell's home on November 16, 1878. Back then, as its website proudly displays today, the Cosmos Club was "the closest thing to a social headquarters for Washington's intellectual elite."[9] This status had to do with a historical moment when several ambitious, broad-thinking individuals held posts in U.S. bureaucracies. Powell was prominent among them, but the Cosmos Club also included Spencer Fullerton Baird, a key figure in the early life of the Smithsonian Institution. Others included Otis Tufton Mason, who helped found the American Anthropological Society in 1879 and was the second curator of the Smithsonian; Grove Karl Gilbert, who joined the U.S. Geological Survey under Powell's directorship and went on to become its senior geologist; Lester Frank Ward, the first president of the American Sociological Association, who also joined the U.S. Geological Survey under Powell and became its chief paleontologist; and WJ McGee, who was also recruited to the U.S. Geological Survey by Powell and, later, followed him to the Bureau of American Ethnology.[10]

The members of the Cosmos Club developed distinctly American ideas regarding the natural and social sciences, often by rejecting British ones. They had a good time of it, too. In fact, Lester Ward described one favorite practice of Cosmos Club members as "Spencer-smashing."[11] Spencer-smashing was fairly straightforward. It involved laying out, and then eviscerating, the arguments of the British social and political theorist Herbert Spencer, especially his idea that evolution reduced to his famous adage: "the survival of the fittest."[12] Spencer-smashing was not limited to the Cosmos Club. It was common practice (though never put in such precise terms) among American pragmatists like Charles Peirce, William James, and John Dewey.[13] As Richard Hofstadter has argued, in the decades following the U.S. Civil War, one could not "be active in any field of intellectual work . . . without mastering Spencer."[14] I return to pragmatism below, because it lingers in the shadows of American water management. For Cosmos Club members, however, Spencer-smashing provided warrant for pursuing a view known as "Earth-making."

Otis Mason, a prominent American anthropologist, was a central figure in developing the concept of "Earth-making." Mason, the second curator of the Smithsonian, was likely influenced by its first, Spencer Baird, who was deeply interested in George Perkins Marsh's ideas of how humans modify the Earth.[15] In fact, in a letter to Marsh, Baird suggested that perhaps humans should be understood of as having produced the Earth (as we now find it), rather than vice versa.[16] This idea seems to have struck a chord with Mason, who used the term "Earth-making" to signal how we might see the Earth as something that was mutually produced alongside human evolution, rather than seeing humanity as something the Earth had produced.

Mason's idea of "Earth-making" took shape in three key essays, beginning with "The Land Problem" in 1892. There, Mason argued the orientation to "land" that prevailed in legal notions of property, and in public policy more broadly, failed to see how human actions modified an ever-evolving environment.[17] Prevailing ideas also failed to see how Earth itself had self-organizing properties, which Mason connected to its capacity to bring about negative or positive effects. In two later essays, Mason argued that a study of "technogeography" should be undertaken to assess how the arts and industries of mankind are in reciprocal relations with Earth processes across the atmosphere, the hydrosphere, and the geosphere.[18] Here, Mason began to link geology and anthropology through the institution of property, which connected both disciplines to land and, from there, to planetary evolution. Mason thought this had several consequences. First, it meant rejecting ideas of a natural order, whether in divine or natural law, as the basis of human ownership of the Earth. Second, it revealed the concept of "fitness" in social Darwinism as contingent because, to the extent that institutions of property were misaligned with evolution, their success was an outcome of chance. Finally, as explored next, Mason thought these problems required new, American sciences to solve the "land problem" by aligning property to Earth-making.

Mason's insight that humans and their institutions were in reciprocal relationships with the Earth prefigured contemporary ecology. But Mason did not stop there. He also argued that the Earth has an intelligence that coordinates evolution, an idea that predates James Lovelock's "Gaia Hypothesis" by over a half-century.[19] Anther Cosmos Club member, Grove Karl Gilbert, also explored how the action of the Earth might be generalized as a basis for agency. Gilbert's arguments in government publications, including two chapters in Powell's famous 1875 survey of America's arid lands, shaped conversations regarding western settlement.[20] The perceived need for a distinctly American response to the "land problem" was formulated in reference to the laissez-faire resource capitalism of late nineteenth century and the British notions of "property" that came with it, which were blamed for the depletion of American resources in the service of corporate interests.[21] In this context, "Earth-making" was not only a political tool that united natural and social sciences to support U.S. institutions and their relations to land. It was also an ethnocentric device: American social and natural sciences just happen to be the types of science that provide evidence for "Earth-making" by connecting American solutions to the "land problem" to the contingent dynamics of planetary evolution.

The Force of Geologic Agency

Earth-making was a species of what Martin Rudwick terms "geohistory": the reorganization of the historical imagination from a view of human history as roughly coextensive with the cosmos to a view of human histories as a sliver of geologic time.[22] Telling geohistory requires conceptual tools that connect Earth history to the histories of human societies. Prominent among these tools is Charles Lyell's notion of uniformitarianism, often summed in the maxim that the present is the key to the past.[23] Conceptually, uniformitarianism posits a consonance between historical and contemporary processes that produce the observed landscape, from savannahs to snowy peaks.

As director of the U.S. Geological Survey, Powell took uniformitarianism seriously. So did McGee, who represented the U.S. Geological Survey at the 1885 International Geological Congress in Berlin. Uniformitarianism became the guiding principle of Earth-making and central to linking the history of geologic action—the agency of the Earth—to the evolution of biological life, the rise of civilization and, ultimately, to the study of civilization: anthropology. This broad project located Earth-making within a unified view of the human and natural sciences and gave a prominent role to the action of water. In fact, one of Powell's key geologic contributions was the idea of "base level erosion," for which he used the Green River in northeastern Utah to show how deep valleys may be cut by the slow march of geology and water's agency:

> We may say, then, that the river did not cut its way *down* through the mountains, from a height of many thousands of feet above its present site, but, having an elevation differing but little, perhaps, from what it now has, as the fold was lifted, it cleared away the obstruction by cutting a cañon, and the walls were thus elevated on either side. The river preserved its level, but mountains were lifted up; as the saw revolves on a fixed point, while the log through which it cuts is moved along. The river was the saw which cut the mountain in two.[24]

In Powell's idea of base level erosion, flowing waters were the teeth of the river's sawing action. The action of water also interested McGee, who focused much of his early work on glaciers. He published studies on the causes of glacial periods, the dynamics of glacial action, the interaction of ice sheets with geologic subsidence, and the formation of glacial canyons.[25] McGee's interest was in landscapes that appear, in geological terms, to be younger than one might expect. Glaciers can help to explain these cases because they can do very focused work on a landscape. For instance, glaciers may form lakes on their surfaces as they warm, with only an ice dam holding the water back. If the ice dam bursts, a large glacial flood can ensue (a jökulhlaup) that scours in a matter of days, weeks, or months what may have taken much longer to achieve otherwise. The "glacial key" to geology was also gaining traction elsewhere, such as in Britain, where water was taking on an increasingly important role in explaining Earth processes.[26]

McGee made both practical and conceptual contributions to geology. Practically, he identified geological formations still in use in the United States today, such as the Potomac, the Columbia, and the Lafayette (or Appomattox) Formations.[27] Conceptually, one of his main contributions was to reclassify what counted as "geological" to include processes, rather than only geological products (e.g., the observed landscape). Reclassifying was important for McGee. His opening salvo in the first issue of the *National Geographic* magazine stated that "scientific progress may be measured by advance in the classification of phenomena."[28] For McGee, advances in classification provided for a "New Geology" that "interprets geologic history from the records of degradation as the old geology interpreted history from the records of deposition."[29] So, rather than classifying as "geologic" only what was deposited over time in stratigraphic layers, McGee's classification scheme included the processes denuding a landscape, such as water's erosive action. As McGee explained:

> The phenomena of degradation were brought into prominence by Lyell, and have ever since maintained an important place in geologic literature. Within the last decade, however, a novel and important cognate idea has been developed: it is now perceived that the processes of degradation are governed by definite laws and leave a legible record of their operation in the configuration of the surfaces upon which they have acted, and consequently that geologic history can be interpreted from the hills produced by degradation as well as from the strata produced by deposition

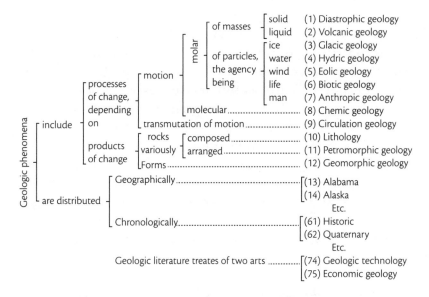

Figure 2.1. Classification of Geology. Source: McGee, "Geology for 1887 and 1888," 232.

in contiguous areas. This discovery, simple as it seems, marks an era in the progress of geologic science, if not indeed the birth of a new science.[30]

Today, the New Geology is known as geomorphology, a field examining relationships among forms and processes. Critically, however, once the conceptual move is made to include processes, it extends geologic action in as many directions as there are ways to degrade a landscape. As McGee's 1890 classification scheme shows in figure 2.1, this results in an abundance of geologic agents, including wind, biota, glaciers, and hydrology. McGee classifies all of these, along with humans (the "anthropic"), as different forms of geologic agency. The interactions among multiple agents were key to the New Geology because it creates the possibility of a unified view of agency and, hence, of the social and natural sciences.

Like Powell, McGee was committed to confronting metaphysical dualisms between humans and nature. The newfound abundance of geologic agents was, for both men, an outcome of Darwin's theory of evolution and the extension of uniformitarianism to natural selection.

Powell believed Darwin had made a great contribution to philosophy by moving the study of life beyond metaphysics.[31] Darwin's bulldog, Thomas Huxley, was held in equal esteem for using uniformity to distinguish science from pseudoscience.[32] In 1901, McGee dedicated his address as retiring president of the Anthropological Society of Washington to Huxley's work, *Man's Place in Nature*, which generalized uniformitarianism into a basis for the social and natural sciences.[33]

According to McGee, Powell also thought geology provided the means for explaining how biological forms of agency evolved without metaphysical intercession. In this sense, the arrival of human agency in the geologic record was simply another episode of Earth-making. As such, it was geologic force, not a unique metaphysical endowment of humanity, that provided the conditions for knowing the external world. As McGee described it,

> Especially notable among [Powell's] possessions was a principle brought over from geology—the principle of interpreting natural phenomena in terms of agency, or primary force (primary, so far, at least, as current knowledge goes). This principle was perhaps the keynote of Powell's work in geology; certainly it became the keynote of his researches in ethnology and general anthropology.[34]

In 1879, Powell became the first director of the Bureau of American Ethnology. After he became the director of the U.S. Geological Survey in 1881, he headed both. This lasted until 1894, when his directorship of the U.S. Geological Survey ended. The year before he had already reduced his workload at the Bureau of Ethnology as the result of poor health, but he remained its formal head until his death in 1902. During the last decade of the nineteenth century, McGee was "director-in-charge" of the Bureau of American Ethnology, a position he held until 1903. After Powell's death, the appointment of a permanent director bypassed McGee and went to William Holmes because the man in charge of the decision, Samuel Langley, didn't like McGee and refused to appoint him after his less-than-stellar record running the bureau.[35] Yet by 1895 McGee had also turned from geology to anthropology.[36] In addition to serving as president of the Anthropological Society of Washington, he was active in forming the American Anthropological Association and served as its first president from 1902 to 1904. Despite this anthropological turn, however, McGee never strayed from his geologic roots.

Agency after Kant

What is the philosophical motivation for Earth-making? The answer is twofold. First, Powell and McGee wanted to work without the Kantian subject in tow; there were to be no metaphysics in geology and none in anthropology. Second, they wanted to confront laissez-faire doctrines and social Darwinism at their roots—in their conceptualization of the individual and an individual's relationship to both society and the Earth. The promise of Earth-making was that it internalized contingency such that the history of the Earth was of a piece with the history of human societies. Both of these histories were conditioned by evolutionary chance, not the laws of nature or of gods. By predicating social science on geology, the stage was also set for a political goal: to secure an exception to British colonialism by securing the history of the United States and its institutions to that of the Earth, not its European forerunners.

In the Powell-McGee account, there were no distinctions of kind to be made regarding agency. All agents affecting the Earth or each other could be classified under a single schema once processes of degradation came into the geological fold. The material basis of geology was aptly termed "Earth-stuff," itself a combination of vitalism, the potential of matter for life, and motility, which characterized matter's motion. McGee's view is slightly clearer, and because he consistently refers to Powell's view, I draw primarily on it. Also, McGee later applied his view when he became "the most vigorous philosopher" of the Conservation movement in America.[37] To begin, recall that this whole set of ideas was touted as a New Organon. With such ambitious ends, a key concern of both Powell and McGee was how to resolve the controversy between mind and matter that Kant, in their view, had failed to reconcile. As McGee wrote,

> After Bacon came other leaders who pictured nature in terms of the mind, or the mind in terms of nature. Newton framed a "Principia" which trains the mind to follow certain processes of nature; Humboldt constructed a literary "Kosmos" in imitation of nature; Kant, Hegel, and Schopen-

hauer limned nature as a mental picture; Spencer wrote a synthetic philosophy in which nature and mind were brought into a single view, yet
effectually sundered by his own bar of unknowability; while psycholo-
gists are interpreting mental operations in terms of natural process; yet
few—surprisingly few, in view of the marvelous success attending Bacon's
essay—have attempted to combine nature and mind in single treatment.[38]

McGee's aim was to escape "that besetting dualism which has clung
to the human mind since the sylvan savage first noted front and rear, or
this side and that."[39] McGee thought the dualism of mind and matter
deeply flawed, principally because it did not pass the test of uniformity
and supposed that one type of agency, either mental or material, must
be rendered in terms of the other. This seesaw battle was wrongheaded
because it was addressed only to its world picture, with mind on one side
and matter on the other. And there nature had sat, from Kant onward,
limned as a mental picture.[40]

To gain a foothold against this view, Powell implicated Hegel and
Spencer as thinkers who "reified the void" by making the Kantian gap
between appearance and reality the basis of philosophic inquiry.[41] This
reification, Powell argued, impounded key registers of scientific inquiry, such as space and time, behind what humans could think. Powell claimed Kant carried over an occult postulate from pre-scientific
thought that keeps metaphysics alive by requiring what exists to conform to what is thought. As he wrote, "According to Kant, space is a
form of thought, not of things."[42] By contrast, Powell held that the existence of things, including space and time, did not depend on a Kantian
subject or on any unique endowment that outfits humans for navigating a universe of mind and matter. For that is not the universe we live
in. Rather, Powell forwarded a version of realism that held space and
time are properties of things (not of thought) and that knowledge of the
world, including the languages used to classify things in it, is part of a
shared evolutionary heritage.[43]

Powell viewed every object as a unit, from pieces of paper to people.
These objects all issued from Earth-stuff that was both mind and matter.
In fact, Powell held that "every particle of matter has consciousness."[44]
From this basis, Powell held that a proper philosophy of science could
explain everything from rocks to plants, animals, complex human so-

cieties and, ultimately, scientific concepts themselves. As combinations of Earth-stuff increase in complexity, there arises a gradually enhanced capacity for higher degrees of consciousness. And, as more innately conscious particles of matter come together in increasingly complex ways, their capacity for self-organization increases. Following uniformitarianism, agency differs only by degree. The vitalism inhering in matter is complemented by something Powell termed "motility," which refers to how matter "feels" its way about and adjusts to the actions of other geological agents. In this regard, Powell's view is remarkably similar to that of pragmatist Charles S. Peirce in his 1892 essay, "Man's Glassy Essence."[45]

Powell's view was not identical to Peirce's or with the more popular vitalism of Henri Bergson, even though he knew of both. In fact, Powell's compatriot at the Cosmo Club, Lester Ward, complained that Bergson's popularity came from capturing the zeitgeist while Ward's own version of vitalism predated Bergson's and was equally competent.[46] Ward's version of vitalism moved between Powell's account of geologic agency and William James's views on psychology.[47] Ward agreed with Powell that Earth-stuff had agency and felt its way about its environment. Yet he also agreed with James that if we ask, "Does consciousness exist?" then we must answer no.[48] Consciousness was a holdover from Kantian philosophy, a solution to a problem that began with mind and matter. In his essay, "The Status of the Mind Problem," Ward compared Powell and James.[49] Powell even introduced Ward on the occasion that he delivered the paper, which runs counter to Donald Worster's claim that Powell seems "never to have looked" at the work of William James and that he'd have benefited if he had.[50] At any rate, in Ward's view there was only one type of Earth-stuff from which the entire cosmos evolved. For Ward, as for Powell, the mind evolved from the interplay of a multitude of agents interacting with one another and feeling their way about over geologic time.[51]

Powell's vitalism had elements in common with Bergson. Both held that creativity arises in lockstep with cognitive capacity and that progress is itself a moment of directed (though not teleological) evolution.[52] Their main difference was Powell's geological view of agency, which contrasted with Bergson's biologically oriented view. For Powell, it was not the human experience of space or time that mattered—as in Bergson's *longue durée*—but, rather, geologic uniformitarianism that provided the basis for claims about reality. Yet this posed a hurdle for a purely scientific account: How did hypothetical reasoning, such as is required for scientific inquiry, come about from geological action? This was especially problematic for phenomena that simply could not be experienced, such as planetary evolution, but that demanded scientific explanation.[53]

Powell thought that, in order to move science beyond metaphysics, it was necessary to accord a higher place to hypothetical reasoning. On this point, Powell was in agreement with Charles S. Peirce, who in 1878 distinguished between deductive, inductive, and hypothetical (or abductive) reasoning before concluding that geology was part of the hypothetical sciences.[54] The question was how to account for hypothetical reasoning and, thereby, to explain "mind" in terms of geologic evolution. For this, Powell relied to significant extent on the work of Grove Karl Gilbert, a fellow Cosmos Club member and colleague of Peirce's at the U.S. Geological Survey. Gilbert was known as the "clerk of the cosmos" after apprenticing in the Cosmos Hall lab in Rochester, New York, which took its name from Alexander von Humboldt's treatise on nature and the history of science.[55] Although Gilbert was not inclined toward grand theories, he introduced an important concept for linking hypothetical reasoning and geological processes: the plexus.

Gilbert's concept of the plexus classified scientific hypotheses as neither inductive nor deductive because he held that many phenomenon are overdetermined by antecedent conditions. As he wrote, "Antecedent and consequent relations are not therefore merely linear, but constitute a plexus; and this plexus pervades nature."[56] Gilbert appreciated non-linear relationships between historical conditions and observed phenomenon, and the plexus was designed to shift scientific methodology toward relational rather than inductive classification. In Gilbert's system, hypothetical reasoning was an inference to the best explanation, which placed the scientist in a specific relation to observed events and to the antecedent conditions that allowed observations to be grouped together. This meant that the scientist was not a disinterested observer but in a specific historical relation to phenomena. The logic for this proceeded as follows:

> Given a phenomenon, A, whose antecedent we seek. First we ransack the
> memory for some different phenomenon, B, which has one or more fea-

tures in common with A, and whose antecedent we know. Then we pass by analogy from the antecedent of B, to the hypothetical antecedent of A, solving the analogic proportion—as B is to A, so is the antecedent of B to the antecedent of A.[57]

Gilbert's logic is remarkably similar to the formulation of abduction Peirce gave in a 1913 lecture at Harvard: "The surprising fact, *C*, is observed. But if *A* were true, *C* would be a matter of course. Hence there is to reason to suspect that *A* is true."[58] Although Peirce and Gilbert worked together at the U.S. Geological Survey, Gilbert stated he never talked to Peirce about these ideas, believing him too metaphysical for practical questions.[59] The point, however, is not just that Gilbert knew and worked with Peirce but that providing a logical basis for the "hypothetical sciences" was part of broader conversations across geology, philosophy, and the upstart American social sciences. In Gilbert's view, hypothetical reasoning was a collective and social exercise because analogical understanding built up over time as multiple individuals generate and test hypotheses.[60] Other geologists, such as Thomas Chamberlin, would take this so far as to reverse Auguste Comte's positivism and set up geology as the comprehensive foundation for all knowledge.[61] Decades later, Chamberlin's idea of "multiple working hypotheses" influenced another key figure in American water management considered in this book, Gilbert White.[62]

The Social Subject

WJ McGee also considered geology a new intellectual firmament. He endorsed the views of Powell and Gilbert but added the twist that time was neither cyclical, as in pre-modern understandings, nor linear, as in secular accounts. For McGee, time was elliptical. His argument drew on a homology with planetary movement: Earth's orbits are not closed because each annual orbit progresses upon those previous, so each is ever so slightly different than the last and is itself open to influence. Likewise, each human generation begins with the heritage of those previous to it, but each travels its own path.[63] In this way, non-linear evolutionary progress is inevitable because the Earth itself, and its manifold agents, are all acting in variations (however slight) over time. Here,

McGee builds on Gilbert's ideas of "collective hypotheses" to imagine a more-than-human social subject because more than just humans affect Earth's geological heritage. The result is an interdependent subject that socializes with a broadly dispersed set of interacting agents across geologic time and through planetary space.

McGee also connected his views to the evolution of hypothetical reasoning. In his essay, "The Earth the Home of Man," he argued that the vital force of matter is the result of complex interactions that mark the difference between life and non-life. This transition from non-life to life requires a relative openness to chemical interaction that at first is "highly unstable."[64] The relatively late appearance of life in the geological record is explained by these delicate and complex interactions, which had many false starts before life took hold. This precarious window defines his vitalism as the "exceeding susceptibility of living things to external forces and conditions."[65] Like Powell, McGee's vitalism is married to motility (matter's techniques of feeling its way about). Together, vitality and motility form the basis for understanding life as precarious adjustment. As life forms adjust in increasingly complicated ways—as life becomes more complex—the faculty of "prevision" emerges as the capacity to "predict the future in terms of the past," and this forms "the beginning and essence of consciousness."[66]

Prevision is uniformitarianism's forward-looking lens. It arises not metaphysically but through the gradual adjustments of an organism's shared and social past with hypotheses about the future. An organism's present is key to its evolutionary past and to its bets on future success. McGee's emphasis on the unstable, open, and contingent aspects of intellectual capacity both grounded cognitive capacity in the vitalism of Earth-stuff and secured an evolutionary basis for understanding life's shared and social capacity for self-direction as differentiated by degree, not kind. McGee offers many examples of prevision: beavers building huts and dams and spiders spinning webs to ensnare prey. For McGee, prevision is not only the result of an Earth full of agency; it is also evidence for how the collective capacity to hypothesize about the best chances for future success arises geologically.

For McGee, once Kant's "occult postulate" was exposed to the light of geology, the picture of nature as separate from humans vanished because subjectivity itself was an outcome of the social interactions of an abundance of geological agents. This argument served as McGee's version of Spencer-smashing, especially the idea Spencer forwarded in his *Principles of Psychology*.[67] Therein, Spencer reduced Darwin's ideas about how organisms were adapted to their "circumstances" (plural) to the idea that there is an "environment" (singular) to which an individual organism had a relationship.[68] It was this organism-environment relationship that formed the basis for social Darwinism, since individual organisms could then be competitively measured for their "fit" with the environment. For McGee, we could never know what is more or less "fit" since Spencer walled off behind nature—now, the "environment"— the social relationships that individual organisms had with everything else and that affected their evolutionary prospects. As such, Spencer closed off precisely the kind of pluralism sought by Powell, McGee, Gilbert, and pragmatists like William James, who also railed against Spencer.[69]

McGee charged Spencer with reformulating the mind/matter dualism as organism-environment interaction. Equally problematic was that Spencer's view was oriented only to the internal relations of an organism but not its external, social relations.[70] This exclusion of social relations made social Darwinism unpalatable because it claimed evolutionary "fit" was only about individual success. McGee, by contrast, held that life was social and that social life depended on other geological agents. As he argued, "There are probably no terrestrial materials known to man which have not been modified by vital action, save, possibly, a few ancient crystalline rocks and a few lavas from the deeper sources."[71] McGee termed this interdependence "the solidarity of life" in which "few—if any—members could maintain separate existence."[72]

McGee's "solidarity of life" is an early forerunner to ecological views of life as interdependent across humans, non-humans, and the abiotic world. The "solidarity of life" is also reminiscent of Albert Schweitzer's famous appeal to reconceive the question Jesus asked his followers: "Who is your neighbor?" In Schweitzer's view, the concept of "neighbor" must be expanded to include all living things if we are to cultivate a reverence for life.[73] But unlike Schweitzer, McGee thought neighborliness a brute geologic fact, not an expression of the will-to-live that Schweitzer had naturalized from Friedrich Nietzsche's will-to-power. Nevertheless, McGee writes,

So no living thing lives unto himself alone, but each aids or injures his neighbors in an endless succession of interactions, and the entire series of living things of the earth is bound together in a single solidarity, and this solidarity of life is the glory of the earth.[74]

From this quote we might ask: Why not have a moral imperative? The "solidarity of life" has a nice normative ring to it. McGee's answer was that the whole thing was haphazard; evolution had a direction, but it did not have any ends. Up to now life exhibited a direction toward more complicated interactions and complex organisms, but as a whole the planet was not consciously self-directed. This is what made Earth-making such an important step. It was a form of self-knowledge that arose from geologic processes that recognized contingency all the way down. It was the next step after Bacon because modern science would now be able to guide the haphazard experiments of evolution in empirical, not metaphysical, terms. As McGee concluded "The Earth the Home of Man,"

The child of human parents is at first a helpless weakling, and must be fed, clothed, petted, nourished, and protected by those stronger than himself, and parents give freely of their life force that the child may be brought to maturity. When the human infant gains man's estate he repays with interest the debt unconsciously assumed in his infancy, supports his parents in their declining years, succors his fellow-men, and feeds, clothes, and protects the succeeding generation; and in this interchange of kindly acts lies the beauty and perfection of human life.

In like manner, mankind, offspring of mother earth, cradled and nursed through helpless infancy by things earthly, has been brought well toward maturity; and like the individual man he is repaying the debt unconsciously assumed at the birth of his kind by transforming the face of nature, by making all things better than they were before, by aiding the good and destroying the bad among animals and plants, and by protecting the aging earth from the ravages of time and failing strength, even as the child protects his fleshly mother. Such are the relations of earth and man.[75]

Taking a step back, one question that arises is: How does McGee's view differ, if at all, from modern theories of the "conquest of nature"? First, unlike the accounts of the "conquest of nature" offered by historians like Carolyn Merchant, there is no "Adam" who has fallen from the biblical Garden of Eden and who is now tasked with gardening the Earth.[76] Second, McGee's view also does not fit with Enlightenment views of the Kantian subject because he situates humans among an abundance of planetary agents that are all unwittingly collaborating without regard for their cumulative effects. For McGee, conquest is a means, not an end. Conquest is required for continued evolution, not something allowed by, or demanded of, the unique metaphysical standing of humans, for they have no such standing. Instead, as the next chapter considers in more detail, the requirements of the philosophy of water management derive from knowledge of haphazard and contingent evolutionary processes worrying an aging Earth.

An additional benefit McGee derived from his view was the repudiation of the individualism presumed in laissez-faire political philosophy. In the late nineteenth century, John Stuart Mill's notion of "purely self-regarding acts" was taken by some as legitimating the exhaustion of what once seemed an infinite supply of resources in the United States.[77] Purely self-regarding acts were heartily endorsed by Spencer, who argued for the fundamental law that "every man may claim the fullest liberty to exercise his faculties compatible with the possession of like liberty by every other man."[78] This was a law Spencer thought would result in individual perfection. Yet in McGee's view of social evolution, Spencer was nothing but a sociological alchemist since individuals had to sprout magically from nowhere, somehow evolving free of social relations and ready-made for acts that were purely self-regarding.

The next chapter considers the "liberal positivism" Powell and McGee used to situate the individual persons described by liberalism in the social, interdependent space of the geological community. Water's agency was critical to that community. Ultimately, water bridges human and non-human agency and provides the fulcrum for dispatching laissez-faire resource economics in the name of national planning. To see why national planning mattered philosophically and politically, however, it is first necessary to see how Powell and McGee set up the United States as an exception to British colonialism by employing their geologically infused anthropology to provide evidence for social progress.

Uniformity and Social Progress

Powell concluded *Truth and Error* by stating, "The philosophy here presented is neither Idealism nor Materialism; I would fain call it the Philosophy of Science."[79] In Powell's philosophy, the latest step in Earth-making was the capacity to purposefully direct geological processes to enhance evolutionary progress.[80] But what counted as enhancing evolution? This question led Powell and McGee to anthropology, which they used to explain the rise of scientific knowledge in a manner consonant with other episodes of Earth-making. Later, this anthropological account underpinned how McGee identified *for whom* water was to be managed. But before proceeding it is necessary to understand what their argument was and why it took hold politically. Not least of all, it was an argument that convinced U.S. President Theodore Roosevelt to institute two of McGee's key ideas: multipurpose river basin planning and conservation.

Imagining Uniformity

At the turn of the twentieth century, the intellectual community in Washington, DC, in many ways led American science across anthropology, geography, geology, education, and social statistics.[81] Members of this community published journals like *Science, National Geographic,* and *American Anthropologist.* During this time, Powell was "the most prominent spokesman" for this community, and his interest in ethnology "was especially concerned with problems of theory in accounting for social evolution."[82] As Michael Lacey argues, Washington intellectuals affected the institutional, economic, and judicial transitions that enabled government interventions in Progressive Era policies under Theodore Roosevelt.[83]

Among Powell's most enduring anthropological contributions were the linguistic studies of indigenous peoples of North America recorded in the Bureau of Ethnology's annual reports. The reports fascinated later anthropologists, and Claude Lévi-Strauss claimed he underwent "some privations" to save enough money to buy them.[84] Powell's orientation to language also rejected metaphysics in favor of measuring cultures based on what individuals do, not what they are. For Powell, a scientific account of culture that remained consonant with uniformity required that definitive cultural features were not located in the constitution of individuals but in socialized habits. Powell was especially interested in habits of thought, and these required language. That being said, neither Powell nor McGee were free of assumptions about physical attributes and their relationship to cultural superiority. In fact, they bet on whose brain was larger (the post-mortem decision went to Powell) as part of the view that psychological capacity increased with more Earth-stuff in one's cranium.

Powell used symbolic systems to differentiate the relative psychic development of groups through stages of savagery, barbarism, civilization, and enlightenment.[85] Language was one part of the symbol systems that enabled social progress, and Powell coined the term "acculturation" to describe this evolutionary process.[86] In Powell's view, the capacity for enhanced symbolic cognition arose as more sophisticated societies passed knowledge from one generation to the next. Powell's was a strange kind of ontological realism. For instance, the science of numbers (or plurality) was a fact about the real multiplicity of objects. Different conventions of measurement reflected alternative pathways for imagining social existence through symbolic systems that classified the multiplicity of objects. Underpinning this view was a claim that language, words, and symbols were also real objects.[87] This becomes important below when Powell attacks Hegel's view of history such that American acculturation is based on evolutionary, rather than historical, habits.

Once symbolic development is set in terms of psychic development, Powell turned to how mental habits arose and what form they took. This was a widely shared topic among many intellectuals with respect to uniformity. For the pragmatist John Dewey, uniformity was a principle that unified scientific claims without falling back on dualisms of mind and matter.[88] For John Stuart Mill, uniformity established a logical basis for scientific inference as a principle that indicated a relation between things and the class they were a part of.[89] Uniformity indexed the relationships, for instance, between individual swans and the category "white." Mill's view caught the eye of Charles Peirce, who thought Mill reduced uniformity to conventions of classification.[90] Peirce thought Mill erred by presuming that uniformity in nature was independent of evolutionary context. Mill's mistake was that he grounded uniformity in idealism, rather than in real objects and their relations, such as the heredity of white swans.

As the next chapter considers, Powell and McGee had an abiding interest in Mill. But they also had an agenda of their own regarding how uniformity fit with social and conceptual development. In Washington, their efforts played out in a circle of which Charles Peirce was intermittently a part. Their connections with Peirce are not straightforward, though almost certain. It bears sketching them out because Powell appears to follow Peirce's cues on uniformity, and, at several points, Powell's writings read as almost thought-for-thought renditions of Peirce. Although Powell never cites Peirce, there are reasons not to discount the influence of Peirce on the philosophy of water management.

Peirce worked for the U.S. Coast and Geodetic Survey for thirty years after graduating from Harvard in 1859.[91] Taught mathematics at Harvard by his father, Benjamin, it was his father who hired him at the Geodetic Survey, which the elder Peirce ran during its critical transition from mapping hydrographic basins for navigation to surveying the baseline for settlement of the American west. While at the Geodetic Survey, Charles Peirce worked with Simon Newcomb, with whom he had studied with at Harvard. Albert Einstein later described Newcomb's work on planetary motion as of "monumental importance."[92] Peirce's work at the Geodetic Survey focused on refining techniques for measuring gravitational force. In 1884, he corrected calculations for predicting rare meteorological events made by Grove Karl Gilbert, who Powell routinely saw in the Cosmos Club.[93] Peirce also published a series of essays in the early 1890s in *The Monist*. One essay, "The Law of Mind," includes virtually every element that Powell later included in *Truth and Error*, including the idea that basic particles of protoplasm—Powell's Earth-stuff—had capacity for consciousness and "feel" their way about.[94]

There are several likely reasons that neither Powell nor McGee cited Peirce, or even William James, who was Peirce's longtime friend and advocate. The first was Peirce's reputation. After leaving the Geodetic Survey for a job at Johns Hopkins University, Peirce maintained an open affair for several years while married. It was Simon Newcomb who alerted the board of trustees at John Hopkins University of this social misstep, which likely led to Peirce's failed academic career there.[95] Peirce had had a fraught relationship with Newcomb since their days at

Harvard.[96] Newcomb, in contrast to Peirce, was an upstanding member of the Washington community. In 1894, Newcomb and McGee were awarded first and second prizes, respectively, for their essays on what elements make up the most useful citizen of the United States.[97] McGee must have had some of these elements because on Valentine's Day, 1888, he married Simon Newcomb's daughter, Anita. It is perhaps not coincidental that McGee's ideas of elliptical time and planetary motion were also developed around this time.

Another reason Powell and McGee would not likely have acknowledged Peirce was his relationship with Samuel Langley, the man who passed over McGee for the directorship of the Bureau of Ethnology. Langley liked Peirce and helped him out when he returned to Washington after being let go from Johns Hopkins. Langley even offered support for Peirce to publish his philosophic work through the Smithsonian.[98] Powell's colleague, Lester Ward, reviewed Peirce's work for its suitability in Smithsonian publications and found it wanting. Once back in Washington, however, Peirce did write an essay for the annual report of the Smithsonian Institution for 1900 entitled, "The Century's Great Men in Science."[99] There he gives special place to geology, arguing that in the nineteenth century the United States had become its home.

This detour into some of the connections among Peirce, Powell, and McGee perhaps helps to explain why, although they lived in shared circles, there was little exchange between them. In fact, it is striking that for synthetic thinkers like Powell and McGee that they would not mention the American pragmatists. One likely reason was appearances. McGee, for instance, would almost certainly have been privy to the ongoing adventures of Peirce since the latter was also good friends with the prominent Pinchot family and even lived at their estate for a time.[100] Their son, Gifford Pinchot, was a key colleague of McGee's as American conservation took shape (which is detailed in the next chapter).

The degree to which Powell, McGee, and Peirce shared a common approach to uniformity is striking. For instance, Peirce's essay on "Uniformity" concludes that "the interest which the uniformities of Nature have for an animal measures his place in the scale of intelligence."[101] Peirce defended this view, in part, by claiming that any group of objects had at least one quality that was common to them (whether a positive, shared character or a negative, absent one) such that, "in any world whatever, then, there must be a character peculiar to each possible group of objects."[102] The view Peirce articulated was the kind of realism Powell could abide: a realism in which differentiating characteristics could be found in any group. As we saw above, Powell differentiated among human groups based on characteristic habits of thought. Likewise for Peirce, who wrote in 1890, "Uniformities in the modes of action of things have come about by their taking habits."[103] For Peirce, the scientific testing of habits was part of our existence as "social animals" and depended on there being real objects to test our hypotheses against. Finally, Peirce also shared a commitment to a social understanding of reality and collective hypothesis testing that led to an increase in knowledge. As he wrote,

> The real, then, is that which, sooner or later, information and reasoning would finally result in, and which is therefore independent of the vagaries of me and you. Thus, the very origin of the conception of reality shows that this conception essentially involves the notion of a COMMUNITY, without definite limits, and capable of a definite increase of knowledge.[104]

Peirce's claim that reality is grounded in COMMUNITY was published in the *Journal of Speculative Philosophy*. Powell would likely have been aware of Peirce's connection of reality and community since Powell's counterpart at the Bureau of Education, William Torrey Harris, was the founder and editor of the *Journal of Speculative Philosophy* and a key expositor of Hegelianism.[105] Powell took special umbrage with Hegel and claimed to have studied German idealism carefully.[106] But whereas Peirce was interested in the logic of scientific inquiry, Powell was interested in the evolution of mental habits. In this regard, Powell believed modern philosophy fit with a grander scheme of classification and that, since Kant, the dualism between mind and matter had set in place linguistic practices that, once classified as social habits, would clarify scientific inquiry. Powell argued against the Hegelian dialectic between being and non-being by claiming that the linguistic particle "non" was simply a device in naming and, at that, it was a device that named Kant's occult postulate: the void between phenomenon and thing. Like Kant, Hegelians emptied space and time of objects and then tried to treat time and space independently of matter, and this smuggled in the mind-matter dualism under the guise of a dialectical synthesis.[107] Powell then argued that no matter how elaborate its metaphysical backdrop for history, Hegelianism could not account for new, geologic habits of thought in America.

The American Exception to Colonialism

Powell thought modern philosophy was entangled in cultural habits of thought that inhibited progress by reifying the gap between appearance and reality.[108] By grounding American social sciences in geology, Powell believed that habits of thought could be classified in evolutionary terms. The implication was that Hegel's historicism, and his accompanying ideas of justice and rights, could be interpreted as an evolutionary moment of acquiring certain habits and not others. Through the new habits of thought made available by U.S. geology, laissez-faire metaphysics could be dispatched once and for all. Powell's view echoed the pragmatist William James, who wrote that "the only objective criterion of reality is coerciveness, in the long run, over thought."[109] The difference between Powell and the famed pragmatist, however, was that Powell set up the American social sciences, notably anthropology, as both the way out of the tangle of modern philosophy and the solution to the "land problem."

In the *Phenomenology of Mind*, Hegel offered a thinly veiled defense of colonialism by arguing that slaves realize their identity as historical subjects through the practice of enslavement (i.e., labor), which reveals their independence and inequality with respect to the master.[110] Through labor, the slave develops a "mind of his own" and thereupon enters into the historical dialectic known today as the politics of recognition.[111] In Hegel's account, colonialism plays its part in the progression of history by raising people out of barbarism and into civilized subjects. Although Powell also believed societies progress from barbarism to civilization, he found Hegel's view unsatisfying because it was not the *historical* fact of labor that led to recognition but an evolutionary moment of self-awareness. The difference between Hegel's historicism and geologic evolution was crucial for Powell because it enabled recognition of the people of the United States, and the habits of thought that led them to develop the New Geology, as an exception to colonial relations of masters and slaves. As next chapter considers, the extension of geology to anthropology meant that the United States had achieved self-awareness in purely evolutionary terms. It was not labor that produced the American exception to colonialism but, rather, the action of geological agents and the unique American insight that humans were geological agents themselves.

The extension of geology to anthropology in the United States allowed for new and improved habits of thought and new solutions to the "land problem." This also served to confront Hegel's claim in the *Philosophy of History* that America had so much space that conflicts would be settled by geographical dispersion and that only when land ran out would the United States enter world history.[112] Essentially, the "land problem" would arise when the frontier closed, at which point America would fall into line with European history. For Powell and McGee, Earth-making was designed to show how a solution to the "land problem" could be found in evolutionary terms. As a result, when the western frontier closed—as claimed by Frederick Turner in 1893—the United States would not enter world history but instead would solve the "land problem" by connecting American institutions to geology. This evolutionary advance would not only solve the "land problem" by allowing for the creation of geologically grounded social institutions, it would also secure self-knowledge to the geologic principle of uniformitarianism, rather than to the metaphysics of Mill, Spencer, or Hegel. As the next chapter considers, water was central to how this philosophy was put into practice. By solving the "land problem" through water management, McGee thought the people of the United States were not only exceptional but had also entered a new evolutionary stage that came after history: Beyond civilization was enlightenment.

Understanding the use of geology to situate agency is central to the philosophy of water management. This is because water's action takes a prominent role in connecting land to social life. To situate water's agency as part of this philosophy, it was first necessary to see how Powell and McGee rejected the notion that there is one unique agent in the cosmos and situated humans among an abundance of geologic agents. Once sole proprietorship of agency is abandoned, the possibility arises for an abundance of agents that act and react with each another to shape shared environments.[113] But a problem remained: Earth was evolving haphazardly and without the guiding hand of self-knowledge to care for it. Conveniently, McGee developed two key ideas—conservation and multipurpose river basin development—that positioned the forms of life of the people of the United States, aided by the American social sciences, as the managers of evolutionary abundance.

3

Managing Water for "the People"

It is in the concept of the river as a power to be controlled
by engineering projects, and at the same time as an agency
of interdependent parts, that the views of the engineer and
the geologist must meet and merge—eventually, if not today.
—WJ McGee

WJ McGee was born in a farmhouse near Farley, Iowa, in 1853. His life
has not been memorialized like Major John Wesley Powell's, in whose
shadow he worked for much of his life. There is one biography of
McGee's life, composed by his sister Emma, that includes descriptions
of his early life, education, and work, but the bulk is a selection of his
writings.[1] Another account can be found in the introduction to a recent
transcription of the field notes McGee scrawled during an 1894–1895
study of the Seri Indians.[2] Other glimpses of McGee's life come from
a memorial service held in December 1913 at the Carnegie Institution
in Washington. There, people like the anthropologist Franz Boas and
the forester Gifford Pinchot offered their candid thoughts. From the
remarks at his memorial, it seems that McGee was not lacking for confidence. Although not religious, on one occasion he was mistaken for
a clergyman and without hesitation delivered an impromptu sermon.
McGee's confidence was also reflected in his contributions to political and intellectual life in early twentieth-century America, the two
most enduring of which are conservation and multipurpose river basin
development. Ideas are not owned, but these two were arguably more
McGee's than anybody else's.[3] As this chapter shows, these two ideas had
an important influence on the Progressive Era policies forwarded under
U.S. President Theodore Roosevelt. McGee, long-suffering from cancer,
died at the Cosmos Club on September 4, 1912.

While a full biography of McGee remains to be written,[4] this chapter details how his ideas of conservation and multipurpose river basin

development were forged in the context of the closing of the western frontier, the causes of which are often tied to the rapacious, laissez-faire capitalism that was fast exhausting an evolutionary store of goods.[5] It was a time, as Carolyn Merchant argues, when the idea of the self-made man was a modern recovery of Adam for a new Garden of Eden in the United States.[6] For Merchant, the political economy of the American frontier united this self-made man to brute evolutionary competition. In her account, conservation in the Progressive Era reigned in laissez-faire capitalism and installed national planning to benefit all humanity, a shift from egocentrism to anthropocentrism.[7] Merchant's account is powerful and ambitious. Yet, in addition to being addressed to an individualist notion of the "subject" that McGee and others rejected, I detect another problem with it. Namely, Progressive Era policies in the early twentieth century were designed to benefit "the People" of the United States, not all humanity. American conservation was ethnocentric, not anthropocentric.

McGee's rejection of laissez-faire philosophies did not translate into a universalized notion of human equality. Rather, McGee extended his geologically informed anthropology to create a superstructure for science composed of "joint knowledge of nature and of knowledge itself."[8] McGee thought science could lift democracy to a higher plane of evolution, and he and Powell even had a special name for this new plane: the demotic.[9] The demotic reckoned the agency of the Earth to liberal democracy on empirical terms that, in turn, demanded an account of how evolution had churned out liberal persons whose social institutions and habits of thought made it possible to unite geological knowledge of nature and anthropological self-knowledge. McGee found his starting point in the first line of the American Constitution, which begins, "We the People of the United States." For McGee, "the People" that existed prior to, and provided the legitimating basis for, the U.S. constitutional state held the key to understanding how the social characteristics of one group had progressed to a new plane of evolution. McGee had a special penchant for writing it precisely this way—"the People"—which wound its way into his own writing and many of the speeches he wrote for President Roosevelt.[10]

McGee's notion of "the People" connected anthropology and geology through water. Following the uniformitarian maxim that the present is the key to the past, McGee interpreted "the People" of the United States as a society whose management of its most vital resource—water—was a self-referential clue to its future success. Although McGee thought that water management practices in the United States had (like the rest of evolution) evolved haphazardly, he also thought "the People" had chanced upon a key principle: that water was public property. McGee then put this accidental insight to purposeful use by uniting resource conservation and multipurpose river basin development in a program of national resource planning expressly designed to benefit "the People." For McGee, national planning was a kind of collective prevision that mirrored how individual organisms had evolved by hypothesizing based on experience. To hold all of this together—from geologic knowledge of Earth, to the self-knowledge made possible by anthropology, to the collective evolution of "the People"—McGee attempted a grand synthesis in which water was the key agent of Earth-making.

Like a braided river, McGee's grand synthesis of geology, anthropology, and water management for "the People" proceeded along several interwoven channels: First, he reformulated the liberal distinction of private and public in accordance with his view of the social subject. Second, he argued that "the People" of the United States are supported by the social agency of water itself. Here, the agency of water bridges life and non-life in a way that McGee then used to naturalize the U.S. Constitution. Third, McGee trenchantly argued for his view to become the basis for national resource planning. He advanced his ideas ardently in his role as secretary and vice chair of the Inland Waterways Commission, which has been described as the most important commission on national planning in early twentieth-century America.[11] In 1909, McGee declared water a resource in a manner that crisscrosses over geology, technology, society, and the health of both "the People" and the planet. Normal water had arrived.

The Public and the Private

In 1898, the United States defeated Spain and gained control over the Philippines, Guam, and Puerto Rico. For McGee, the acquisition of territory raised anew the question of how the material expansion of land affected habits of thought. Writing in the *National Geographic* magazine,

McGee argued American territorial expansion was good for the world because it created more space for individual enterprise.[12] But the expansion of the United States also demanded an examination of how territorial gains affected national character and the social institutions that enabled individual success. McGee's assessment was that the United States led the world in all ways save seafaring. Later, in a "sweeping geopolitical brief," McGee wrote to President Roosevelt, arguing that water projects like the Panama Canal were necessary to securing the United States as the first post-colonial power and to ensuring that American engineers would surpass their British and German counterparts.[13] Eventually, however, McGee turned from engineering saltwater passages to consider how the inland freshwaters of the continental United States should be harnessed to create the conditions that enhanced its liberal democracy.

Recall that Powell and McGee rejected John Stuart Mill's notion of purely self-regarding acts. For Powell and McGee, there are no such acts because there are no corresponding subjects to which they could appertain. In their view, to exist is to exist socially. Yet neither Powell nor McGee completely rejected Mill's liberalism. McGee, in particular, thought there was a place for Mill's view if it was viewed as a stepping-stone: Mill had identified valuable features of liberal individuals, but he hadn't considered carefully enough either their social context or their social existence in the solidarity of life. Further, McGee viewed the abundance of geological agents as part of a moral heritage that liberal societies, and the United States in particular, must now direct as part of ensuring their future success.

Michael Lacey describes the responses of Powell and McGee to Mill as a "liberal positivism" that used the positivist methods of the social sciences to understand the social conditions that produced liberal individuals.[14] In short, "liberal positivism" examined what Powell described as the processes through which "man has transferred the struggle for existence from himself to his institutions."[15] Likewise, McGee's view was that human development began with individuals but passed to the collective institutions that societies established to govern themselves and their relationships to the natural world.[16] From the perspective of liberal positivism, the aim of an enlightened society was to master the institution of property at the social level through institutions that would promote collective happiness across the evolutionary spectrum. It was not "nature-conquest" but a mastery of the subject-world relationship. For McGee, it was yet another way to weld the concept of uniformity to anthropology:

> A nation of free minds will not be selfish or cruel; and the sense of uniformity in nature finds expression in national character—in commercial honesty, in personal probity, in unparalleled patriotism, as well as in the unequaled workmanship which is the simplest expression of straight thinking. Every step in our national progress has been guided by the steadfast knowledge born of assimilated experience.[17]

In McGee's first presidential address to the Anthropological Society of Washington, he reformulated the public/private distinction in his peculiar brand of thought. He began by incorporating geology into anthropology through what he termed the five cardinal principles of science (McGee and Powell were as obsessed with fives as Peirce was with threes). The first principle was developed in Lavoisier's chemical investigations, and the second was the physics of motion. McGee seems not to have cared much about the historical succession of ideas since the third principle was Darwinian evolution and the fourth principle was Lyell's uniformitarianism. The fifth principle was the conscious organization of scientific knowledge by society. This "science of man" was McGee's vision for anthropology, and it enabled scientific thought to feed back upon evolutionary process through a principle he called the "Responsivity of Mind."[18]

The Responsivity of Mind thesis bears a striking, if warped, resemblance to American pragmatism. The idea is that there must be some test that scientists apply that gives them confidence in their results but that does not appeal to metaphysics. McGee proposes two procedures for this. The first refers the source of confidence to experience. The second is the conscious organization of experience, which he termed "mentality."[19] In McGee's argument, "mental working" is what links the gradually enhanced cognition of Earth-stuff in complex organisms to the principle of uniformity. Mental work thereby becomes the vehicle through which improved habits of thought ultimately come to inflect more highly developed societies. Furthermore, mentality accumulates through a non-linear progression of knowledge from one generation to another. This is another way that McGee accords with Powell's rejection of Hegel's view of "mind" as historical and proposes instead that the Responsivity of Mind reflects the social habituation of an individual to collective evolutionary experience. In the most advanced societies, collective experience is codified into democratic institutions.[20]

In his second presidential address to the Anthropological Society of Washington, McGee extrapolated on Thomas Huxley's *Man's Place in Nature* to detail how the principles of science fit uniformity.[21] Consistent with his own geological ideas, McGee held that Huxley confirmed that human knowledge persists from one generation to the next in a manner similar to the law of conservation of matter. There was some intellectual entropy, but there was always a great deal that the new generation learns from their ancestors, which implied every cultural group progresses through stages of knowledge accumulation. This begins with a matrilineal form of savagery before progress is made to a patrilineal stage of barbarism. A third stage emerges when societies become organized based on laws of property. Finally, enlightenment is reached when laws are based on "the right of the individual to life, liberty and the pursuit of happiness." For McGee, the culmination of human progress in the language of the American Constitution had a scientific basis that was revealed through American anthropology. The ability to master property, in McGee's view, depended on the geologically infused anthropology that solved the "land problem" through a systematic classification of geologic action that could marshal the "assimilated knowledge" of American experience into alignment with the agency of the Earth. McGee thought this version of enlightenment, grounded in geology, was made possible through the American experience of overcoming colonization.

McGee stitched this view together by arguing that since Francis Bacon modern science had become stuck on the idea of scientific mastery, or "nature-conquest." Scientific mastery, however, was limited because it fixated on the control and manipulation of variables and ultimately only offered an account of man as the "highest animal."[22] But with the advent of colonization, scientific mastery must now be positioned with respect to "world conquest" that "served to raise thought concerning mankind to a new plane."[23] Following Powell, McGee thought that this new plane was psychic—having to do with habits of thought that affected the "disposition of daily conduct" of social individuals.[24] It was not the "manipulation of variables" that produced enlightenment but the conscious, synthetic organization of knowledge. For it was the power of thought to raise social organization into the complex form of the post-colonial nation-state that demonstrated not only scientific mastery but also the mastery of society's evolutionary conditions.

The new American geology, and the social sciences that accorded with it, allowed for "world-conquest" through the mastery of the conditions of cultural life. Of course, these new disciplines and the knowledge they produced had the added benefit of placing "the People" of the United States at the helm of evolution. Politically, "world-conquest" also rebutted Mill's argument that colonies could hardly be considered countries and were properly understood as the hinterlands for the established political community of the colonizers.[25] In an important sense, then, McGee's notion of "world-conquest" extends hypothetical reasoning in geology (discussed in the last chapter) to the democratic testing of ideas in liberal societies. Here, "nature-conquest" is supplanted by a form of "world-conquest" that is grounded in the new kinds of knowledge produced by, and tested within, the post-colonial condition. Furthermore, the evidence for this superiority is not found in Mill's nominalist metaphysics but in the actual social institutions of the United States.

McGee knew his view was at odds with other anthropologists, especially Franz Boas, who did not believe in evolutionary stages of development and did not base explanations for how individuals or groups interacted with their environment in the principle of uniformity. In fact, McGee and Boas worked together to form the American Anthropological Association. In 1901, Boas had distinguished between mental processes and materials of thought, a position that opened the way to cultural relativism in anthropological research.[26] Their disagreement created a fissure in early American anthropology that was never bridged. Even at McGee's memorial service Boas could not hold back from denouncing his views as too deductive.[27] In this, Boas was right; McGee deductively coordinated everything under uniformitarianism. That is why he could not abide the claims of Boas that there was a distinction between mental processes, which may be common across cultural groups, and the materials with which humans thought. For

McGee, this would reopen the door to metaphysics by suggesting the possibility of private cultures whose different "materials of thought" needn't conform to evolutionary accounts of social development. Perhaps more critically, Boas's view suggested that science itself could be rendered in cultural, rather than evolutionary, terms based on its own materials of thought.

In the wake of his controversy with Boas, the intellectual tide began receding on McGee. His tenure as president of the Anthropological Society of Washington ended in 1901. Powell passed away the next year, and McGee was passed over as director of the Bureau of American Ethnology after mismanaging funds and not showing diligent care with valuable documents during his decade as director-in-charge.[28] His term as president of the American Anthropological Association ended in 1904, and, looking for his next assignment, McGee took a position as director of the Anthropology Department of the St. Louis World's Fair and moved to Missouri.

In 1905, McGee became the director of the St. Louis Public Museum. The following year he attended the Deep Waterways Conference in St. Louis, where people were organizing to get support for an inland, deep-water port. While attending the conference it dawned upon McGee, "as in the sudden sunrise of the desert," that the full development of water was a uniquely federal task.[29] In national water planning, McGee saw the possibility for linking geology and anthropology in a way that could not be relativized through the "materials of thought" because water was universally necessary. In water, McGee would also solve the "land problem" and move U.S. institutions beyond the colonial shackles of "nature-conquest" and firmly into a new phase of "world-conquest." It was a grand vision, and McGee wrote to President Theodore Roosevelt recommending the creation of a federal planning program. Never lacking for confidence, McGee sent Roosevelt not one letter, but two. The second only required the president's signature to invite McGee back to Washington to get started.[30] Roosevelt agreed to the proposal, so McGee resigned from his position in St. Louis and became the expert in charge of soil water in the U.S. Department of Agriculture. In 1907, Roosevelt created the Inland Waterways Commission. At its first meeting, McGee was elected secretary and vice chair; positions he held alongside his post at the Department of Agriculture until his death.

Social Water

When McGee returned to Washington he set to work articulating his vision of conservation, which explicitly relied on water as the premiere agent in Earth-making and, consequently, as vital to the progress of "the People." Even more than this, the profound role of water in shaping planetary evolution meant that, for McGee, it was through the social nature of water that social subjects accorded with the principle of uniformity. The upshot of harnessing social waters through the social institutions of "the People" was that McGee thought America had progressed to a new evolutionary stage beyond European civilization because the mastery of water was, in fact, mastery of evolutionary abundance. This new stage was enlightenment. Of course, McGee knew that American institutions had evolved under European influence, but he also thought the liberal democracy in the United States could now surpass them. As such, managing evolutionary abundance was a material and symbolic fulfillment of Jean-Jacques Rousseau's claim that, "with liberty, wherever abundance reigns, well-being also reigns."[31]

As the epigraph to this chapter suggests, McGee envisioned a future in which geology and engineering merged in conscious recognition of water's interdependent agency.[32] This merger put a heavy burden on American water management, and McGee took a dual strategy that began with the idea of resource conservation and was enacted through multipurpose river basin development.[33] His contemporary and counterpart at the U.S. Forest Service, Gifford Pinchot, credited McGee as the "scientific brains of the conservation movement all through its early and critical stages."[34] McGee's vision shaped the agenda of the Inland Waterways Commission, which coordinated planning among the Bureau of Soils, the Forest Service, the Reclamation Service, the Bureau of Corporations, and the Army Corps of Engineers.[35] As secretary and vice chair, McGee had considerable reach and was described as "the trusted and effective adviser in every branch of the Commission's work."[36] One of the recommendations in the Inland Waterway Commission's preliminary report to the U.S. Congress was to nationally coordinate resource conservation and to thereby improve upon the water development models of Germany, France, Austria-Hungary, Holland, and Britain.[37] For his part, McGee became a driving force behind a 1908 conference to develop a unified vision for resource conservation in the United States. The conference was no small affair. The entire 60th Congress attended, as did justices of the U.S. Supreme Court and the president. It was the first time all three branches of the U.S. government were in the same room to discuss national resource planning. Scientists and social scientists were there, too, as were virtually all state and territorial governors. Some fifty thousand copies of the conference proceedings were distributed, and, as recording secretary, McGee shaped much of the message.[38]

The 1908 conference led to the creation of the National Conservation Commission (chaired by Gifford Pinchot) and to the National Waterways Commission, both of which inspired McGee to further articulate his vision. Although conservation affected forestry, agriculture, and energy, it was water that sewed the concept of conservation to a broader philosophical basis. Through water, McGee built his evolutionary arguments into the moral and material basis for national resource planning. But he refused to reduce water to an abstract unit on the latter half of a dualism of society and nature. Quite the opposite: For McGee, water was the planetary agent that provided the evolutionary conditions for the U.S. state and supported its ability to master property relations and, thereby, to escape the shackles of colonial thought once and for all. Furthermore, the extension of geology to anthropology made it possible to design social institutions for resource planning that could guide and direct evolutionary abundance for social progress. McGee's writings at this time show how his vision was articulated as the basis for a tradition of resource conservation that had immense impact on national planning in the United States and, later, international development.

In his 1908 article, "Outlines of Hydrology," McGee situates water's agency within geology. He even describes water as the "mineral" that forms the hydrosphere and, as such, takes up a key role in shaping the planet:

> Viewed as a whole the hydrosphere takes on a significant, or at least suggestive, character which may be likened to the automacy [sic] . . . of the organic world and the autonomy of the human world—it assumes a semblance of self-activity in its changes of state and movements in space which tends to facilitate its own working and perpetuate its own efficiency as a planet-shaping agency, for example, in that its presence

is necessary to the temperature of the planet which in turn regulates its changes and movements.[39]

Once positioned within the hydrosphere's planet-shaping agency, McGee builds an account of hydrology that links water to society through Earth-making. He starts by arguing that, "as part of the hydrosphere, the stream exists and moves; as an agency, it works; as a worker, it modifies its environment and itself."[40] The agentive work of the stream, argues McGee, reflects a "continuous adjustment" between the chaotic internal movements of water and the external relations it has to other forces, such as geology and organic life. In this sense, water's agency is a vital source for, and active force upon, the landscapes that enable life itself. Water, although a social object like any other, is also the condition for the relations of life in general. For instance, McGee writes that water is

in its movement and changes of state the leading external agency of earth-making, it first brought forth and then gave form to the continents; and the organisms developed within it to reach higher estate on land depend on it both for the chief part of their substances and for all their vital processes. A growing and living world without water is unthinkable.[41]

McGee's focus on water's agency does not of itself defeat the claim that he was a reductionist, where water was only H_2O. To defeat that claim, we must see how McGee characterized the dynamics of water's behavior. It is here that McGee offers one of the first attempts to synthesize hydrology and hydrodynamics, and he did so in a way that fit his commitments to vitalism and motility. Synthesizing hydrology and hydrodynamics was no small aim, especially because throughout the nineteenth century the scientific and mathematical developments in hydrodynamics were often in tension with practical advances in hydrology.[42] However, as the epigraph reveals, McGee thought it essential to link a geological account of water's agency to hydrological engineering. This had long been a concern for McGee, who wrote as early as 1891 that American approaches to flood control had yet to account for the room that rivers demanded.[43] At that time, U.S. flood control proceeded largely on hydrographic surveys made by French geologist Joseph Nicollet in 1843.[44]

In McGee's understanding of the New Geology, simply mapping water's geography was not enough. Rather, water's behavior needed to be synced with the coevolution of American society and the mutual adjustments that water and society made to the actions of each other. For him, this link came through a social notion of "water modules." McGee held that "the discrete particle involved in stream movement can not be a single molecule" because this would not allow water to have sufficient magnitude to undergo changes of state, to have adequate surface tension, or to exhibit the behaviors it does.[45] In this sense, H_2O was a social unit. As he stated,

> Since the unit so conceived is the ultimate quantity of H_2O capable of functioning in the characteristic ways and is at the same time the prime determinant of the rhythmic movement of H_2O in masses, it is the natural measure and modulator of moving water and can hardly be denoted otherwise than as the *module* of H_2O.[46]

McGee did not hold a reductionist view of water, but before considering how McGee fit "water modules" to society, it is important to highlight three things. First, McGee's view was that water had agency across all aspects of the hydrosphere. Second, McGee sought a union between geology and engineering as a means to understanding water's behavior. Finally, I am not presenting this evidence to support of McGee's views. In many ways, he was profoundly misguided. Nevertheless, it is important to consider how, in the U.S. case, water management was understood as an issue of social policy. The next section argues that McGee's notion of water's agency, and the way it functioned as a basis for conservation, are critical to understanding how water management fit with liberal democracy in the United States.

Water and the Natural Nation

In 1909, McGee published an essay that declared water a resource.[47] Together with a 1911 article on "Principles of Water-Power Development," the declaration of water as a resource allowed McGee to render water within social space and in accordance with the nation-state.[48] On one hand, water's social and planetary agency created social space for all geological agents while, on the other, the conscious organization of relations to water by "the People" directed evolutionary abundance. For McGee, water management was evidence of a confluence of internal and external relations in the "solidarity of life." That is, societies whose habits of thought enabled them to master the institutions of property for the common good of "the People" were precisely those who saw that mastering water was the solution to the "land problem." It was through water—not land—that human and Earth agency could be combined. By linking water's agency to the knowledge and know-how of enlightened societies, McGee hoped to engineer the conditions for liberal abundance. It is not exaggerating to say that, in his attempt at a grand synthesis, McGee's ultimate aim was to naturalize the U.S. Constitution and to thereby secure it to a scientific basis that would conserve natural resources for posterity.

McGee's 1909 and 1911 essays have features typically identified as "modern." The 1909 declaration of water as a resource provides a national inventory of water, shows how an economic valuation of water can lead to increased efficiency and productivity, and compels the reader to view water, qua resource, as a wholly owned subsidiary of progress. The 1911 essay views water resources as part of an evolutionary heritage of the United States, replete with legal and ethical norms that are themselves justified by virtue of the unique characteristics of "the People" and their institutions. These essays provide a glimpse into McGee's reasoning during his work at the Inland Waterways Commission, a period in which his publication on potable waters in the eastern United States "was in great demand and undoubtedly had a wide influence on the development of water supplies and in guarding them from pollution."[49]

The connection McGee forged between his vision of social water and of "the People" begins with a critique of state rationality, particularly the water-blind U.S. Constitution. In McGee's view, nothing could be more vital than water, yet it appeared nowhere in the American Constitution. This reinforced his view that it was evolutionary luck that institutions of public water ownership had evolved in the United States. An enlightened view, by contrast, would direct this evolutionary good fortune to establish water as the basis of individual life and the social relations of the constitutional state. Here, McGee sought to naturalize the liberal tradition that, following John Locke, established an individual's inalienable property in their person.[50] Applying his view of individuals as social subjects, McGee argued that no individual could alienate the right to water without harming the conditions that allowed "the People" to prosper:

> As the prime necessary of life—the ultimate basis of existence for each of the individuals united in the nation—the water of the country is, under that leading principle of our national existence that all men are equally entitled to life, liberty and the pursuit of happiness, the common and indivisible possession of all—a possession in equity inalienable and indefeasible since no constituent of the nation could alienate or divest himself of his share without surrendering his right to life and so weakening the nation.[51]

McGee solidified the link of water to "the People" through empirical evidence of U.S. institutions, especially the 1908 judgment of the Supreme Court justice Oliver Wendell Holmes, Jr., in *Hudson Water Co. v. McCarter*. In McGee's assessment, Holmes's ruling provided a template for linking the history of American institutions to his own evolutionary account of resource conservation. Holmes's judgment was also evidence of how U.S. institutions (e.g., the Supreme Court) were evolving to codify the chance outcome of social relationships into public water ownership that supported "the People." Moreover, the judgment of the court was, for McGee, a moment of public self-reflection: a conscious recognition that evolutionary chance had produced a principle of public water ownership. McGee found all of this in Holmes's judgment, which affirmed the public ownership of water based on the structure of American federalism. This structure did not mirror the center-periphery model of British colonialism but rather affirmed that each state in the union was part of a national community. This judgment was made all the more palatable for McGee, no doubt, by Holmes's 1905 affirmation that Herbert Spencer's views were not supported by the American Constitution.[52] As such,

> The people of the state collectively have a residuary right in the intrastate waters . . . a manifestly valid doctrine which requires nothing but application in other states with respect to their intrastate waters, and extension

to the concomitant federal authority over interstate waters in their nature as navigable streams or as sources of such streams, to work a great public benefit.[53]

For McGee, the "ultimate basis" for national wealth and individual welfare was provided for by water. In one essay he classified "desert thirst" as a disease.[54] So adamant was McGee on using water as the ultimate basis for value that he even calculated how to replace the gold standard for American currency with water. McGee's calculation was fairly clever. He summed the total value of all U.S. property in dollars. Then he took that dollar value and applied it to the total of all U.S. water as measured by acre-foot (the amount of water required to cover an acre of land with a foot of water). Since the hydrological cycle varies from year to year, McGee used the seven-year average of surface runoff. Each acre-foot of water could then be given a monetary value based on the gold standard's relationship to property values. Now as valuable as gold, water could provide a material basis for naturalized economic institutions. As he reckoned, this put "the value of the water reserve . . . at $150,000,000,000 in gross, *i.e.* $3 per acre-foot."[55]

McGee's attempt to employ water as the U.S. currency standard may have been a response to the doctrines of the Yale economist Irving Fisher, who Roosevelt had also appointed to the newly created conservation commission in 1908.[56] Roosevelt had asked Fisher to prepare a report on the "conservation of human life," and Fisher later made recommendations on the economic value of a federal public-health service.[57] Fisher was enamored with using mathematics and statistics to make economic calculations abstractly. But abstract calculations were only half of the equation that McGee thought necessary to unite mental processes with the "materials of thought." For McGee, the other half of mastering the property relationship required a shared material basis for the characteristics of the community that gave legitimacy to the U.S. state, which he found in water. Geology met anthropology precisely in the social nature of both water and liberal society. As a result, the ownership of water inhered in the rights of any and all individuals that were party to "the People" who established America by constitution.

Throughout his 1911 essay, McGee insists that water is a community resource that should be governed in the public interest. In just fourteen pages, he uses the term "public" no fewer than twenty-two times and references water to the common good not less than ten times. His vision troubles accounts of high modernism that argue state rationality or idealized norms about "populations" are the basis for U.S. water planning. For McGee, the task of water management is to maintain and, where possible, to enhance the conditions that make it possible for the characteristics of the American people to evolve. To do so, McGee reformulates liberalism in evolutionary terms and in line with the example set by "the People." And this reformulation of liberalism leads to a reformulation of utilitarian ethics in geological terms in which water is to be managed in the "public interest in accordance with the righteous principles of the greatest good to the greatest number for the longest time."[58]

Gifford Pinchot later acknowledged that McGee convinced him of the need to extend utilitarianism to natural resource planning in general. In his role as the chair of Roosevelt's conservation commission, Pinchot entrenched this geological extension of utilitarianism *for the longest time* in Progressive Era policies and, as first chief of the U.S. Forest Service, in American approaches to forest management.[59] It is difficult to say, but McGee's description of this extended utilitarianism as "righteous" may well have been done to appease Roosevelt's religious beliefs.[60] Whatever the rationale, the result of extending utilitarianism was to position American liberalism in a register in which managing the abundance of geological agency was central to conserving natural resources and maximizing the utility derived from them.

To appreciate the consistency of McGee's view, it is worth tracing it out in a bit more detail. Recall that McGee's view was that modular units of water provided the building block for seeing river systems as complex units in which multiple agents mutually adjusted to one another. In this way, the river basin became the preferred unit for planning because it reflected the coevolution of multiple human and non-human agents and relations among them. This was the case because river basins were the geological units that directed water flows. Since social relationships between humans and water, and between water and everything else, were what supported social progress, institutions should be designed so as to reflect this natural accord. In this, McGee reflected Powell's vision of direct democracy on a basin-by-basin basis.[61]

Far from ignoring the coevolving landscape between 'the People"
and U.S. territory, McGee held that previous efforts to design American institutions were precisely those that needed to be positioned in a
geological register. From this position, McGee mercilessly criticized the
American Constitution because it was founded without regard for water.
For instance, the "Proceedings of the Anthropological Society of Washington" on October 12, 1909, record a paper entitled "Conservation in
the Human Realm," presented by McGee. The summary of that paper as
found in the minutes for the meeting are as follows:

> At first water was neglected as a mere appurtenance to land; and now that
> it is recognized as the primary resource—that on which all life depends,
> so that it gives value to all the rest—it also is passing under a monopolistic
> control whereby all citizenship will tend to merge into industrial depen-
> dence on centralized power. The situation is one of the gravest ever con-
> fronted by any people in the world's history, graver than any ever survived
> by a nation; and it behooves those possessing the advantage of scientific
> training and knowledge of principles to give it earnest consideration—
> and to aid in defining the interrelated duties of the individual, the fam-
> ily and the state in ways tending toward the perpetuity of our people. A
> lengthy discussion of this paper closed the meeting.[62]

The notion that water was a "mere appurtenance to land" was, for
McGee, as it had been for Powell, a misguided basis for statecraft. But
McGee pushes this line farther, arguing that the exclusion of water from
the political geography of the state was mistaken because water was the
primary geologic and social agent of development. As such, an individual's right to water ought to be reflected in the constitution because water
provides the conditions for the community constituting "the People" of
the U.S. state. Moreover, the incorporation of water, as public property,
into state institutions provided a solution to the "land problem" and secured the post-colonial step to enlightenment by aligning a chance evolutionary principle into purposeful policy. Conservation, therefore, was
part of capitalizing on the moral luck of "the People" to overcome the
laissez-faire metaphysics of extractive capitalism. Managing water managed chance and provided a basis upon which to direct evolution. For
McGee, four key principles grounded conservation such that it could

keep the as-of-yet unfulfilled promise of fraternity under the American Constitution. These, as he enumerated in an essay on "The Conservation of Natural Resources" were

1. The equal rights of all men to opportunity.
2. The equal rights of the People in and to resources rendered valuable by their own natural growth and orderly development.
3. The equal rights of present and future generations in and to the resources of the country.
4. The equal rights of citizens to provide for the perpetuity of families and States and the Union of States.[63]

Securing individual rights to water in a water-aware state focused McGee's conservation ideas on the laissez-faire resource economics of the nineteenth century.[64] As the earlier quote summarizing his paper to the Anthropological Society suggested, McGee saw corporate, industrialized control of water as the gravest threat ever confronted by any nation. For McGee, consolidating water within institutions of collective and public ownership was a safeguard against economic exploitation. This helps to make sense of how liberal U.S. institutions fit with McGee's scientific positivism. The latter gave a scientific account of the social interactions that had produced liberal individuals and provided a geological rationale for resource management by showing how America had happened upon a new plane of evolutionary development *despite* the lack of mastery over property. Since there was no guarantee that this chance outcome wouldn't be overrun by colonial monopolies or powerful corporate interests, McGee held that evolutionary progress required nothing less than naturalizing the U.S. Constitution.

Following Lester Ward and Major Powell, McGee sought a new kind of civic republicanism based on the idea that the role of government was to create and enhance the conditions for individual success.[65] In so doing, he followed a distinction that Powell had made between major and minor regulations, which were reformulations of liberal distinctions of the public and the private but within the intersubjective register of Powell's institutional views of sociology.[66] Therein, no strong divide between "public" and "private" existed in the classic liberal sense dividing the "man" from the "person" because even habits of thoughts and belief were socially transmitted. Working with this distinction, McGee claimed that it was necessary to rethink the relationship of citizen and state when it came to the material basis for the health of the nation.[67] It was water conservation, McGee argued, that was awakening "the People" to a new sense of their shared social existence and collective interdependence. This awakening had already started to cultivate a new kind of civic engagement, in his view, for which both the 1908 conference of the governors and the earlier St. Louis Lakes-to-the-Gulf Deep Waterway Association provided evidence. Conservation merely named the awakening of a society whose characteristics and institutions national resource planning served.

McGee described the new "Cult of Conservation" as providing a sure empirical footing for the American people. Conservation would rectify the "legislative ineptitude and administrative apathy" inaugurated when the founding fathers referenced the American Constitution only to land and ignored water. Under conservation there were four material foundations for coordinating the nation: land, forests, minerals, and finally,

> Water is coming within ken as the basis of prime value on which all others must depend, and as an inalienable birthright of the People—a common heritage for the common interest, to be administered by Nation and States jointly as befits its interstate character, but never to be withdrawn or withheld from direct control by citizens for their own common good.[68]

Managing Abundance

If we bring these streams of thought together, we can see how McGee's view regarding the mastery of property gets reformulated by first seeing water as a social object and then interpreting the U.S. experience as evidence for consciously directing water to social ends. It was the match of modular units of water to social subjects that ensured the health of individuals and the nation. Since McGee's view of water's agency is overwhelmingly dominated by metaphors based on the actions of streams (i.e., not of the ocean), it is not surprising that the river basin became the preferred unit for ensuring that individual development and national security are secured as part of a mutual adjustment of institutions and the environment. As the Lakes-to-the-Gulf Deep Waterway Association submitted to McGee's memorial:

He regarded a river system as a unit from source streams to the sea; and that its problems should be treated as a whole, so as to develop in one solution all the collateral utilities—not only regularity in flow and fixation of beds and banks, but also reclamation, waterpower, and sanitation.[69]

McGee's vision of conservation was designed to work hand in glove with multipurpose river basin development to enhance the evolutionary prospects of "the People." Rivers required development, in McGee's view, because their vital relationships had evolved in haphazard fashion. Yet rivers could not simply be harnessed and directed for single ends, such as flood control, because the evidence of evolution pointed to a different fact: namely, that providing an abundance of opportunity for liberal individuals was the surest path to enlightenment. From McGee's geological perspective, caring for an aging mother Earth required organizing the planet's vital water resources to ensure that enterprising individuals would continue to build the social institutions—ultimately the world—that linked people and planet in purposeful progress. Fully developing the nation's waterways would link commerce, agriculture, and industry as a means to taking up and securing this evolutionary project.[70] Although his vision was not fulfilled in his own lifetime, McGee nevertheless provided foundational ideas that, as later chapters consider, were cemented—quite literally, in the case of dams—in water management practices linking resource conservation to multipurpose river basin development.

McGee's vision of linking social water to social subjects was not premised on an idealized "population," as suggested by high modernism. Rather, he enrolls the characteristics of 'the People" as warrant for further enhancing the prospects of their own forms of life. McGee's view is remarkably tidy: Geology evolves through American insight, which is then extended to the American social sciences. Then American social sciences show how "the People" have evolved the scientific, legal, and institutional bases for rendering water a resource that, when conserved and fully developed, can direct and enhance geological processes. Yet in affixing on "the People," McGee's anthropological gaze is thoroughly ethnocentric in its dismissal of alternate forms of life, such as those of North American indigenous societies. The most striking example of this is that, after his laudatory remarks regarding Holmes's decision regarding public rights to water, McGee is completely silent on Holmes's support for the 1908 decision in *Winters v. the United States*, in which the U.S. Supreme Court acknowledged a prior right to water for indigenous peoples.[71] For McGee, the U.S. case was not an idealized example that found justification in social or natural laws, nor was it justified by abstract ideals of rationality. Rather, it was an empirical case based on conclusions deduced from a strange brew of uniformity across social water, geologic agency, and anthropological explanation. From all of this, McGee distilled a general formula for governing water that anticipates ideas of harmony and subsidiarity in water governance that are made explicit in global water governance a century later. As he wrote,

> It follows that the inherently progressive development in the use of water attending the natural growth and orderly development of the people can best be fostered by combining individual and institutional agency in the highest practicable degree—*i.e.*, by effective cooperation among individuals and both business and civic organizations, including corporations, communities, municipalities, states and federal agencies.[72]

McGee's governance schema was derived in reference to his account of water as a social object that belonged to "the People." He may be one of the best exemplars of what Charles Taylor terms the "modern social imaginary," in which a pre-political "people" are imagined as the basis for the moral and material legitimacy of the constitutional state.[73] McGee, in fact, is adamant on this point and once stated that with the constitutional utterance of "We, the people of the United States" the ages of mysticism gave way to a humane foundation for government.[74] This persistent orientation to the American experience laid the foundation for normal water. Through McGee's influence, water became an object upon which geologic, social, and technopolitical arguments could crisscross in ways that would remove it from the domain of metaphysics and secure it to the health of individuals, the state, and the planet. That is, water became a resource. By solving the "land problem" through water, McGee believed American society was lifted to a new plane of enlightenment. Indeed, McGee thought that this new evolutionary stage created a burden for the evolutionary "strong man" who must engage in a different kind of colonialism—on an evolutionary plane beyond the white man's burden—in which the aim was "world-conquest" in which other races were no less human but nevertheless needed to be guided, educated, and even policed into the next stage of progress.[75]

McGee's view culminates in the language of the constitutional state. It was water that gave value to everything else and explained why the bonds of fraternity were greatest in the United States.[76] It is precisely this type of language that has been remarked upon by political theorists for how it requires alternate forms of life—which would be found only at "lower" stages of development in McGee's view—to conform to the language of the state as a condition for recognition. This view is, in a word, monological. It is also, in another, inaccurate. Particularly so in the United States, where subsuming the experience of "the People" under a dominant cultural norm does not reflect the dialogic treaties or agreements reached (although less often respected) with indigenous peoples regarding land, property, or water.[77] Rather, and given McGee's certain knowledge of cases regarding indigenous land and water rights, the ideas of conservation and of water resources management provided cover for dispossession.

McGee linked conservation to multipurpose river basin development, notably in the Inland Waterways Commission.[78] He connected both to social progress, which later became commonplace in water management and in the connection between conservation and international development. So persistent has this influence become that the evolutionary extension of utilitarianism guided U.S. water policy for a century, while McGee's arguments regarding future generations—the equal rights of present and future generations in and to the resources of the country—received almost verbatim recitation in 1987 under the guise of sustainable development.[79] Of course, antecedent concepts of sustainability were not only McGee's, yet his vision of liberalism linked resource conservation to water development that served the collective fate of nations, not of individuals alone. It was on this new plane of evolution that the United States had reached "the demotic" by reckoning the agency of the Earth to liberal democracy. America, as the first post-colonial state, had cleared a path for evolution writ large. As such, the project of normal water made water public everywhere it traveled. This required weathering a battery of objections regarding which society water management enhanced when, later, normal water was enrolled in the project of international development.

PART II

Scarcity

4

America's Post-colonial Model of Development

An American democracy can serve the world only as it dem-
onstrates in the conduct of its own life the efficacy of plural,
partial, and experimental methods in securing and maintaining an ever-increasing release of the powers of human
nature, in service of a freedom which is co-operative and a
co-operation which is voluntary.
—John Dewey

I have tried in these pages to express my confidence that
in tested principles of democracy we have ready at hand a
philosophy and a set of working tools that, adapted to this
machine age, can guide and sustain us in increasing opportunity for individual freedom and well-being.
—David Lilienthal

For some American historians, John Wesley Powell's idea of dividing
the American west into watershed-based constituencies lingers as a
kind of forgotten wisdom.[1] History has been less kind to WJ McGee.
His attempt to naturalize the U.S. Constitution through water management is all but forgotten. Even where the ideas of Powell and McGee
are cited, they are rarely (if ever) connected to the broader philosophy
of Earth-making that took shape among members of the Cosmos Club.
Forgetting this philosophy started early. By 1920, the enabling legislation for the Inland Waterways Commission was repealed while, under
new federal administration, comprehensive resource management in the
United States largely went dormant, a dynamic reinforced by political
rivalries among federal agencies, such as the Bureau of Reclamation and
the U.S. Army Corps of Engineers.[2] Obituaries of America's Progressive
Era often identify the lack of a clear political ideology for conservation
or its faith in resource efficiency as causes for its demise.[3] Yet, as I am

arguing in this book, the progeny of Powell and McGee's philosophy—conservation and multipurpose river basin development—lived on and remained effective, not as ends in themselves, but as means for connecting contingent geological and social forces to American democracy.

This chapter argues that the ideas of Powell and McGee persisted (in revised fashion) into later iterations of American liberalism. Politically, conservation was never totally forgotten and, because it provided rationale for government interventions into economic planning, it offered historical precedent for dealing with later crises. In 1921, for instance, the benefits of comprehensive water management led Henry Ford to seek federal funds for hydropower to run his factories.[4] Ford planned to create a "new Eden" using the Wilson Dam site near Muscle Shoals, Alabama, which was initially designed during World War I for the war effort. For political reasons, Ford's plan was unsuccessful, and the dam wasn't completed until 1924. However, when comprehensive water management returned triumphantly in 1933 under the New Deal, the Wilson Dam site was incorporated into the newly formed Tennessee Valley Authority (TVA).[5] The TVA, especially under its second director David Lilienthal, rekindled the philosophy of water management in more politically savvy, but only slightly less hyperbolic, terms than the New Organon. In Lilienthal's words, "The TVA is probably the best known single demonstration of modern American democracy."[6] As the epigraph from Lilienthal suggests, the TVA forged the links among democracy, engineering, and the Earth that Powell and McGee foresaw but did not achieve.[7]

The ideas of Powell and McGee also persisted as water managers retold the story about the national characteristics of "the People" in geopolitical terms. Drawing on American pragmatists like John Dewey, these retellings added to the claim that there are no metaphysical subjects a second idea: that there are no unique "People" for whom Earth's water should be managed. The exit from colonialism taken by Powell and McGee proved only a first step because, although it addressed America's external relationships to European influences, it did not confront colonialism's domestic remnants, such as the inequality between America's industrial centers and its resource hinterlands. Lilienthal proposed a second step that positioned normal water at the base of a global project in international development that was modeled on America's claims about its own successful domestic development beyond colonialism. His argument was that the promise of liberal democracy was global precisely because the characteristics of the American people were not unique. What Americans had chanced upon was a universal method for progress. Drawing inspiration from Dewey, and as the epigraph suggests, America's democratic water management methods were what mattered for moving into the post-colonial era.[8]

This chapter does not retell the TVA's history or detail how American expertise was exported internationally, yet both feature in its argument regarding how water's abundance became linked to claims that water was becoming scarce. Ultimately, the TVA provides the model that buries abundance. I mean this literally: many possible avenues for evolutionary abundance are now buried under the reservoirs held by the large dams needed to support, and in many ways to prove, liberal democracy. When the TVA became the model for international development, more of evolution's potential abundance was buried as water behind dams was released in accordance with liberal management norms. Other dams were built at a voracious pace to prove the worth of other systems, like communism. To compete, the TVA also had to bury abundance culturally by using its water management methods to ensure water was not managed to support competing forms of life. This produced a peculiar American response to post-colonialism after World War II, a time when the TVA became the model for international development. Explaining how abundance was buried and how water scarcity arose continues into the next chapter. Here the aim is to show how normal water shifts into a geopolitical register that naturalizes water resources to a new iteration of American liberalism that claims to rectify the residual, spatial inequalities of colonialism through regional water development.

The TVA: The March from Uniformitarianism to Unity

The creation and form of the Tennessee Valley Authority resulted from several factors: an economic depression that began in 1929, controversy over what to do with the plant at Muscle Shoals, the New Deal era of federal economic interventions in America, efforts in "grassroots" democracy, and political battles among federal and state governments over flood control, agriculture, power, navigation, and forestry.[9] These factors and others, such as controlling malaria, contributed to the design of the TVA. On its face, the TVA appears to fit the "high modernism" of state-led projects.[10] But the TVA also affected what counts as modern, especially as it reformulated American conservation and multipurpose river basin development. The TVA was not the expression of a pre-formed institutional vision or of an overarching program of modern rationality. Rather, the TVA took shape through contests over how (sometimes if) it served American democracy, foreign policy, and the free market.[11] A key figure in these contests was David Lilienthal, the TVA's second director.

Lilienthal was a TVA booster if ever there was one. He studied law at Harvard under Felix Frankfurter—who later advised president Franklin D. Roosevelt on New Deal policies—and counted the pragmatist and U.S. Supreme Court Justice Oliver Wendell Holmes among his mentors. On Frankfurter's endorsement, Donald Richberg hired Lilienthal to work at his Chicago law firm. In Chicago, Lilienthal helped to draft the Railway Labor Act in 1926, which gave railway workers the right to be represented by their own organizations. In 1931, Lilienthal agreed to chair the Wisconsin Public Utilities Commission, where he was widely regarded as a success. In 1933, he was invited by Franklin D. Roosevelt to sit on the advisory board of the newly created TVA. Just thirty-four years old, Lilienthal was put in charge of power policy alongside the president of the University of Tennessee and agricultural expert Harcourt Morgan and the TVA's lead engineer and first director Arthur Morgan.[12] Lilienthal served at the TVA until becoming chair of the Atomic Energy Commission and later testified in the hearings of Robert Oppenheimer.[13] After leaving public life in 1950, Lilienthal traveled the world as a consultant and even coined the term "multinational corporation" in his 1953 book on the new global era of "big business."[14]

When Lilienthal left public service to establish his own private firm, he used his political connections to forward TVA-style water management as a solution to international development challenges. According to his biographer Steven Neuse, later in his career Lilienthal was willingly instrumentalized by President Lyndon Johnson to support the Vietnam War because he thought it a precursor for TVA-style development.[15] Trained as a boxer, Lilienthal doggedly advanced his ideas regarding the TVA, often in the face of considerable criticism. In fact, only months into his 1933 appointment he came under fire from a senior republican, Wendell Willkie. Willkie was a left-leaning Republican, but even he thought the TVA was too socialist.[16] Lilienthal first met Willkie in a ring deemed neutral ground: the Cosmos Club.[17]

Lilienthal and the TVA

After Lilienthal was appointed to the TVA's board of directors in 1933, it did not take long for conflict to arise. The animosity between Lilienthal and Arthur Morgan was particularly intense. Morgan differed with Lilienthal over how the TVA fit with American liberalism and human values more broadly. Later in his career, Morgan described his view as more fully capturing the philosophical impetus Roosevelt spoke of when he said the TVA "touches and gives life to all forms of human concerns."[18] For Morgan, this meant the TVA should use water management to bring a suite of cultural changes regarding social and moral order. To this end, Morgan used his position as director to create model communities for TVA employees, with specific educational curricula in schools and libraries that the TVA also ran. These were far from perfect and often reinforced racial divides. Nevertheless, the TVA became a showcase for foreign observers, from India's Prime Minister Jawaharlal Nehru to the French philosopher Jean-Paul Sartre.[19]

As lead engineer, Morgan significantly shaped the TVA in its formative stages, but he was not long at the helm. Just five years into his tenure as director Morgan was fired by the president after having accused Lilienthal of wrongdoing without furnishing adequate proof. Lilienthal was subsequently named the TVA director and his vision came to dominate its institutional culture and international reputation. In his view, the TVA was a showcase for how resource conservation through regional development worked for public benefit.[20] Lilienthal also forwarded his vision of the TVA with a sense of history. In his book, *TVA: Democracy on the March*, he frequently referenced conservation's early figures, such as Theodore Roosevelt and Gifford Pinchot.[21] Oddly, McGee is nowhere mentioned. But if McGee could have read Lilienthal's book, he would have nodded along enthusiastically, given its emphasis on the moral imperative of viewing the river basin as a unit, identifying the common heritage and destiny that society shares with water, and inaugurating a fundamental change in resource management that "begins . . . at the beginning, *in the minds of men*, in the way men think and, so thinking, act."[22] Further, Lilienthal in many ways fulfilled McGee's aspirations to link the agency of water to engineering. In one of Lilienthal's grander flourishes, he detailed the great cycle of intertwined movement that takes shape as water runs from rills and rivulets to rivers and then into the huge steel tubes and turbines that put water into the service of mankind:

> Such a cycle is restorative, not exhausting. It gives life as it sustains life. The principle of unity has been obeyed, the circle has been closed. The yield is not the old sad tale of spoliation and poverty, but that of nature and science and man in the bounty of harmony.[23]

Lilienthal's rhapsodies were not explicitly linked to geology, but they are not quite a vision of rivers as an "organic machine," either.[24] Rather, Lilienthal exchanged the temporal undulations of geological uniformitarianism for a spatial unity between water, national territory, and the economic and development prospects of American liberalism. Lilienthal did not reject earlier ideas of conservation for "the People" but instead universalized the natural fit of water resources to liberal forms of life. To do so, he turned to the task of showing how the methods for linking water to American democracy can be universalized. It was through democratic methods that social water was united with social institutions—a much less arduous task than naturalizing the Constitution. Lilienthal captured the spirit of democratic methods through the metaphor of "the march." It is the march of democracy that, for Lilienthal, provides the moral order to the TVA's material aims of unifying the movement of water with social progress. So whereas McGee emphasized that "the People" occupied the apex of evolution, Lilienthal reworked normal water geopolitically, arguing that the TVA spoke "in a tongue that is universal, a language of *things close to the lives of people.*"[25]

Lilienthal's version of democracy began at the "grass roots," where development must always "meet the test of the question: Does this activity in furtherance of unified development employ *methods that bring in the people*, that give the people themselves, in this fundamental task, the fullest opportunity for the release of the great reservoir of human talents and energies?"[26] To meet this test, Lilienthal was adamant that the authority of the state be divorced from the administration of authority and decentralized across institutions. Decentralization was what would allow the American motto of *E pluribus unum* (out of many, one) to become reality because it would afford the state a neutral position with respect to the different substantive goods that "the many" might hold. For Lilienthal, neutrality could not be achieved through state planning. Neutrality required methods that enjoined individuals in a common moral purpose of planning for their future—through everyday means like contracts, partnerships, and negotiations—at the grass roots.[27] Lilienthal thought planning mattered, and he followed John Dewey's lead in viewing every planning event as an experiment with democracy. In fact, Lilienthal cited Dewey frequently, such as in the passage below from Dewey's *Freedom and Culture*, which Lilienthal used to position the TVA as a model for democratic renewal *within* the United States and which (as shown below) he later extended as a universal model of development:

> The conflict as it concerns the democracy to which our history commits us is *within* our own institutions and attitudes. It can be won only by extending the application of democratic methods, methods of consulta-tion, persuasion, negotiation, communication, co-operative intelligence, in the task of making our own politics, industry, education, our culture generally, a servant and an evolving manifestation of democratic ideas.[28]

Despite his reliance on Dewey, Lilienthal either did not grasp, or did not care to entertain, the radical nature of Dewey's social liberalism.[29] Nor, perhaps, did he fully appreciate the moral philosophy that under-wrote Dewey's reconstruction of democracy as experience.[30] Lilienthal was, however, almost certainly familiar with Dewey's criticisms of the nitrogen and munitions plant at Muscle Shoals. Regarding this project, Dewey had argued that the "great accumulation of water power" was redundant because modern society was changing at ever-accelerating speed.[31] Dewey argued that when the acceleration of a technological society combined with techniques of mass production, long-standing beliefs regarding the nature of community were undermined by changes to the conditions in which social relationships were forged. For Dewey, this produced a public with a new set of problems for which the old axioms of democracy were inadequate. So accumulating more water power was redundant because it did not solve the problem of accelerated social change and, if anything, accentuated it. By appropriating Dewey for his own purposes, however, Lilienthal responded to such criticisms by uniting the material conditions of society, especially water, to new forms of technological coordination and democratic pursuits of the freedom of opportunity. For Lilienthal, Dewey was wrong when it came to water because it was precisely through the TVA that public problems could be solved through democratic methods.

Appropriating Dewey also helped Lilienthal on two other fronts. First, although Lilienthal conceived of the government as removed from the administration of the TVA, this was never achieved. Controversy and political interference dogged the TVA, especially from those who regarded this gem of the New Deal as too close to the social planning of totalitarian states and not aligned closely enough with liberal economies.[32] Even among those willing to accept some state planning, there was debate between whether planning should be top-down or bottom-up. These debates were reminiscent of Lilienthal's earlier feud with Morgan over a planned approach to social change versus Lilienthal's "grassroots" democracy.[33] Lilienthal had hoped that institutional design could prevent political interference in the enhancement of individual freedom. The role of the state, for Lilienthal, was to secure the material conditions for liberal democracy while leaving decentralized management experiments to grassroots decisions.

Second, the design of the TVA provided the institutional conditions for social progress at the regional scale and, through this, demonstrated how liberal democracy structured the social space that created an abundance of opportunity. This reflected the tenor of McGee's earlier desire to combine individual and corporate agency at the highest degree possible. In the TVA, however, deductive norms of uniformitarianism were replaced by methods that united the well-being of the region to the liberal persons forming the "grass roots." The implication was that the state does not reflect the national characteristics of "the People" but instead ensures the equality of opportunity for the ongoing democratic experiments of freely associating individuals. This fit broadly with a conception of the TVA as a distinctly American form of modernization that ran counter to other modernizing states, especially Russia and Germany.[34] On this point, Lilienthal was adamant that the TVA be seen as producing public goods, such as electricity, that were owned by the public and designed to enhance their economic opportunities, not that of state planners.[35]

Lilienthal contributed to normal water by revising it to pace new geopolitical realities. Recall that Powell and McGee were keen to ensure that water be directed to best enhance evolutionary abundance, which required defending American exceptionalism and was part of securing water to "the People" who came together under the American Constitution and, in so doing, stepped out of the colonial era. Especially for McGee, "the People" were an evolutionary fact; a hard won victory in the elliptical orbits of progress. For Lilienthal, however, the claim of American liberalism against external forces of colonialism was not in doubt. Rather, the task was to ensure that resources and wealth within American liberalism did not perpetuate colonial inequalities. Like McGee, Lilienthal ignored how the United States dispossessed indigenous peoples of their territory and, instead, vaulted America's experience in overcoming colonialism as the key to understanding successful water management. How Lilienthal frames this subversion reveals how the philosophy of water management naturalizes the unity of democratic methods and American liberalism:

> It is folly to expect Americans clearly to see the tragedy, *for the world*, of an intense nationalism until restrictive sectionalism *within the nation* is also seen as a self-defeating policy. A demand for an end of a colonial system far from home is not nearly so important as an understanding of the colonial system within the United States, and the reasons why it is so injurious to this nation's interest. And colonialism, or exploiting the hinterland, is substantially the basis upon which the South and the West have been so long predominantly a raw-materials source for the dominant manufacturing regions of the North and Northeast.[36]

Leaving the implications of a tragedy "for the world" for later in this chapter, Lilienthal's understanding of colonialism emphasizes the spatial relationships that produce domestic inequality. This appears to be the most important lesson that he took from Dewey's exhortation that American liberalism look within its own institutions and attitudes for democratic renewal. When Lilienthal examined American liberalism he saw that the long march of democracy had not yet weeded out all of the remnants of colonialism. In fact, he maintained that much of America remained a hinterland, predominantly in the west and south, which provided raw goods to the north and east. Lilienthal was not alone in his interpretation of America's colonial hangover. Arthur Goldschmidt, a director in the Department of Economic and Social Affairs at the United Nations, made a similar argument in 1963. Goldschmidt argued that that, because the regular path of out of colonialism (independence) wasn't available for individual American states, the federal government was obliged to enhance the economic welfare of the south and that the TVA provided the model for rectifying what amounted to a continued, quasicolonial relationship of America's industrial and financial centers to the hinterland.[37]

Lilienthal and Goldschmidt later advised President Lyndon Johnson on how rectifying colonialism domestically could be marshaled as a model for foreign policy. Before moving to those arguments, it is important to note that situating colonialism's center-periphery relations "within the nation" naturalized political space at the scale of the river basin (or watershed). This new iteration of naturalization was layered on top of the geological register that Powell and McGee had developed to counter external influences of colonialism. Lilienthal's addition, however, was decidedly geopolitical in that progress would now be achieved through river-basin development that targeted spatial inequalities within American territory. As Franklin Roosevelt said regarding the TVA: "If we are successful here we can march on, step by step, in a like development of other great natural territorial units within our borders."[38] But the naturalization of watersheds to national territory is not straightforward. Nor does the division of authority from the administration of water management mirror the division of powers between federal and state governments. These two asymmetries embroiled the TVA in legal challenges that nearly crippled it. The fact that the TVA survived further instilled in Lilienthal the value of his democratic vision.[39] Yet to reconcile his vision with American federalism Lilienthal required a new social space that did not rest either on the watershed per se or on national territory. Producing this space drove the concept of regional development. Through the "region," water management bridged between political orders, their colonial legacies, and the material conditions of progress.

Regional development simultaneously naturalized both democratic methods for water management and the watershed, qua region, as a territorial unit. This twofold naturalization was designed to correct domestic inequality that had persisted since colonialism. Yet it had its own colonial effects because it forced other social groups to adopt the language and practices of the state as a condition for participation in the "grass roots" of water management. So while the philosophy of water management began to cultivate an appreciation of democratic pluralism in theory, it did so to the exclusion of different practices, different sources of authority, and the administration of authority from those sources. In this regard, the U.S. state was not neutral. Rather, the focus on America's colonial experience provided both impetus and catalyst for American rhetoric in the post–World War II era of international development and the emerging project of post-colonial state building. The rhetoric of regional development naturalized American water management while burying the idea that water's abundance was to be directed towards maintaining other social possibilities. Once naturalized, water resources provided for an abundance of liberal opportunity. Seen through the TVA, water resources were "nature's constant gift."[40]

Regional Water Development

As regional development rose in prominence, planners began to ask how multiple views and multiple potential purposes for water should be balanced. Gilbert White, who features prominently next chapter, has argued that this question drove planning for regional water management in the United States.[41] Initially, this question was answered through arguments about the correct way to think about water management—the right way of "beginning . . . at the beginning," to recall Lilienthal's exhortation. Correctly thinking about water management began by interpreting domestic lessons from the TVA in the political context of post–World War II America. In this regard, the TVA had proved vital to the war effort and remained central to ensuring that democracy could survive and flourish within a secure national territory. For instance, the prominent historian and public intellectual Arthur Schlesinger explicitly tied

the TVA to the evolution of "American liberalism" that was being formulated as the nation's political philosophy was refashioned in light of
the post–World War II world order.[42]

In the years after World War II, the TVA came under intense scrutiny for the amount of government financing it received as Uncle Sam's
"Billion Dollar Baby."[43] Defending the TVA fell to Gordon Clapp, who
became director when Lilienthal left in 1946 to chair the Atomic Energy Commission.[44] The need to defend the TVA came not only from
critics of federal spending but also from the 1947 Hoover Commission,
which took its name from former president Herbert Hoover, who was
appointed as chair by then-president Harry Truman. The commission
released its findings in 1949 and declared American resource development a national emergency. It was an emergency similar to the one earlier conservationists identified: wasteful use and degradation of natural
resources compounded by the lack of coordination among various government agencies. Later in 1949, the Department of the Interior convened a "National Emergency Conference on Resources." There Clapp
used the TVA to reinforce the link between regional development and
the benefits to both local and national interests.[45] He enumerated the
economic benefits of the TVA, especially the increased tax revenues for
the federal budget.[46] He also identified the TVA as key to American
success in World War II owing to its quick construction of dams and the
steady supply of energy it provided to manufacturing plants serving the
war effort. Perhaps his most explicit defense of the TVA's role in America's security apparatus, however, was a 1953 interview broadcast on CBS:

> And I think, most important, and one that we mustn't forget, is that [the
> TVA] has made a great contribution in National Defense. This area was
> where the first atomic bomb was made at Oak Ridge and it was power
> from the TVA dams that made that possible. It's a great aluminum man-
> ufacturing center. And during the war, the fact that we had electricity
> available made it possible to expand aluminum production and get our
> airplanes in the air faster, and we think contributed to bringing the war
> to that much closer or similar end.[47]

While Clapp spearheaded the defense of the TVA, its connection to
national security was also promoted in reports and pamphlets connect-

ing it to the emerging Cold War. Especially important were the TVA's contribution to America's nuclear arsenal, its guided missiles program, and the synthetic production of phosphorous used in bombs.[48] In short, Clapp's argument was that the TVA was essential to America's military arsenal and as important as ever given the security threats of the Cold War. The propaganda produced by the TVA during this time played on popular concerns regarding the need to fortify the American way of life, perhaps to the chagrin of the "nervous liberals" who were wary of the effects of propaganda on democracy in America.[49] But the military retooling of the TVA also fit the motif of "arming mother nature" that grew throughout the Cold War.[50] And it is in this shifting geopolitical context that I would like to pick up on Lilienthal's idea that it would be a tragedy "for the world" if nationalist projects were based on relationships that subjected individual freedom in one region to interests elsewhere.

In post–World War II America, there was a certain allergy to nationalism just in case it was construed as implicit support of communism or fascism. Among scientific communities, these concerns co-produced a particular cultural brand of objectivity.[51] Bryan Norton has described the effects on resource management as inaugurating a shift toward methodological individualism in which societies are understood as the aggregate of individual interests rather than reflecting national characteristics.[52] This contrasted with Margaret Mead and other anthropologists who, throughout World War II, had worked on understanding national characteristics—cultural patterns—with the hopes of navigating cultural difference and technological modernization for post-war peace.[53] The views of Mead and others were not taken up, however, as liberals like Lilienthal promoted universalized notions of democracy and intellectuals at elite American institutions pushed "modernization theory" as the basis for U.S. foreign policy.[54] Karl Wittfogel, who was developing his own view of water and "total power" around this time, described Mead's view as "diaperology" because of its reliance on interpreting cultural patterns through psychoanalysis from childhood onward.[55] When it came to water, the path through these debates was to deploy the TVA as a model of "modernization" that captured—and where necessary produced—a universal and peaceful path to development based on the coordination of democratic individuals.[56] This mirrored at the international level the domestic shift in the United States from bureaucratic utilitarianism to individualist utilitarianism in water management. In the former, a collective notion of agency, or at least political identity, defines the public good. In the latter, the public good is sought through a methodological individualism that seeks to ensure individuals can act in their own interests.[57] This shift mobilized water management without reference to the characteristics of "the People" while still supporting American liberalism.

The judgment that allows regional water management to reproduce procedural norms and territorial units without reference to any particular social context operates between two poles of naturalization. Recall from above the asymmetries between democratic methods and the administration of authority, on the one hand, and between national territory and the aggregate of watershed units, on the other. These asymmetries created a new space—the region—that fit uneasily with the liberal promises of grassroots democracy in the United States. This led the TVA into numerous legal conflicts, which I left to the side in order to highlight how that space was bridged through a happy union that (1) reinterpreted regional development as a democratic response to internal conflicts that remained from colonialism, and (2) took up an institutional mission that made the TVA essential to U.S. territorial security. By combining these two considerations, the TVA was set up to advance post-colonial development domestically and, if applied elsewhere, to create liberal opportunities worldwide that linked individual preferences and state security under a view that challenged the "nationalisms" of totalitarian states.[58] Yet it also naturalized water resources to the liberal promise of an abundance of opportunities and universalized America's response to colonialism as a model for post-colonial development. In short, it created a model for post-colonial development based on American settler-colonialism.

Normal Water and International Development

In his inaugural speech on January 20, 1949, U.S. President Harry Truman declared that the path to peace lay in enhanced prosperity for the "underdeveloped areas" of the world.[59] Widely known as "Point 4" because of its placement in his speech, Truman's declaration kicked off a massive program of international development in the mid-twentieth century.[60] Of course, the United States had already been working on development projects for decades in China and elsewhere.[61] So, too, had other countries, non-governmental organizations, and religious networks. Even for Truman, Point 4 largely reiterated his 1946 statement to UNESCO regarding how the relationship of natural resources to war was tied to the need for resource conservation:

> The real or exaggerated fear of resource shortages and declining standards of living has in the past involved nations in warfare. Every member of the United Nations is deeply interested in preventing a recurrence of that fear and of those consequences. Conservation can become a major basis of peace.[62]

Truman's blanket category of "underdeveloped" covered roughly two-thirds of the world's population, which was presented as ripe for the project of international development. Under UNESCO's first director general, Julian Huxley, the TVA was constantly promoted in reference to development, and Huxley thought the TVA should be the United Nations's development model in general.[63] After visiting Russia, Huxley toured the TVA before concluding it was a success of social science that reconciled liberty in the U.S. south with American democracy and provided clear evidence of cultural progress.[64] For Huxley and Truman, the success of the TVA model, and of continued progress, resided in successful resource conservation.

Truman's 1946 letter to UNESCO was written in reference to the UN Conference on Resource Conservation and Utilization. After that conference, which was broadly viewed as a success, the immediate problem was flood control in developing nations, yet the Americans "stressed the need for viewing the problem not solely in terms of flood control but also in terms of multiple-purpose river basin development."[65] This link of conservation to multipurpose river basin development, long held since McGee's time, was subsequently advanced through newly created regional commissions, such as the Economic Commission for Asia and the Far East. Through these and other channels, the TVA model rose to near hegemony such that to think "development" was to think of the TVA.[66] Through the reframed colonial logic of Lilienthal, the TVA provided for domestic success while funding this model of development through new institutions, like the World Bank, furthered American interests internationally. The TVA was a weapon of modernization "which, if properly employed, might outbid all the social ruthlessness of the Communists for the support of the people of Asia."[67] Already by 1945 over fifty thousand translated copies of Lilienthal's *Democracy on the March* had been distributed by the Office of War Information in China alone.[68] Tens of thousands more were distributed elsewhere in the years that followed, signaling broadly that international development came part in parcel with American liberalism.[69]

In 1950, Truman established the President's Water Resources Policy Commission. The Commission did not include Lilienthal, even though he had left the Atomic Energy Commission that year. The President's new commission reaffirmed the critical role that the Inland Waterways Commission played in combining conservation and multipurpose river basin development. For the President's Commission, this history formed the basis for ensuring national expenditures were made "for the good of the Nation as a whole; and nothing less than the whole country can be the unit considered in the formulation of federal policies."[70] Yet water development in the United States now also needed to serve an "expand-ing economy" while bearing in mind that "'planning' in the American sense means planning to maintain and strengthen free competition."[71] The economic thrust did not depart from the earlier ethos of water devel-opment—in which the aim had always been to enhance the prospect of liberal individuals. Rather, and in line with economists like Friedrich von Hayek, national policies increasingly sought to reduce the centralization of planning in government agencies.[72] For Hayek, no single perspective, such as that of the state, could have the requisite knowledge required to rationally plan for optimal resource allocation.[73] It was likewise so with water. And the President's Commission specified that government in-terventions should only be made to enhance competition but that it was "not in accordance with the American system, nor is it any part of the purpose of the plans for water development proposed in this report, that the Federal Government should itself become a great monopolist."[74]

The idea that governments cannot know or determine the public good reflects a broader shift in economic thinking post World War II. Timothy Mitchell has argued that "the economy" was itself formed as an object of knowledge during this period.[75] It is worth pursuing Mitch-ell's idea because of what it implies for thinking about how western democracy in the twentieth century emerged in response to resources and technologies and their management. In Mitchell's account, the global attempt to prevent an abundance of oil from getting to world markets led a cadre of actors to render oil scarce by controlling key bottlenecks in world trade networks: ports, pipelines, roads, and so on. Through a series of interventions, these actors made the path for oil and the American dollar to act as the basis for the global currency system. A key conceptual move, according to Mitchell, was from a material basis for economic analysis, such as natural resources or labor, to an analysis of the circulation of money. This shift rendered economics "a science of money" that operated in a "not-quite-natural, not-quite-social space that came to be called 'the economy.'"[76]

In Mitchell's account, examining the uneasy fit of 'the economy' with wholly natural or social spaces presents an opportunity to see how economic processes were naturalized to the state.[77] As Neil Smith showed, geographers were active in shaping new geoeconomic formations and in reifying state territory as the natural unit of economic processes.[78] Mitchell goes on to suggest that the Bretton Woods institutions established in July 1944, especially the World Bank and the International Monetary Fund, played a special role in the project that linked "development" to the proliferation of new forms of political and economic power. For instance, Mitchell notes that John Maynard Keynes had proposed another institution that would have established a reserve of key commodities to balance out swings in the prices of natural resources. Even Hayek had agreed there should be a stockpile of key natural resources held in trust by the government, but this never came about.[79]

Debates about whether "the economy" was a material object or not hearkened back to McGee's disagreements with the Yale economist Irving Fisher.[80] As Mitchell points out, arguments for economics, the "science of money," to be conceived of in non-material terms followed Fisher's lead to create an abstract monetary system. Yet from what was a non-material monetary system abstracted? In application, development theorists like W.W. Rostow later reinterpreted stadial theories of evolutionary development as a fortification against communism during the Cold War.[81] Yet this does not explain how a non-material "economy" was given expression without appealing to the unique characteristics of "the People" whose form of life "the economy" aligned so closely with. My position is that the "science of money" had no need of the commodity storehouse that Keynes, Hayek, and others wanted because it connected political and financial security to the industrial infrastructure required to create and capture liberal notions of an abundance of opportunity. As with oil, water needed to be rendered scarce just in case it could be used to serve and support alternate forms of life (e.g., communism).

Mitchell acknowledges that several key moments in the emergence of "the economy" came through the financing of large dams, primarily from the World Bank, which focused much of its early investment on water. This made for a happy union between the conservation of natural resources and the project of international development. Both took the TVA's regional approach as the model, which helps to explain Wolfgang Sachs's later complaint that conservation and development are practically indistinguishable.[82] On one side, the material supply of water and the benefits to be derived from TVA-style management were embedded in a broadly liberal view of individuals while regional development was forwarded as a model for addressing legacies of colonialism globally. On the other, the monetary requirements to develop water on an industrial scale required deep pockets, and large dams became precisely the kind of projects that the World Bank was interested in financing.[83] The World Bank's first loan to a developing country was for hydroelectric development in Chile (1948) and then to Mexico (1949), where hydroelectric development and power regulation were explicitly referenced to the TVA.[84] These loans precipitated a remarkable global transformation of the Earth's surface. In the last half of the twentieth century thousands of large dams (dams higher than fifteen meters) were built, and untold—in many cases, uncounted—millions of people were displaced. Today, there are more than fifty thousand large dams on Earth, and many more planned.[85]

In the mid-twentieth century, "water management" began to crystallize as an object that operated between the territory of the state and the goal of enhancing regional development in a post-colonial era heavily shaped by American intervention. If economics was emerging as the "science of money," water management was emerging as a "science of supply" that enhanced national interests without being based on national characteristics. Large dams were a door for "regional planning" that provided good return on investments loaned to developing nations. If managed properly—that is, through liberal norms—dams increased liberal opportunity to the benefit of individuals and the state. The TVA emphasis on regional development as a bridge between individuals and national economies fit this social and political space uniquely, no doubt because it helped to produce it.

Normal Water Goes Global

In 1951, David Lilienthal visited the Indus Basin that straddled India and Pakistan. Relations between the two countries were tense, and Lilienthal wrote in *Collier's* magazine that the TVA model could be applied to the Indus Basin to develop water and prevent political crisis.[86] His timing was perfect. The World Bank had already tried to negotiate an agreement between the two countries without success. Recounting the arrival of Lilienthal, World Bank historians described him as a deus ex machina arriving just in the nick of time.[87] The World Bank seized on Lilienthal's proposal to broker a deal, and even though a final settlement was not reached until 1960, his influence was part of state formation in the post-colonial era.[88] For Lilienthal, even competing nationalist projects on international rivers were solvable through regional development.[89] In retrospect, the Indus Basin proved only the beginning. Throughout the 1950s, the World Bank developed strategies for financing water projects in many international watersheds.[90] Eventually, the TVA would become virtually synonymous with American foreign assistance while Lilienthal gained the moniker "Mr. TVA."[91] By the time Lilienthal revised *Democracy on the March* in 1953, he could list the influence of the TVA in Palestine, India, Puerto Rico, Peru, French West Africa, Mexico, Brazil, China, Uganda, Turkey, Chile, and France, to name a few.

U.S. foreign aid and the World Bank did not always work hand in glove. One such case was the Aswan High Dam in Egypt. There, on behalf of the World Bank, the U.S. Foreign Operations Agency financed an engineering study of what was to be a "century storage" scheme.[92] At the time, the World Bank had plenty of enthusiasm for the TVA and its potential to transform the Middle East.[93] The Foreign Operations Agency took the TVA as its model and was part of what Timothy Mitchell describes as the "rule of experts,"[94] shorthand for how the properties of some thing, like water, and the technologies needed to support a particular form of life, like liberalism, are both registered within and throughout political formations affecting development. This was no doubt taking place in the case of the Aswan High Dam. But more than the rule of experts was in play. For instance, remarks from the 1956 hearings of the U.S. Senate Committee on Appropriations on the financing of the Aswan High Dam explicitly detail costs and technological aspects of the project in reference to the "Soviet challenge."[95] The committee minutes also detail how the decline of wealth in the American south after the abolition of slavery had cut revenue to cotton producers, which led some southern senators to reject U.S. aid for Egypt's new dam unless there was a guarantee that newly created water supplies would not grow cotton and compete with their constituencies.[96] Ultimately, America did not finance the dam, and Russia did.

The push and pull of politics affected the spread of American water development throughout the twentieth century.[97] Domestically, the TVA was never reproduced in the United States, in no small part because Lilienthal himself blocked new proposals out of fear that the TVA would lose its unique status if new water authorities were created and then grouped together under the Department of the Interior.[98] Internationally, tensions within the TVA were replayed, such as in the Damodar Valley Commission in West Bengal, where Lilienthal and his rival Arthur Morgan offered competing advice on the same project.[99] Lilienthal was also active in Iran, where he continued to pursue his moral vision of achieving liberal democracy through water management.[100] Lilienthal also explicitly endorsed the views of Walter Lowdermilk, who argued in the 1940s that TVA-style water management in the Jordan Valley would create the conditions for a new state of Israel.[101] U.S. Vice President Henry Wallace endorsed Lowdermilk's proposal, which began a new set of politics as water abundance, scarcity, and (later) security were tied to Israeli identity and settler-colonial practices.[102]

It was not until the mid-1960s that the international importance of the TVA reached its peak.[103] By then, the TVA had achieved remarkable influence, while the confluence of development financing and technopolitical expertise spread its unique brand of American modernization.[104] American efforts also pedaled the TVA using channels other than the World Bank, such as the U.S. Bureau of Reclamation.[105] The Bureau, which had been established in 1902, is often linked to the larger-than-life figures who engineered its grandiose projects and shaped irrigation across the American west.[106] Internationally, the Bureau was wielded as a technopolitical weapon, particularly in the Mekong region, where Lilienthal was later invited to advise development projects by President Lyndon Johnson.[107] Throughout this period, normal water expanded its remit. Consider, for instance, how the 1957 Economic Commission for Asia and the Far East contextualized its conclusions on the development prospects for the lower Mekong River:

> Since a river basin, from headwaters to the sea, should be regarded as a single dynamic and organic system, it is desirable that planning for the optimum use and conservation of water resources should cover an entire river basin, including the main river and its tributaries.[108]

In the 1960s, President Johnson was operating in the context of the Vietnam War and being advised by the likes of Arthur Goldschmidt to use water management to resolve the conflict. Goldschmidt had published a paper on the development of the American south in which he drew a direct parallel between the north-south relations in the United States and "the economic development of the former colonial regions of the world."[109] Johnson later thanked Goldschmidt for drawing out the similarities between the global legacies of colonialism and the prospects of applying lessons from American economics to post-colonial development.[110] In a 1965 speech at Johns Hopkins University, Johnson pledged $1 billion to develop the Mekong River Basin on a scale that would "dwarf even our own TVA."[111] Yet by the time Johnson made his pronouncement to model his "water for peace" initiative on the TVA, several important developments in the field of water management had also come about. These ran squarely into the work of another key figure, Gilbert White, who had expertise both in the Mekong region and domestically in the United States. White's influence, as we will see in the next chapter, was key to taking the philosophy of water management global in a way that would later allow it to keep pace with changes to international development and growing environmental concerns.

Headstones

When David Lilienthal died in 1981, his obituary ran on the front page of the *New York Times*.[112] By then, the TVA had achieved enormous influence and was tied to the rhetoric of creating opportunity, for individuals and the nation, based on a unity of watershed management and democratic methods. The TVA promised to advance the common good at the scale of the region, where the grass roots democratically pursued their own ends, and the nation benefited as a result. The TVA did not employ an exclusively temporal register that had infused early conservation policies. Rather, the TVA kept up the march of progress through a spatial configuration in which regional development broke the colonial relations chaining resource hinterlands to financial centers. As America universalized the TVA as a post-colonial model, it also inaugurated a geopolitical shift in which the science of water supply was increasingly aligned with the science of money. Lilienthal worked to ensure that American liberalism was seen in universal terms, in which underdeveloped nations were not so because of any individual or social characteristics but because they lacked the conditions for success enabled by democracy and modernization.

The upshot is that evolutionary possibilities have been impounded behind the great headstones of modernity: the large dams that foreclose on the abundance of social and ecological evolution in order to create an abundance of liberal opportunities. Of course, dams were also built for other political projects, and none ever achieved complete hegemony. Yet by impounding water's evolutionary abundance behind a new iteration of American liberalism, normal water layered onto the geological claims of Powell and McGee a claim to unity among watersheds, democracy, and territory that operated without reference to any particular social characteristics. By burying abundance, supply-side water management provided a material corollary to an emerging world order that would come to operate in terms of scarcity. Dams were not storehouses of commodities to moderate the cycles of capitalism. They were storehouses for liberal opportunity—with the added benefits of allowing international financial backers to extract rents from the loans needed to build them. All of this, however, was not sufficient to establish that water was scarce. For that, normal water would need to forge a new sensibility that could naturalize regional development with the spatial inequalities of water's global distribution. In short, normal water needed a new geography.

5

The Space of Scarcity

I should say that geography has to do with all those aspects
of social life which are concerned with the interaction of the
life of man and nature. . . . Any fact, then, will be a geographical fact in so far as it bears upon the dependence of man
upon his natural environment, or with the changes introduced in this environment through the life of man.
—John Dewey

Because oceans cover seven tenths of the earth's surface, it is
evident that a major part of precipitation falls directly into
the sea; it has passed through the hydrological cycle without
having been a natural resource at all.
—Gilbert White

Gilbert Fowler White was a perennial figure in American water management and international water policy during the latter two-thirds of the
twentieth century. Also a member of the Cosmos Club, White provided
in his work a foil for understanding how the philosophy of water management globalized a pragmatic, situational approach to the task of human
adjustment. It is through the work of White and others that water management, as a science of supply, became a space where demand was also
factored in. This required formulating new stopping rules, particularly
from hydrology, through which the philosophy of water management
sought to bypass its ethnocentric heritage. As hinted at by the epigraph
from White, cultural circumvention came via hydrologic circulation; just
as water could rain out over the ocean and never become a resource,
water scarcity was a planetary phenomenon because every society shared
in the contingent, dynamic aspects of global hydrology.[1] Hydrological
variability in time and over space meant that all societies needed to rationally manage water in ways that would allow them to adjust to change.

As abundance was buried behind large dams, the shift to scarcity appeared to happen in short order. So quickly, in fact, that when water was declared globally scarce in 1977 at the UN Conference on Water in Mar del Plata, Argentina, it had the appearance of a crisis. In reality, the rise of water scarcity and its accompanying spatial sensibility had a longer gestation. The roots of U.S. water management in the uniformitarianism of John Wesley Powell and WJ McGee were not denied. Instead, the spatial sensibility that globalized water scarcity refracted the naturalization of water to "the People" through a spatial view of global hydrology that found a unity distinct from any particular social characteristics, much like other co-productions of scientific objectivity during the Cold War.[2] The co-production of water scarcity alongside this form of objectivity befit the "renascent liberalism" being articulated by pragmatists such as John Dewey. For renascent liberals, social planning directed industry and finance into the service of both cultural liberation and individual growth.[3] The testing ground of social planning was experience and the cultivation of democratic ways of learning from social action.

The priority given to experience also supported water management's search for a new geography. As the epigraph from Dewey suggests, environmental interactions produce geographic facts.[4] Dewey's take on geography was not too far from Franz Boas, who argued that the affective importance of geographic phenomena made them worthy of study in a register unconcerned with attempts to extract general laws from them.[5] As earlier chapters showed, American water managers had a longer history with pragmatism, and this continued with Gilbert White. His contribution was to link a geographic sensibility regarding the unequal distribution of water resources to what he called the "broader bases of choice" that managers needed to develop in order to not prematurely limit how experience informed decisions.[6] For White, the material and moral hazards of too much or too little water rendered human-water relationships precarious and required enhanced techniques for "human adjustment"—a phrase White was fond of. White's version of human adjustment nuanced normal water in a way that fit evolving ideas of liberalism. In White's view, human adjustment mirrored at the level of social agency the sort of evolutionary adjustments McGee saw as defining the way all life forms feel their way about. White's was adjustment at a social scale: just as adjustments by individual agents were not unique to humans (because agency was not unique), neither was social adjustment unique to any particular group of humans.

The search for a new geography for water management was facilitated by American anthropology, which was increasingly open to other social sciences when it came to human-environment relationships. In 1955, the Wenner-Gren Foundation funded a conference on "Man's Role in Changing the Face of the Earth."[7] Held at Princeton, the list of conference speakers read like a roll call of environmental thought in the United States. Luna Leopold was there, as was Abel Wolman, the renowned professor of sanitary engineering at Johns Hopkins University. Sol Tax, the University of Chicago professor and editor of the journal *American Anthropologist* was in attendance. So was Karl Wittfogel, fresh off his castigation of anthropologists like Margaret Mead and ready to test run his notion of "hydraulic civilizations" that he published two years later.[8] There were also zoologists, like Marston Bates, and the Yale botanist Paul Sears. Pierre Teilhard de Chardin was scheduled to attend but passed away earlier that year. His paper was delivered in absentia and built on his ideas about the noösphere, which a decade earlier had shaped Vladimir Vernadsky's notion of the biosphere. Other broad thinkers were at the Princeton conference, too. The Berkeley geographer Clarence Glacken delivered a paper on the changing ideas of what constituted a habitable world. It foreshadowed his monumental work, *Traces on the Rhodian Shore*, which anticipated many of the issues in the Anthropocene that arise when western cultures reimagine life without their version of nature.[9]

Fittingly, the book produced from the conference was dedicated to George Perkins Marsh. Tellingly, Marsh alone did not inspire the conference because his views were deemed too ethnocentric.[10] A second influence was the Russian geographer Alexander Woeikof, whose ideas regarding human transformation of the Earth had gained traction in Europe. It was astute to situate the conference as both critical of American ethnocentrism and more open to geography. On the one hand, American anthropology had a history of engaging geography, and, on the other, American geography needed help. Harvard had closed its geography department in 1948, and closures at Stanford, Yale, and the University of Pennsylvania soon followed. Meanwhile, one of America's most prominent geographers, Isaiah Bowman, was working closely with the U.S. government to ensure post-war geopolitics facilitated American economic globalization.[11] The shared unease over ethnocentric environmentalism and geography's alignment with U.S. foreign policy coalesced on issues of international development. As the Berkeley geographer Carl Sauer put it, "In the spirit of the present, this mission is to 'develop the underdeveloped' parts of the world, material good and spiritual good now having become one."[12]

Sauer's critiques were particularly relevant because his focus on regional difference contrasted sharply with Tennessee Valley Authority (TVA)-style development, which universalized the "region" to fit the post-colonial space the United States claimed for itself. Using the TVA as a model of post-colonial development, however, could not be referenced to any particular society without appearing flagrantly ethnocentric, a critique felt acutely in water management—the bread and butter of the development model. Over the next several decades, water management was refashioned by a new geography that claimed to be universal without being ethnocentric. Key to this new geography was the International Hydrological Decade (IHD). Launched in 1965, the IHD linked all regions to the global water cycle in a seemingly natural way. As this chapter considers, the IHD did much more than this, it also linked human impacts on the planet's water in particular way—one that connected resource conservation and international development to an understanding of global hydrology that positioned liberal forms of life as best suited to manage water's variability and to structure the task of human adjustment. Managing water in this new planetary space required a pragmatism that eschewed theory for experience and that oriented water management to predicaments that could arise for any society. This space was established in numerous ways, and a figure key to many of them was Gilbert White.

Water Management and Gilbert White

Gilbert White steadfastly contributed to American water management from the New Deal through to the beginning of the new millennium. While David Lilienthal and others were popularizing and promoting the TVA as a model for development, White and others were advancing new approaches to river-basin development to address increasingly complex management challenges. White was not one for the limelight, and his Quaker beliefs imbued him with humility and sympathy for others. Yet his accomplishments were numerous. In 2000 alone he was awarded the U.S. President's National Medal of Science, the Public-Welfare Medal from the U.S. National Academy of Sciences, and the Millennium Award from the International Water Resources Association.[13] Like McGee and Lilienthal, White operated in the halls of power in Washington and, later, in international circles. Wherever he went, he deployed the training he received from America's first geography department, established in 1903 at the University of Chicago.

White was never as philosophically explicit as Powell, McGee, or Lilienthal. Yet he shared much with them, particularly the engagement with American pragmatists, which White was exposed to in Chicago when he attended the Lab School created by John Dewey. As the epigraph suggests, Dewey conceived "any fact" geographic if it affected human-environment relationships or their modification. This is not too far from McGee, who thought "human geography" dealt with the distribution of humans, their activities, and artifacts on the Earth.[14] Some of this similarity may reflect the fact that both Dewey and McGee were responding to Thomas Huxley. We have already considered McGee's view of the precarious adjustments organisms make to the environments produced by other geological agents. In 1898, Dewey argued that there was no perennial conflict between man and nature as presumed by social Darwinists.[15] In Dewey's view, those who were most "fit" in evolutionary terms were not identical with those who were most ethical, so there was no natural alignment of moral and material progress. He believed the conflation of evolutionary fitness and moral worth by social Darwinists (and even by Huxley) should be reversed such that "fitness" would be another name for the capacity to adapt and readapt to the environments individuals live in and, collectively, modify.[16]

Dewey's influence on White is best seen methodologically, through the former's project-oriented educational models and ideas about how human ecology was mediated by individuals and institutions.[17] As James Wescoat has thoughtfully mapped, many of Dewey's ideas likely came to White through his graduate supervisor, Harlan Burrows.[18] For instance, Dewey's definition of geography in the epigraph anticipated Harlan Barrows's 1923 attempt to make geography into a discipline of human ecology that focused on human adjustment to evolving environments.[19] As Dewey had previously written, "The unwritten chapter in natural selection is that of the evolution of environments."[20] In his plural understanding of environments, Dewey also rejected Spencer's atomization of individual relationships to a single "environment" and instead advanced a social view of environmental space that was acted on, and responsive to, interacting evolutionary forces. George Santayana criticized Dewey for construing environments anthropocentrically, as though human sociality was the only relevant domain.[21] In response, Dewey claimed that Santayana reified the idea of a "human" in the foreground and set against a background of "nature" that smacked of the sort of metaphysics his naturalism could not abide. He then argued that the foreground/background distinction was best handled, not by denying the distinction, but by arguing there are many foregrounds and backgrounds.[22]

In Dewey's pragmatism, the method of experience is part and parcel with a unified view of the human and natural sciences. In this view, adaptations and readaptations—the whole suite of human adjustments— should never foreshorten inquiry based on a priori distinctions of mind and matter or nature and culture. In fact, they shouldn't even attempt to satisfy dogmas that divorced humans from nature. For Dewey, it was critical that the full range of possibilities be maintained in order to adjust and learn from experience, and this required cultivating democratic habits through fair institutions and attitudes.[23] In many ways, Gilbert White's work paralleled Dewey's view that life is precarious and that the human experience is shot through with chance.[24] Even White's acclaimed doctoral dissertation was entitled, "Human Adjustment to Floods."[25] Further, just as Dewey rendered "environments" as part of a social world, White's preeminent concern was with the social dynamics of human adjustments to both the everyday circumstances and extreme hazards that humans, in part, created.

Although White was not given to philosophical or theoretical writing, he did acknowledge the influence of the pragmatist William James, notably his work *The Varieties of Religious Experience*. For James, the test of belief in religion was no different from that in any other domain: Beliefs were those convictions upon which a person was willing to act.[26] This test of belief elevated experience above doctrinal authority and was largely congruent with White's Quaker beliefs. In secular terms, such as in cases that dealt with beliefs about things extended in as many directions as the "environment," James even granted experience primacy over universal accounts in the social and natural sciences.[27] Although the interpretation of experience may seem to rely on theory (i.e., a theory about what experience entails), the pragmatist view is that learning from experience comes about through the habits of truth testing by a community. Like Dewey, James held that experience was what allowed for a methodological unity in the testing of claims across the social and natural sciences.

White Goes to Washington

Gilbert White used his educational and religious training to forge a link between development and water management that allowed American ideas to travel internationally. The route to this global influence began in 1934 when his graduate supervisor, Harlan Barrows, asked White to accompany him to Washington, DC, as part of a project on the newly created National Resources Planning Board under President Herbert Hoover.[28] Memories of the devastating 1927 Mississippi floods were fresh, and the TVA had been created just a year earlier. Once in Washington, White reported on public works and natural resources, particularly land and water, for the Water Planning Committee.[29] Seen in retrospect, the Water Planning Committee set the tone for domestic U.S. water planning for nearly four decades.[30] A key element of the committee's work involved a long-standing controversy over how to develop rivers in a way that balanced flood control with land management in headwater regions—indeed entire watersheds—where many "little waters" were influenced by individual actions that the government could not reasonably hope to control.[31] Luna Leopold later summarized the flood control controversy as revealing how a whole suite of concerns established the need for integrated water management and development, better institutional alignment at the federal and state levels, and a clearer appreciation of the effects of river development on both social and environmental systems.[32]

White's assignment in Washington was originally supposed to be a six-month stint, but he stayed in the Bureau of the Budget until the onset of World War II. During that time, he observed the inner workings of government bureaucracies and political offices, particularly during the crafting of the Flood Control Act of 1936, which created formal require- ments for cost-benefit calculations in U.S. water planning.[33] After World War II, White completed his PhD on human adjustment to floods. In it, he explicitly links his ideas back to George Perkins Marsh, through McGee, to his own research on flood control and water management.[34] Remarkably soon after, White became president of Haverford College in Pennsylvania, a position he held from 1946 to 1955. While at Haverford, White continued to have an important role in American water manage- ment. In 1948, he was named vice chair of Harry S. Truman's Presidential Water Resources Policy Commission. The three-volume tome pro- duced by the commission covered legal aspects of water policy reform and used ten case studies from across the United States to advocate for new approaches to water management. These new approaches to water management included the use of both structural and non-structural ap- proaches to developing water and included more explicit engagements with cost-benefit economics and political analysis. As the report sum- mary stated, "There is a sobering finality in the construction of a river basin development; and it behooves us to be sure we are right before we go ahead."[35] Published in 1950, the commission's report came just a year before the political scientist Arthur Maass published his doctoral work from Harvard on the U.S. Army Corps of Engineers. White later recounted that Maass's book, *Muddy Waters*, marked the start of a new era in economic and political techniques in U.S. water management.[36]

Several factors that raised water's political profile help to account for White's increased role in domestic water concerns in the United States. One was continuing controversy over flood plain management, which led to the creation of the Water Resources Council in 1961, of which White was a member.[37] Another was the activity of some U.S. Senators, like Frank Moss, who warned of a looming "water crisis" while campaigning to rewrite laws governing how bureaucracies like the U.S. Army Corp of Engineers should operate (if they should continue to exist at all).[38] Such warnings were not new. Already in 1952, the climatologist Peveril Meigs had warned of growing water problems in the United States.[39] But in the 1960s the rhetoric ramped up. What Moss had termed a "crisis" oth- ers rendered a coming "water famine."[40] Concerns over water shortages were often referenced to advances in hydrology, such as the 1962 report of the U.S. Federal Council for Science and Technology.[41] All the while, Arthur Maass and others at the Harvard Water Program were developing increasingly sophisticated techniques for cost-benefit analyses.[42] White hoped that these techniques, together with improved hydrological science, would allow for "broader bases for choice" and enable more sophisticated adjustments to water resources that built on America's experience with the Inland Waterways Commission and the TVA.[43]

White thought that "broader bases for choice" would help ensure that options for human adjustment were not unnecessarily curtailed and that water management would remain open, in principle, to whatever register adjustment might most adequately be achieved through. Science, technology, infrastructure, economics, and policy were all fair game when it came to adjusting to water resources. White's pragmatism fit the notion of "multiple working hypotheses" that the geologist Thomas Chamberlin had developed to keep theories from guiding inquiry.[44] Indeed, a signature feature of White's work is that the extremely different conditions in which humans interacted with water needed to be connected to water's own extremes, which humans could also affect. There were many possible hypotheses for understanding how different moral orders, whether new techniques of economic valuation or traditional ideas, could provide broader bases for choice that expanded options for human adjustment. White's view was that singular responses to social or environmental extremes (i.e., dealing with floods solely through infrastructure) were prone to exacerbating problems and curtailing possible solutions by dismissing contrary views out of hand. Summing up his position in 1963, White wrote, "I am not interested in staking out professional claims [in geography]. What does seem important is to recognize intellectual problems which call for solution, and which because of their relation to spatial distributions and human adjustment to differences in physical environment are of interest to geographers."[45]

During the 1950s, 1960s, and 1970s, White gained a remarkable repertoire of experience through involvement in domestic and international initiatives. In 1955, White resigned as president of Haverford. The move was prompted, at least in part, by a dinner conversation with Margaret Mead, who had coolly remarked that, if White continued on as president of Haverford, he would be on a "one-way street" of university administration and likely never return to research.[46] He subsequently returned to the University of Chicago and later moved to the University of Colorado. White's academic work was complemented by his efforts with a Quaker peace initiative that had begun convening diplomats from around the world for conferences. The accomplishments of the initiative are impressive, involving over twenty-five conferences that brought together five hundred and fifty foreign ministry officers from more than fifty countries that "read like a Who's Who of the world's most distinguished diplomats at midcentury."[47] Such initiatives formed a key part of American diplomacy throughout the Cold War, and when it came to water, the situation was no different.[48]

White's appreciation of water as an issue of international development and of human adjustment to change that involved economic, political, and social choices became key features of water management. White chaired the sessions on integrated river-basin development at the first UN Scientific Conference on Resource Conservation and Utilization in 1949.[49] From 1953 to 1956 he also chaired UNESCO's Advisory Committee on Arid Zone Research, which was hailed a success.[50] These established him among a growing, global network of environmental experts and positioned him well to contribute insights regarding how to integrate multipurpose river basin development and multiple points of view when the United Nations convened an expert panel on integrated river basin development. In 1958, White co-authored the expert panel's report, which cited the American experience in the TVA as well as numerous other instances in which cooperation over river development yielded benefits.[51] Interestingly, in the report's section on the "Origin of the Concept of Multi-purpose Development," water's agency is recognized as part of the process of rendering water within social space:

> A river is a living entity providing a source of wealth which ought to be shared equitably, as a legacy amongst its beneficiaries. When by development the potential riches of a river have been realized and apportioned among the people, it may be said that the initial river, wild and often destructive, has disappeared; but it lives again as a new domesticated river bringing only beneficent results.[52]

From 1961 to 1962, White chaired a Ford Foundation consulting group set up to study options for the lower Mekong region in Southeast Asia. Building from the Economic Commission for Asia and the Far East report in 1957 (discussed last chapter), and in a similar vein as David Lilienthal and Arthur Goldschmidt, White thought that the integrated development of water in the Mekong could help secure regional peace among Vietnam, Laos, Cambodia, and Thailand. He subsequently drafted his arguments for a "fourth course" in Vietnam based on water development.[53] He circulated over 1,100 copies of the manuscript and used his contacts in the White House to get a copy to Lyndon Johnson.[54] White's ideas were timely, given the president's 1965 speech at Johns Hopkins and the pledge to fund something bigger than the TVA. Like others, White's recommendations trucked in the language of the TVA, but with a broader view of having a United Nations–backed process for international coordination. There had been a UN arrangement known as the Mekong Committee since 1957, but it had been conceived of primarily as a political coordination mechanism.[55] White's intervention tabled a broader suite of options by arguing for enhanced technical, social, and political capacity in water management. His approach applied the concept of multipurpose river basin management in the context of international development and fit broadly with the "Water for Peace" initiative launched by President Johnson in 1965.

The International Hydrological Decade

While the United States strategized about how water programs might support its position in the Cold War and the Vietnam War, domestic concerns were also pushing America to consider international issues in water management. These concerns precipitated the establishment of the International Hydrological Decade from 1965 to 1974. The IHD significantly changed how water managers understood water's global distribution, especially when the Soviet Union's committee for the IHD published the *Atlas of the World Water Balance* in 1978.[56] The atlas included global and regional maps of water distribution and was the culmination of a new spatial sensibility about human-water relationships that made it possible to calculate any country or region's deviance from a normalized distribution of water on Earth. By providing a baseline for estimating water's uneven distribution, the atlas presented a horizon that came into view for coordinating development challenges under a global scheme. It was not the idea of the hydrological cycle that was new but the comprehensive picture of its global distribution that aligned the material order of water with a moral order for management.

The global, spatial sensibility crafted through the IHD affected normal water by creating new practices—new stopping rules—that were not backstopped by the characteristics of any particular society. Rather, a narrative took shape through work by UNESCO and others around how the scientific rise of hydrology over the last three centuries could link the practices of ancient societies to contemporary concerns and the emerging Earth sciences.[57] The integration of historical experiences and new scientific methods introduced the claim that the challenges identified by contemporary water management techniques had been going on for a very, very long time. Indeed, they conditioned the rise of civilization. This subtle shift veiled the ethnocentric dimensions of water management by suggesting that contemporary challenges were not the outcome of any particular set of ideas because all societies had managed water in some sense. As such, water management challenges were a natural part of social coordination. The evidence for this was to be found in the history of hydrology, which indexed normal water to water's spatial distribution on Earth in a manner largely consistent with how the history of geology before it placed humans in evolutionary time.

The U.S. influence on the IHD emerged, in part, from its response to the "little waters" controversy in which flood control needed to be linked more closely with land use (which is reminiscent of the "land problem" and the need to link social institutions to geologic processes). In 1963, the National Academy of Sciences in the United States published the results of an Ad Hoc Committee on International Programs in Atmospheric Sciences and Hydrology.[58] Gilbert White, Luna Leopold, and other American experts formed the committee, which repeatedly emphasized the need to understand the "land phase" of hydrology in which water, plants, soils, and geological processes interacted with, and were acted upon by, human activity. The committee's concern with the "land phase" of hydrology echoed the claims of other U.S. experts, such as Raymond Nace, who also called for international attention to hydrology owing to the fact that there was no hydrological "cycle" in a single sense but, rather, a "hydrologic geocycle" in which water circulated at multiple temporal and spatial scales affected by human activity.[59] Because human actions changed the "land phase" of hydrology all around the world, any national interest in hydrology had to consider the effects of international land use on water's many cycles. The result of the American push to modernize hydrology alongside the emerging Earth sciences then taking shape was that, when UNESCO adopted the resolution approving the IHD, it did so with "substantially the wording proposed by the United States."[60] Through the IHD, Nace argued that hydrology, though once a "laggard," would take its place as an "interdisciplinary Earth science."[61]

The IHD started down the path of linking domestic water management and international hydrology when, in 1967, Raymond Nace framed water resources management as a "global problem" that had "local roots."[62] Nace, a former colleague of White's on UNESCO's Advisory Committee for Arid Zone Research, worked for the Water Resources Division of the U.S. Geological Survey and chaired the National Academy of Sciences's National Committee for the International Hydrologic Decade. Nace's global-local reasoning augmented the deductive formula of uniformitarianism by comparing different slices of evolutionary time in order to reveal both water's finitude and its uneven distribution within a balanced water system. Today, this formula is routinely used to situate water "crises" in reference to the total amount of water on Earth—a lot—that is winnowed away through calculations of how much water is actually available: Most water is salty, a small fraction is fresh, but most freshwater is locked up as ice or so deep underground that the actual amount of useable freshwater is a mere sliver of the total. The practiced use of this formula is now a customary part of codifying water scarcity. It is also a habit of thought routinely used as a stopping rule that provides a backdrop for water challenges all around the world and that has decidedly spatial implications: We need to rethink water management everywhere.

The combination of water's finitude and its uneven distribution was reinforced by the IHD and the global picture it painted of human-water relationships. Tellingly, Nace entitled UNESCO's 1969 report on the IHD *Water and Man: A World View.*[63] Nace's account of the history of "water and man" told of the progress of hydrologic science and how water could not be reduced to H_2O because many subspecies of water existed.[64] Alongside advances in hydrology, Nace fashioned water management into a global story of lessons learned from previous civilizations in Sumeria, Mohenjo-Daro and Harappa (Indus Basin), Greece, Rome, and Egypt. The collective experience of previous civilizations provided warrant for gathering human-water relationships into a view of the world that could not be gainsaid by complaints that hydrological wisdom reflected only the views of a particular society. Why? Because the rules explaining management experience were found in a shared human capacity to adjust to hydrological realities in space and over time.

Nace was not alone in retelling the histories of human-water relationships. In 1970, Asit Biswas published the *History of Hydrology*, which reproduced a similar narrative arc.[65] Biswas, who went on to advise numerous governments on water development and later founded the Third World Center for Water Management, tied the history of hydrology to the history of western thought beginning with Thales, through Plato, Aristotle, and into "modern science." Biswas extended this eurocentric account to include Korea and China as well. But he reserved a special place for the United States, noting that the U.S. Geological Survey deserved special credit for systematically collecting and publishing data, which he claimed "has probably become the greatest boon the engineering profession has ever been handed."[66]

Others were also telling grand stories about humanity and hydrology. Norman Smith at Imperial College argued in his book, also titled *Man and Water*, that the history of hydrotechnology was critical to social, managerial, and organizational order.[67] Even the U.S. Bureau of Reclamation got in on the action after its assistant commissioner, Gilbert Stamm, called for increased social science research on water development (i.e., dams) in 1969.[68] It took a while, but in 1977 the Bureau of Reclamation approved an independent study, also titled *Man and Water*, that critiqued the planning focus on "*Homo economicus*" and argued that economic emphasis came at the expense of other ways of understanding social relationships affecting water.[69] By the 1970s, White's initial optimism regarding cost-benefit analysis was also waning. In his chapter of yet another book entitled *Man and Water*—one that gathered essays from across the social sciences—White upended economic appraisals that "chiefly served to buttress conclusions arrived at by other paths [and] rarely modified radically the investment patterns or design procedures of government agencies."[70]

Before considering the outcomes of the IHD, it is important to see how normal water's spatial turn buries ethnocentric assumptions about what is being managed: water resources. The plot is prepared by crafting stopping rules that identify a broadly shared hydrological experience with what the management of water entails. In this way, water resources are subtly advanced as not being peculiar to any particular time or place and as having persisted from time out of mind as water circulates through the global hydrological cycle. This is evident in the combined social, technical, and geological evidence regarding the health of previous civilizations. Of course, as the epigraph from White to this chapter reveals, at any given moment not all water is a resource. But, if every society shares in the experience of managing a small and unevenly distributed fraction of the Earth's total hydrologic endowment, then successfully managing water resources is, as it has been through all of human history, the working out of local solutions to this global dynamic. As such, contemporary advances in hydrology offer self-knowledge for how these dynamics work: a literal *worldview*, just as Nace claimed in 1969.

It is remarkable how new histories of hydrology gained global purchase as UN agencies, the World Meteorological Organization, and a global network of scientists coalesced to develop a planetary view of water resources. These histories also reveal the staying power of normal water and the capacity of water resources to crisscross social, technical, and geological registers affecting the health of people and planet. The health of Earth had become a going concern throughout the 1960s, notably after Rachel Carson's publication of *Silent Spring* brought attention to the negative impacts of industrial society on land, water, and other species.[71] For his part, Gilbert White was not interested only in global dynamics. For instance, he was also a driving force in a large and carefully crafted study of the relationship between local drinking water choices and household health in East Africa.[72] Raymond Nace, too, was keen to ensure that the work of the IHD was seen as connecting humans to the Earth system. In fact, he chastised Asit Biswas's account of hydrology as more of a "chronicle" than a history.[73] Nace argued that the uniformitarian maxim of the Earth sciences—"the present is the key to the past"—was the sounder guide, not only for linking human history and hydrological science but also for guiding future decisions.[74] Nace's view is a mere stone's throw from McGee's earlier arguments that geological "prevision" is what justifies successful geological guesses of the past to be counted on when comparing hypotheses about, and planning for, the future.

What is also remarkable is why there was so little academic contest over the historical rewrite of hydrology to fit universal stories of "water and man." For it was not as though there weren't alternatives. In fact, another geographer, Yi-Fu Tuan, provided one of the most interesting, if less well known, counterpoints to this rising narrative. In *The Hydrological Cycle and the Wisdom of God*, Tuan remarked that a "geoteleology" indexed the acceptance of scientific claims about global hydrology to a set of cultural concerns about forms of rational explanation.[75] Tuan's analysis followed the works of early naturalists, like John Ray, to consider how notions of a divine economy made subtle inroads into nineteenth-century hydrogeology. Right up to Huxley, Tuan discerned a thinly veiled Judeo-Christian view in understandings of water's role in Earth processes. Unfortunately, Tuan did not take his analysis into the twentieth century. Yet these ideas no doubt continued, both in the notion of an "Earth in Decay" that pervaded nineteenth-century geology in Britain and in McGee's call to help the Earth as one would an ailing parent.[76] Why wasn't this history taken more seriously? One reason is that, following the rejection of the subject in the early twentieth century, there was a subsequent effort to do without references to any particular society. This was not a phenomenon unique to hydrology. Throughout the Cold War there was a concerted effort to establish objective accounts of scientific phenomena, and even the logic of science itself, that did not depend on social characteristics.[77]

Mar del Plata: Management Meets Development

The IHD ended in 1974 amid the rising tide of environmentalism that had been washing ashore since the 1960s and an upstart environmental justice movement galvanized by the effects of America's toxic Love Canal.[78] In 1969, the International Council of Scientific Unions had created a Scientific Committee on Problems of the Environment, which Gilbert White became a member of in 1970 and served as president of from 1976 to 1982.[79] In 1972, the United Nations convened the Conference on the Human Environment in Stockholm, where the Canadian

Maurice Strong served as secretary-general. In Stockholm, White contributed his expertise on arid regions and was named as an expert who should be approached to review recommendations of the Stockholm action plan for land and water management.[80] In 1969, White's book, *Strategies of American Water Management*, became part of the canon for understanding water management in the United States.[81] In the broader world of water management, White's reputation among diplomats, scientists, and government officials positioned him uniquely for the first UN Conference on Water, held in Mar del Plata, Argentina, in 1977. It was there that normal water decisively took into its fold the proposition that water was scarce.

In 1975, the year after the IHD ended, the United Nations adopted Resolution 3513(xxx) to set the Mar del Plata conference in motion.[82] The timing for the event built upon the IHD and emerging national water laws. The United States had passed the Clean Water Act in 1972.[83] Across the Atlantic, civil engineers interpreted Great Britain's Water Act of 1973 as establishing a "national industry" for hydrology that paved the way for its incorporation into water management.[84] Under the auspices of the International Institute for Environment and Development (IIED), White provided one of the first global water assessments that linked the findings of the IHD to water management, law, and policy—and the IIED's founder, Barbara Ward, later became a driving force behind the concept of sustainable development.[85] In preparation for Mar del Plata, the IIED published reports and sponsored conferences that laid the groundwork for a broad effort to merge international development and water management.[86] One of these conferences met in Vancouver, Canada, in June 1976 to outline how achieving "Clean Water for All" fit with other goals, such as those of the UN Conference on Human Settlements (HABITAT).[87] In Vancouver, participants like Maurice Strong built on growing international momentum to connect international development, human-environment relations, and water management. Gilbert White's co-authored assessment of the world's water situation was included in the conference proceedings, and White, on behalf of the IIED, sent recommendations to the UN secretary-general for the Mar del Plata conference, Yahia Abdel Mageed.[88]

The UN Conference on Water in Mar del Plata included representatives from 116 governments and numerous other institutions and agencies. The conference proceedings fill four volumes with perspectives from around the world on water management and issues of climate, groundwater, ecology, economics, hydrology, law, policy, pollution, poverty, sanitation, and more. Owing to the impressive coverage given to the world's water situation, it is difficult to distill a coherent philosophical approach to water management from the experiences of different countries—difficult, that is, if the presumption is that there was not already a philosophy in play, one that could assemble different experiences in way that is universal but that avoids the appearance of ethnocentrism. With such an understanding embedded in the notion of water as a resource, and buoyed by a planetary account of the world's water, however, the idea of water scarcity quickly rose to become a grounding proposition for linking the many competing concerns affecting water. Ultimately, White's co-authored assessment of the world's water featured as the opening essay in the conference proceedings and an edited volume summarizing the conference.[89] In this way, White helped shaped linkages between the world's water and the prospects for regional water management.

The rise of water scarcity as a proposition of water management began by eschewing older ideas of water as a "free gift" or as replenished from an eternal source. Not only was abundance now anathema, but explicitly rejecting it was part of ensuring water management could move from global assessments to local decision making. As part of the transition from abundance to scarcity, the idea of "Rational Planning" ascended at Mar del Plata. In part, Rational Planning was supposed to keep water management from veering into neo-Malthusian arguments that suggested that industrial society and population growth were on a collision course with limited water resources.[90] Rational Planning's solution was to incorporate water demand more carefully into calculations of efficiency. In short, there was enough water—but not if this scarce resource wasn't valued correctly. Two reports at Mar del Plata were especially influential in this respect. The first was a comprehensive report on "Policy Options," and the second was a World Bank paper on the use of pricing mechanisms to control water use.[91] Together, these two documents were formative for integrating water development (often financed though international development institutions) with regional water management across contexts. Before that could happen, however, both development and management needed to adhere to a common logic.

Rational Planning was the initial vehicle for securing spatial assessments of the world's water to the regional development challenges of water scarcity. Rational Planning aligned itself with the classic tenets of rationality: universality and necessity.[92] In this model of rationality, universality refers to how individuals with the same information will reach the same conclusion provided no logical mistakes are made. In this way the standard of rationality is independent of any person or group. Second, a necessary connection between premises and conclusions explains *why* individuals who begin with the same information will reach similar conclusions. Under this model, Rational Planning began with a large effort in data collection to allow for clear frames of reference regarding the information upon which regional development would proceed. Here, the scientific networks established through the IHD provided the basis for what later became the Mar del Plata Action Plan.[93] Through reports from agencies like the World Meteorological Organization, the Action Plan connected the quantification of water at a global level to national scales in ways that provided common data for planners. In this, things were different than McGee had envisioned. With a global data set, legislation did not need to naturalize state constitutions to national water endowments. Instead, legislation needed to be scaled up—to global hydrology—and crafted in ways that would coordinate any given country's institutional agencies.[94] Rational Planning thereby left wiggle room for regional differences, geographical contexts, and different legal traditions under the banner of establishing broader bases of choice in water management based on the data available to decision makers. It was a path that was deemed universal, but not ethnocentric.

At the national level, Rational Planning was supposed to lead to laws, policies, and economic development plans that created logical supply-and-demand scenarios. Provided with the right hydrological data, it was thought, any region's water endowment could be rationally managed. Experts expected that water availability would vary from year to year. Overall, however, these variations fluctuated in an envelope of stability provided by the balance of the global hydrological cycle, which mirrored steady-state assumptions in ecology.[95] Within this framework, supply-and-demand scenarios could be operationalized to characterize the challenges of water scarcity without appealing to the characteristics of societies or to cultural practices. Rational Planning was, in its own way, a spatial counterweight to the deductive reasoning of uniformitarianism that preceded it. Under the constraints of water scarcity and a new iteration of liberalism, the temporal, evolutionary register of progress gave way to spatial arguments that married the internalized "colonial" logic of regional development (pushed internationally by Lilienthal and others) to the field of international water management that had emerged out of the attempt to link domestic concerns with global hydrology. With the data from the IHD in hand, there was now a way to align political, economic, geographic, and hydrological data with a single model of decision making.

Rational Planning did not explicitly align management with the geologic temporalities of Earth-making; instead, it fit human-water relationships to assessments of the planetary distribution of water that rendered it scarce. This made water management a unique political challenge:

> Confronted by that dilemma, people were learning that the earth's resources were not limitless, that water was a scarce asset and that millions in the world suffered from a lack of it while other millions were wasting such a vital resource; and that the present-day heirs of the situation must now undertake the communal task of administering in justice and in harmony with nature an element which was of such vital importance for life.
>
> In these circumstances, in which the use and conservation of water could not remain isolated problems or problems that could be solved by a specific sector or region—since they constituted a single theme: water management as man's heritage for promotion of the common good—the United Nations Water Conference could thus mark the start of a new era, that of water rationally used, conserved and harmonized with the human environment and with nature.[96]

Bespectacled

After Mar del Plata, water scarcity brought into focus the worldview that pictured relationships of "man and water" envisioned under the IHD. On a planet in which water is scarce, demands strain limited and inequitably distributed resources in ways that require changes to management.

In his introduction to the edited proceedings from Mar del Plata, Asit Biswas built on his hydrologic history to argue that "from the beginning man tended to treat water as a . . . 'free' resource" and that squandering this abundance was now being confronted by increasingly urbanized, industrial societies.[97] Biswas juxtaposed the sullied history of water abundance against the realities faced by the poor in rural hinterlands, whom he thought were likely worse off than the urban poor. Critically, for Biswas, the demands of industrial society operated not only as impetus for Rational Planning in water management but as a catalyst for developing a shared view of scarcity across socialist, liberal, and communist nations. That is, industrialization was a universal model for development while water scarcity was a fact about human-environment relationships, not about specific social or political orders.

Imagining human-water relationships from the "local roots" to "global problems" depended on a belief that these relationships remained constant across scales, an idea that further served to link water to imaginations of "industrial societies" in which economic development proceeded according to rational plans.[98] If water was to function like other units of industrial production, it needed relationships that were uniform. The IHD found evidence for this possibility in the global hydrological cycle itself. It was balanced at a planetary scale, and yearly variations or regional differences did nothing to alter that fact. The stability of water's relationships fit the Rational Planning model for modernization and industrial development, such as was being pushed by the World Bank. Successful modernization became increasingly important by the late 1970s, as the United States started to shift its development efforts from direct forays into places like southeast Asia to indirect mechanisms of economic and institutional development supported by financial institutions, non-governmental organizations, and other non-state actors. The World Bank itself had long favored more latitude. Way back in 1954, David Lilienthal recounted a lunch with the head of the Bank, Gene Black, who wanted to create pathways for private capital to move through the Bank and directly to development projects without host governments, or even the U.S. government, being involved.[99]

When dealing with a world in which water was scarce, private economic transactions were better. The World Bank was even willing to securitize private development loans, rather than having them backed by host governments in developing countries.[100] Often, however, the World Bank's securitized loans were not put in place. Instead, loans were backed by host governments and tied to broader programs of structural adjustment to industrialize resource sectors—of which irrigated agriculture was often key—to bring developing countries into the global economy. This had deep consequences politically, culturally, and economically for water management in places like Iran and elsewhere.[101] But there was also a rift over what, in this rational scheme of supply and demand, water scarcity actually was. In fact, the first metrics of water scarcity to circulate globally do not appear until a dozen years after Mar del Plata, in 1989. As the next chapter considers, it turned out to be exceedingly difficult to connect local and global hydrology under an industrial model. Water scarcity was not rational, after all. It was a judgment and, at that, a judgment that still had to be taught as part of normal water's broader project of bringing water's possibilities into a single planetary story. Likewise, practices for reaching this judgment had to be developed if scarcity was going to function as a stopping rule that gathered together a contingent (if stable) hydrological cycle, vastly different cultural and ecological histories, and evolving demands of industrial societies—that is, if scarcity was to be a be a propositional truth in the worldview of "man and water."

Residue

The sequence from abundance to scarcity issued from the retelling of water management as a story of human-water relationships in which hydrologic histories explained how water had been managed from time immemorial and, now, how the mismanagement of water was a significant problem. This remains a frequent departure point for the water-meets-modernity story. It is a story that creates the common-sense reference point for water scarcity and that frames the apparent abundance of the world's total water supply in spatial terms—at a given moment of geological time—before revealing the minute fraction available for human use. But telling the story this way hides its cultural roots. It is simply not the case that all of the political, social, or legal options—or their fit with certain forms of geologic or hydrologic explanations—are considered in Rational Planning. As we have seen, White's search for "broader bases for choice" is always mediated by a cultural orientation to water as a certain kind of geographical fact: a resource that fits the proposed union between management practices and development agendas. This fit is no coincidence, and it depends on the model of the TVA that united management and development and that itself had its roots in American conservation and multipurpose river basin development. Yet it is remarkable how quickly a supporting narrative of modern hydrology was crafted that made this all quite natural and in which water resources found a natural home in an emerging, global sensibility.

Despite the international effort to develop a planetary view of water, problems remained. Notably, water resources did not fit naturally into a pre-formed container; rather, water resources fit with a particular project of international scientific collaboration that co-produced assessments of the world's water while also naturalizing hydrology through histories of "water and man." The upshot was that the global space in which water is scarce took shape in response to American concerns over how to manage the "land problems" that arose as multiple agents affected the "land phase" of the water cycle. So, despite the fact that the post-colonial experience claimed by the United States was by no means universal, and that concerns in other post-colonial places manifestly did not parallel that of the U.S. south, America shaped much of the international program that linked hydrology to the Earth sciences.[102] The favored workaround was to link regional differences to the global water cycle in a way that forwarded development while maintaining the economic path that inspired it. But power dynamics configured the social space of the region in a particular way, namely, by using water scarcity to walk the line between explicitly ethnocentric views in which America was a model for post-colonial development while still supporting forms of industrial growth and globalization that supported American liberalism. The displacement of other forms of life in the new geography of water management thereby continued to bury abundance as one cultural view of water—as a resource—linked planetary hydrology to development. Water scarcity does not reject "the social" outright or attempt to displace embedded social relationships through economics.[103] Rather, under water scarcity the new geography of water management sought to operate without reference to cultural difference by positioning water resources to mediate social relations.

A second, related problem arose over the cumulative impact of development agendas—what Ken Conca calls "pushing rivers around"[104]—which came to be seen as undermining the conditions for liberal abundance, too. This was not entirely new to normal water; its philosophy always held that these sorts of "human adjustments" were likely as people and other geologic agents modified the Earth. That is why "broader bases for choice" was such a prudent position. What was new, however, was that growing concerns over environmental impacts combined with ongoing issues regarding resource conservation and international development at a time when liberalism was again undergoing heavy revision. It is vital to keep this in mind so the developments in water management after Mar del Plata can be situated with respect to evolving notions of liberalism that emerged in the late twentieth century. As the next part of this book argues, the rise of water security is best explained through a situated account that works out how the sites of what is often termed "neoliberalism" affect normal water.

PART III

Security

6

The Globalization of Normal Water

Given the fact that life is based on myriads of water flows—
through every single plant, every animal, every human
body—and that it is globally circulated in the water cycle
with which man continuously interacts by land use and by
societal activities, *sustainable development must be a question of sustainable interaction between human society and the
water cycle, including all the ecosystems fed by that cycle.*
—International Water Resources Association

Ten years after Mar del Plata, there was still no consensus on how to
measure water scarcity. Then, in 1987, the landmark report *Our Common
Future* introduced the world to sustainable development. Also known
as the Brundtland Report, *Our Common Future* barely mentioned
water, and this, as the epigraph highlights, prompted an international
response from water experts who emphasized the links among water,
development, and sustainability.[1] In retrospect, the Brundtland Report
both galvanized an emerging network of global water experts and laid
bare some persisting problems. On the one hand, only two years after
the Brundtland Report the first metric of water stress received general
acceptance.[2] On the other, no complete consensus on water scarcity has
ever been achieved because competing metrics make different assumptions about socioeconomic contexts, data gathering and aggregation,
and environmental variability.[3] The difficulty of agreeing on how to calculate water scarcity was not only that metrics came on the back end of
the judgment that water was scarce but also that even variables shared
across competing metrics are often weighted differently, which cast
doubt on the seemingly natural fit between water scarcity and Rational Planning.[4] Further, the role of judgments regarding how to measure
water scarcity troubled the idea that any metric could be a non-arbitrary
measure. Every metric makes judgments about social habits, rights,

politics, economics, and ecological contexts in determinations of water scarcity, yet no social or ecological context can provide a universal template for others.[5]

The difficulty of objectively defining water scarcity can be assuaged somewhat if the idea that water is scarce is relieved of the requirement that it function as a rational premise. Water scarcity can, after all, also function as a proposition. For the purposes of management, this is an appealing prospect because propositions are declarations about what may be true or false regardless of how they are expressed. Across turns of phrase, languages, and idioms, propositions declare what is or is not the case. For example, the proposition, "The water is frozen" is true or false regardless of whether it is expressed in Japanese, Bengali, or by pointing at a thermometer. As a proposition, water scarcity likewise conveys truths about water regardless of social convention. So differences across metrics are not fatal; they are simply different ways of declaring the same truth: water was mismanaged under the era of abundance, and adjustments must now be made to an era of finite and unequal supply in the context of competing demands. The practices that shift water scarcity from premise to proposition allow the search for justifications of any particular metric to come to an end. When these practices are extended, water scarcity can even identify mismanagement in places where water was never abundant.

The difficulty of measuring water scarcity without privileging particular meanings of water led to a third stopping rule—after water abundance and water scarcity—for water management: water security. Water security draws on both conservation and development to argue that there is no single perspective that is intrinsically better positioned with respect to the judgments that water scarcity inevitably entail. In this sense, water security is a self-effacing proposition—it retires within the crisscrossing geological, social, technical, and health claims of normal water the fact that liberal forms of life are what water resources support. Just as previous iterations of liberalism installed abundance and scarcity without unique subjects or unique social relations, this third iteration installs water security without reference to unique symbolic ends. What distinguishes water security is that it at once forwards normal water's program to deal with the implications of water scarcity regarding potential international conflict, human development, or ecology, while at the same time water security shrouds the fact that water resources, and their attendant forms of life, are what mediate all water threats, be they from want or from overflow. This proceeds in two steps.

The first step is a "procedural turn" in water management.[6] The procedural turn parallels, to some degree, what political theorists term "the exchange of the right for the good," where the state seeks a neutral position regarding the substantive goods held by individuals or groups.[7] On the ground—as this and the next chapter demonstrate—various methods arise for transitioning the state from adjudicating substantive goods (such as through Rational Planning) to "setting the rules" for addressing water scarcity via economics, decentralized institutions, and stakeholder participation, to name a few means. Hopeful environmental philosophers have argued that emphasis on fair, democratic procedures even retain a (revised) notion of rationality in resource management.[8] On closer inspection, however, the procedural turn is also what enables water management to pace evolving forms of liberalism, which helps to explain how liberal, utilitarian norms subsequently condition international water management.[9] Although often referred to as "neoliberal," I argue below that the iteration of liberalism that water security takes shape within operates on the same logic of "doing without" that characterizes earlier liberal approaches to subjectivity and social relations and that continue to forward water resources as the basis for connecting people and planet.

In a second step, procedural mechanisms are employed to "integrate" development and management with the environment without appealing to the symbolic goods held as intrinsic ends by any particular group. This form of integration gave rise to what became known as "integrated water resources management" (IWRM). Through networks of global expertise that expanded after Mar del Plata, and were reinvigorated by the Brundtland Report, IWRM took hold of the sustainable development agenda when it came to water. Throughout the 1990s, networks of global water experts gained considerable clout, enough that, only two decades after the practice of IWRM was formally adopted in 1992, 64 percent of all countries applied some version of it.[10] The global hubbub over IWRM was not without its difficulties. Rather than adjudicate these, I show how the judgments that align IWRM with liberal forms of life render criticisms of it as a primarily technical endeavor mute—IWRM has always been a deeply political project. But the judgments that legitimate IWRM are themselves troubled by several late twentieth-century dynamics, especially anthropogenic climate change, which undermine assumptions of a globally stable hydrological system. To deal with human activity potentially undermining the conditions for liberal forms life, water management takes up international development's long-standing concern with security at a time when the welfare state is on the wane.

The upshot of these two steps is that water security comes to function as a third stopping rule for normal water. The mismanagement of water abundance and the problems of water scarcity mean that integration is not to be linked to anything intrinsic regarding how different groups conceptualize or imagine relationships to water. Different meanings for water all still exist, but water is managed without reference to them. In place of cultural pluralism, water security links interstate and individual health to social, technical, and planetary considerations without appealing to the competing symbolic goods different communities or groups may hold. To wit, and as the epigraph to this chapter emphasizes, the problem of sustainable development is one of linking "*human society*," writ large, to the water cycle. As water security gains momentum into the twenty-first century, the contradictions identified at the beginning of this book over the human right to water gain civil status. As the next chapter considers, this comes into full view when water security is linked to concerns over the precarious web of relationships among water, energy, food, and the climate in the Anthropocene. It is also then that "Water for Life" is chosen as the title for the UN Decade for 2005–2015. It is a self-effacing slogan designed to encompass any meaning for water while appealing for legitimacy to none.

The Procedural Turn

After Mar del Plata, the United Nations announced the International Drinking Water Supply and Sanitation Decade. The new decade was a direct outcome of the Mar del Plata Action Plan. Throughout the 1980s, it also became clear that water resources were central to sustainable development. As one report later put it, "Water resources are essential agents in the development of agriculture, industry, power regulation, waste disposal, human health and other areas. . . . These areas are not independent and, for effective management of water and sustainable use and development, some degree of integrated management is indispensable."[11] From the perspective of water experts, the long-held notion that water resources are "essential agents" linking development to management was key to aligning water and sustainable development. This is what made it so jarring when the Brundtland Report all but ignored water. Malin Falkenmark, the lead hydrologist on the team that defined the 1989 metric of water stress, described the Brundtland Report as "water blind."[12]

Despite the Brundtland Report's hydrological blind spot, advocates of sustainable development had their eyes open to the difficult prospect of maintaining development while conserving natural resources. In the case of water, however, joining the two was not going to happen by itself. The eventual union took shape under the paradigm of IWRM. Integrated water resources management is an offspring of the attempt to unite environment and development, which was a broader aim of the UN environmental agenda that began with the 1972 meeting in Stockholm and continued into the 1980s.[13] Yet when water went all but missing from the Brundtland Report, it became evident to the international water community that linking water, development, and conservation required a host of changes. Ken Conca has ably shown how putting water on the sustainable development agenda involved a whole spectrum of activity: the expansion of expert networks and the creation of new ones, global water summits, new scientific journals, professional organizations, and a discourse in which to articulate IWRM.[14] Before considering how these activities reinforced normal water, however, we need to look at several shifts prior to the consolidation of IWRM in the early 1990s that are important for seeing how it evolved alongside an iteration of liberalism that took shape in the 1980s.

Economic reforms in the 1980s are often called "neoliberal" and are frequently referenced to policies that reregulated the governance of natural resources to reduce government oversight and increase the role of free markets in environmental and social policy.[15] Wendy Brown's trenchant critiques argue that neoliberalism did not simply reregulate goods formerly excluded from market exchanges but also extended economic rationality into new domains, such as law, and thereby conditioned social relations and institutions in ways that continue to shape how efforts to live differently may proceed.[16] In the water sector, as elsewhere, the intellectual forces behind neoliberal reforms were economists like Friedrich Hayek and Milton Friedman but sometimes also include Ayn Rand.[17] These reforms, however, weren't particularly novel. They followed the same logic of "doing without" that characterized earlier iterations of liberalism. The difference now was that to manage water without reference to any symbolic ends, the commonsense "gut feeling" that water was vital to individual and national health could not be seen as favoring liberal forms of life. The explicit "American liberalism" advocated by the likes of John Dewey, Arthur Schlesinger, and David Lilienthal needed to go. Elizabeth Povinelli has compellingly argued that one factor weighing on this latest iteration of liberalism was the failure of multiculturalism under the "politics of recognition" that rose to prominence in in the 1970s.[18]

Over the course of this chapter and the next I argue that the latest iteration of liberalism was—and remains—one of social pretense. No longer is government a collective expression of subjective will, for those kinds of subjects have been done without. Neither does government reflect the will of a pre-political community (i.e., "the People") because earlier iterations of liberalism have waylaid anything unique about social relations. Social pretense therefore consists, not in indirect forms of governance, but in forwarding the direct governance of contingent goods—like water resources, but not limited to them—that have their life within liberalism. The social pretense consists in the claim that contingent goods can be directly governed without appealing to any form of life while nevertheless linking technical, social, and geological concerns to the health of individuals, societies, and ultimately the planet.

In an era of liberal pretense water resources continue to form the bridge between life and non-life, just as they had for WJ McGee. Yet, rather than advocating that these resources result from the characteristics of "the People" or the democratic methods of American democracy, an effort is undertaken to naturalize contingent social and geological processes to a social world that appears to operate free of place-bound claims regarding subjectivity, social relations, and now symbolic goods. A turn of phrase in the Brundtland Report succinctly captures this sentiment when it states, "The Earth is one but the world is not."[19] Indeed, a key goal of sustainable development—and of the latest iteration of liberalism—has been to consolidate multiple social worlds to a single view of the Earth. Whether trick or illusion, what matters in the latest iteration of liberalism is that the things mediating the consolidation of many worlds to one Earth (i.e., water resources) are not recognized as issuing from any particular social world.

The iteration of liberalism in the late twentieth century continued to align a particular form of life with planetary processes, while governments retired from explicitly adjudicating among the goods that different communities or constituencies may hold with respect to the manifold processes that water supports. The task of governments was to "set the rules" for acquiring water and other resources in a way that allowed contingent social and environmental processes to play out fairly—not through the haphazard dynamics of evolution—and within the bounds of sustainability. As the International Drinking Water Supply and Sanitation Decade got under way, a key concern was how to evaluate different policy options. Just what was fair? The Mar del Plata Action Plan had boldly called for rational laws and policy, but these would mean little if they could not be delivered upon and, however rational they may be, could always be criticized for benefiting some at the expense of others. Meeting these challenges increasingly relied on two procedural shifts in the 1980s: a first regarding objectivity, and another regarding institutional arrangements.

The Search for Objectivity

The call for Rational Planning at Mar del Plata followed a tradition of comprehensive water management—Gilbert White's broader bases of choice—that aimed to include as much relevant information as possible in order to rationally decide what was best. In 1981, the UN Environmental Program's deputy executive director Peter Thacher offered a "master plan for the watery planet" that linked land, coastal, and marine management to complex and global environmental problems.[20] Thacher later acted as senior advisor to Maurice Strong when the latter was secretary-general to the 1992 UN Conference on Environment and Development in Rio de Janeiro. But in 1982, the UN Environmental Program (UNEP) had just published its own assessment of the world environment from 1972 to 1982, which was co-edited by Gilbert White.[21] Thacher's copy of that book and many of his personal records were donated to Harvard University. Maurice Strong's records are archived there as well. Together, these archives offer a unique perspective on how the attempt to implement the Mar del Plata action Plan led to the creation of IWRM.

Ideally, Rational Planning in water management was to be backstopped by national laws and policies. Following White's ideas about comprehensive planning, these laws and policies would provide a framework for regulating complex water development projects to the best ends.[22] But what criteria for "best" should be used? And how should competing views be compared? There were at least three objections to appealing to law and policy for Rational Planning. One was that some governments lacked the capacity to fulfill or enforce regulations. A second was that any law or policy produces winners and losers, so regulation cannot be considered a neutral tool. Finally, since many watercourses are shared between nations, laws that served the interests of one nation may be at odds with others. As Jerome Delli Priscoli, a senior advisor to the U.S. Army Corps of Engineers has stated, the ensuing tension in international water management was a "dialectic between two philosophical norms; one, the rational analytic model, often called the planning norm, and two, the utilitarian or free-market model, often couched in terms of privatization."[23] The tensions between planning and economics in water management were not, however, dialectical. Rather, these tensions were over two ways of advancing liberal, utilitarian aims: one that reflected the bureaucratic model of water management (the planning norm), and another that reflected later transitions to methodological individualism (free markets and privatization). Nevertheless, the idea that there would be laws that met a non-arbitrary standard of rationality came to be seen as increasingly implausible.

To address the impasse between planning and economics, increasing attention was paid to cost-benefit analysis, which had been part of economic arguments regarding water management since the Flood Control Act of the 1930s. In the 1960s, Allen Kneese and Blair Bower had argued that cost-benefit analysis formed one part of the technological and institutional reforms needed to manage water quality.[24] Their arguments were cited frequently in the second intergovernmental group meeting on cost-benefit evaluation of environmental protection held in Paris in 1979.[25] The purported advantages of cost-benefit analysis were both political and practical. Politically, cost-benefit analysis assessed water use decisions without reference to any particular community. In this sense, cost-benefit analysis was objective because it did not judge the desirability of competing water management options. This had the practical effect of allowing governments to take an initial step away from deciding among the goods of different constituencies. Different players, such as municipalities, irrigators, or industry, would all be subject to the same procedures through which costs and benefits were measured.

Adopting cost-benefit analysis, however, proved more complicated. On the technical side, the French experience revealed the difficulty of linking accounting practices for water resource management to ecological and sociocultural variables.[26] Since variables for measurement were chosen from a large set of possible indices, cost-benefit analysis had to justify choices regarding which indicators were used, at what temporal and spatial scales, and how they were incorporated into decision making. There were also challenges regarding what types of water quality indicators should be part of cost-benefit analysis. What sorts of outcomes were being sought and for whom? But a subtler challenge beset cost-benefit analysis. Namely, a particular political community was making the choice to pursue cost-benefit analysis in the first place. Douglas Kysar has made one of the most thoroughgoing critiques of how cost-benefit analysis in environmental regulation scripts political and ethical norms into the language of objectivity.[27] I am in broad agreement with his assessment; cost-benefit analyses have the pretense of objectively managing resources, but they cannot escape the value judgments that shape the decisions over what is to be measured, how measurements should be taken, and how those measurements fit with the ends of the political community that employs cost-benefit analysis.

Throughout the 1980s, the risks to drinking water and sanitation sat uneasily with cost-benefit techniques for international development. Risks to water supply and sanitation led the Food and Agricultural Organization, the World Health Organization, and the UN Environmental Program to set up an expert panel on Water Management for Vector Control to try to connect water risks to resource management. When it came to malaria control techniques, the expert panel referenced the TVA model in the United States for one way to develop water and reduce risk.[28] For his part, Gilbert White was also increasingly concerned

with risk and, after returning from a trip to Russia, argued that understandings of risk are likely to be inadequate if they do not grasp the
social structures in which people make decisions.[29] By this time, White
had less enthusiasm for cost-benefit analysis, yet it was also the period
in which water became the sort of economic good that fit with the form
of liberalism evolving in the late twentieth century.

Water's economic value had long been recognized, as earlier parts
of this book show. What is unique in the 1980s is that water becomes a
certain type of economic good. It is not the material basis for currency,
as McGee had hoped. Rather, water became an economic good that fit
the abstract "science of money" to water management's "science of supply" by using water scarcity to add the demand side of the economic
equation. Such was the claim at a January 1992 meeting in Dublin, Ire-
land, when water was declared an economic good that had an economic
value in all of its competing uses.[30] The World Meteorological Organization and the UN Environmental Program had initiated the Dublin
conference in coordination with other agencies to prevent the sort of
"water blind" approach to sustainable development that characterized
the Brundtland Report. One of these other agencies was the UN Commission on Environment and Development (UNCED), which was then
doing preparatory work for the 1992 Rio conference, where integrating
environment and development would later take center stage. Maurice
Strong was the secretary-general to the Rio conference, following up on
his leadership at the 1972 Stockholm conference.

Strong named Richard Helmer to be UNCED's representative on the
steering committee for the Dublin conference. Helmer had been active
with World Health Organization projects on water quality during the
International Drinking Water Supply and Sanitation Decade, and it was
Helmer's work that Strong drew upon to advance the idea that water
should be thought of as an economic good in his speech at Dublin.[31] Although Strong didn't deliver his speech in person, it expressly connected
the integration of water management, development, and the treatment
of water as an economic good.[32] In context, this link of water management and development was an instance of how the 1989 UN resolution
to integrate environmental policy with development was taken up under
the guise of objectivity. Of course, others also advocated for the treatment of water as an economic good. I've highlighted Strong's perspec-

tive because of his role at major international conferences. Later, Strong would draw on these experiences to address water experts, as in June 1996, when he gave a keynote address to the North American Water and Environment Congress. There he linked the American water management experience to opportunities in the developing world and to global economic institutions, such as the World Bank.[33] Strong also took his wealth of experience and network of global connections to his role as a board member of the World Economic Forum in the 1990s, which later published its own perspectives on water security.[34] To objectively govern water as an economic good, however, several institutional challenges needed to be overcome.

Institutional Arrangements

Economic instruments like cost-benefit analysis were designed to keep governments from entering the messy process of adjudicating among symbolic goods by allowing individuals or groups to make decisions that satisfy their own preferences. Philosophers, such as Mark Sagoff, have argued that this is a strange goal because it announces ex cathedra that public policy is only about one type of social good: individual preference satisfaction.[35] Of course, earlier iterations of American liberalism had already tapped into the idea that managing water as a social good could provide a wellspring for liberal individuals. What is of particular interest here is how, after Dublin, economic valuations of water resources were aligned with a broader suite of reforms that cultivated a view of public institutions that purported to enhance individual preference satisfaction.[36] This required a whole suite of reforms that affected common understandings of water across many domains of social life and even other economic views of water. In short, adjustments were required for entire forms of life.

Managing water to enhance opportunities for individual preference satisfaction rehashed the problem of human adjustment all over again. This time, however, adjusting to water resources required transitioning from water use practices that were explicitly tied to community goods to those that were not. This sort of adjustment was not limited to the developing world, where policies of structural adjustment used foreign aid to create a uniform system for an increasingly globalized economy. Rather, adjusting from community goods to individual preference satisfaction also affected the United States. For instance, even though McGee's notion of "the People" was passé, the idea that water was part of a public trust had been revived alongside growing environmental concerns in the 1960s. The legal scholar Joseph Sax, and numerous other water experts, argued that the public trust doctrine in the United States was directly relevant to water management and to maintaining the government's role in ensuring that community water values were supported.[37] Harvard's Arthur Maass, together with Raymond Anderson, had also argued for more public engagement with water in the 1970s and recommended that control of water be devolved to the local level.[38] By the mid-1980s, Helen Ingram and others had incisively argued that water management in the United States could not be divorced from institutional challenges.[39] In 1990, Elinor Ostrom published her landmark work on governing the commons, which considered (among other things) how local institutions could enhance understandings of collective action problems in U.S. irrigation.[40] Throughout this time, numerous American water scholars reinvigorated understandings of water as a public good.[41] As a result, doing without earlier, explicit conceptions of the public, or the symbolic goods that linked community values to water, required a major adjustment.

A first step down the path of adjusting to water as an economic good was taken when federal funding for water research was dramatically cut under the Reagan administration in the 1980s, and at precisely the time when increasing interstate conflicts over water, such as the conflict over the Rio Grande, required it.[42] This funding slash was complemented by the National Research Council's efforts to introduce water markets. The National Research Council's Water Science and Technology Board positioned its arguments in the tradition "of the distinguished student of water policy, Gilbert F. White," whose work (in the view of the National Research Council) had both accurately predicted growing water stress and introduced the need to consider environmental values.[43] In 1992, the National Research Council published its report, arguing that American doctrines like prior appropriation (first in time, first in right) were compatible with using water markets to transfer water to uses of higher value. It was a strange claim, especially because prior appropriation rights were originally designed to counter capitalist speculation on water by explicitly not functioning like property rights.[44] In remaking the past to suit the present, however, the National Research Council also ignored how existing rights to water did not simply reflect previous decisions regarding the public good but had also created community goods by virtue of the particular upstream-downstream relationships these rights supported.[45] So, even if the present arrangement needed improvement, one could not simply treat rights as though they existed only abstractly. Compounding the difficulties with this bit of historical revisionism, and the "free-market environmentalism" then emerging in the United States, was the continuation of the long tradition of ignoring rights held by indigenous peoples—often done so as to not disturb "non-Indian expectations."[46]

The reinterpretation of water rights within the United States was not an existential claim: The claim was not that communities did not exist. Rather, the claim was that water should be managed without privileging any particular set of community goods. To open the door to revisiting who comprised "the People" would crack wide a troublesome fault line regarding why indigenous peoples—or ecological communities, for that matter—could not be part of a revised and renegotiated vision of "the public" and potentially achieve clearer legal standing.[47] These domestic dynamics were mirrored internationally in multiple contexts in which existing community goods were set aside in favor of individual preferences. This took place most profoundly in Chile, where marketable water rights were introduced in 1981 under Augusto Pinochet.[48] There was and remains considerable debate about the Chilean case.[49] Elsewhere, the overtly American liberalism that had characterized earlier efforts in international development had given way to broader programs of structural adjustment, in which foreign aid came with conditions regarding how to "adjust" governance institutions.[50]

Yet to take any case of economic reform to water management global, as an example of failure or success, was also to operate within a system of ideas in which arguments have their life. In the United States and elsewhere, this system of water management ideas increasingly took up the formula agreed to in Dublin regarding the foundational principles required to integrate water, as an economic good, with broader concerns regarding the conservation of scarce resources and sustainable development. This formula crystallized into what are known as the Dublin Principles:

(1) Fresh water is a finite and vulnerable resource, essential to sustain life, development and the environment.
(2) Water development and management should be based on a participatory approach, involving users, planners and policy-makers at all levels.
(3) Women play a central part in the provision, management and safeguarding of water.
(4) Water has an economic value in all its competing uses and should be recognized as an economic good.[51]

The Dublin Principles neatly mark the procedural turn in water management because the achievement of these principles holds priority over the institutional agencies that deliver them. All options for adjusting social institutions were on the table so long as they fit the principles. As the preparatory report linking the Dublin Statement to the 1992 Rio conference argued, the integration of water management, development, and the environment required four main components. None of the four components emphasized an explicit role for government. Rather, they mirrored the divisions of authority from its administration that Lilienthal's vision of grassroots democracy required, such as (1) political credibility to harmonize policy with administrative authority; (2) organizational structures flexible enough to respond to the progressive developments foreseen by effective management; (3) processes and mechanisms for integration that would cover planning, pollution control, economics, and enforcement; and (4) an organizational culture and participant attitude conducive to integration across agencies, staff, and IWRM participants.[52]

In preparation for Rio, the changing role for government in water management was increasingly aligned with the units created by river basins (or watersheds). In the main, states retained formal authority while procedural mechanisms were employed to coordinate management. Market transactions were sometimes part of new procedural mechanisms, but the politics involved meant that markets were usually highly, and idiosyncratically, regulated. This marked the beginning of a long-standing mismatch between the aspirations of IWRM and its implementation, where one body (usually government) was setting the rules for coordination while those doing the actual coordinating (i.e., by making market transactions or taking part in decentralized institutions) had to play by those rules as a condition for participation. This normalized many unequal power relations under the guise of participatory water management.[53] The mismatch of IWRM's aspirations and its implementation was not wholly bad from a political point of view. Although it meant that there was no straightforward application of IWRM, it also allowed IWRM the sort of ambiguity required to straddle problems across a wide, potentially global, set of contexts. Already by 1988, Maurice Strong had explicitly linked the interdependence of nations on a shared environment to the economic and ecological issues necessary for achieving "common security."[54]

IWRM and the Rise of Water Security

In 1992, at the UN Conference on Environment and Development in Rio de Janeiro, IWRM was explicitly linked to water scarcity.[55] Even after all the work following the Brundtland Report, however, water was still not given the emphasis many experts would have liked. So they continued their push, and did so quite successfully. Through the 1990s IWRM ascended into the dominant framework for global water policy. In 1993, the potential for water scarcity to lead to political conflict or to negatively affect human security provided the World Bank with the rationale for pursuing integrated management that conserved water resources in ways that supported international development.[56] By 1995, a World Bank report on the need for IWRM in the Middle East and North Africa expressly linked failures in arresting water scarcity to political and human insecurity.[57] The dual concern of scarcity and security not only provided further rationale for IWRM; it also suggested the need for new financial, institutional, and governmental arrangements. And while the lack of agreement on water scarcity metrics still posed a barrier, the growing appreciation of climate change soon began to sediment water scarcity in broader concerns about the insecure environment that human activity was bringing about.

In 1989, Peter Gleick—then at the Pacific Institute for Studies in Development, Environment, and Security in Berkeley, California—linked hydrology, general circulation models of the climate, and water resources management.[58] Gleick's work was part of a broader project that carried the momentum of International Hydrological Decade through into understandings of Earth system science that arose alongside the rapid advances in computational simulations and emerging models of "normal" climate.[59] Gilbert White, for instance, also linked the notion of water resources to the emerging Earth system sciences not only in his role at the Scientific Committee on Problems of the Environment in the 1970s but also in the follow-up conference to the 1955 Wenner-Gren meeting (see chapter 5). In fact, the 1987 follow-up conference, "The Earth as Transformed by Human Action," purposefully played on the title of George Perkins Marsh's famous book as it took stock of the last three centuries of human activity with respect to global environmental change, regional consequences, and social theory. White chaired the scientific advisory board for the conference, which also included Paul Crutzen, to solicit papers for the conference and guide its content across the sciences, social sciences, and humanities. When the volume was published in 1990, White contributed a co-authored chapter on the accelerating human appropriation of freshwater since the industrial revolution (see fig. 6.1).[60] Normal water was bringing the "great acceleration" of the Anthropocene into view.

The year after Rio, in 1993, Gleick's edited collection, *Water in Crisis*, became a key work for linking hydrologic and climatic data to water management and development.[61] Drawing on normal water's long history of linking social, technical, and geological claims to human and planetary health, this collected work reinforced the commonsense wisdom of water managers and applied it to the sustainable development project of aligning "many worlds" to one Earth. As Gilbert White wrote in the foreword to *Water in Crisis*, "Only with sane realistic recognition of the physical and social characteristics of water can sound water policy be expected to emerge on a global scale."[62] *Water in Crisis* also positioned water management as part of broader concerns about security, especially the prospect that a degraded environment would increase pressure on key resources and lead to political conflict.[63] Subsequent critiques, however, argued that cooperation, not conflict, was the historical norm for international water sharing.[64] Nobody in the "water wars" debate denied water security was of paramount concern but, in the post-Rio context, emphasis was also placed on international instruments that encouraged cooperation through institutions that drew on

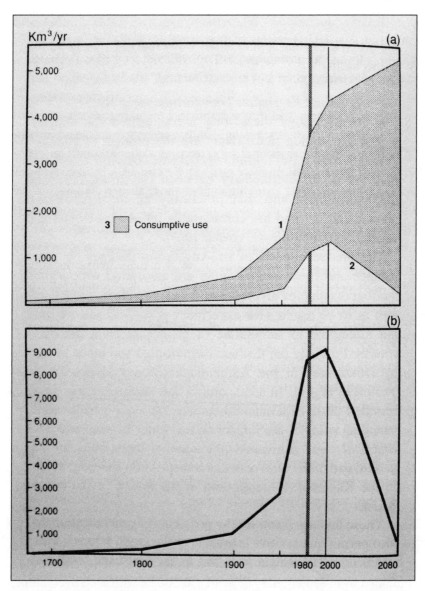

Figure 6.1. "The Chronology of water consumption for 400 years. Chart (a) shows (1) water intake from all sources; (2) waste water returned to streams, and (3) consumptive use. Chart (b) shows the volume of river runoff polluted by waste water. Both charts represent projections of all four parameters from 1680 to 2000 and from 2000 to 2080, assuming drastic measures are adopted to reduce waste-water discharge." Figure and caption are reproduced from L'vovich and White, "Use and Transformation of Terrestrial Water Systems," 248, fig. 14.16.

histories of cooperation.[65] While the debate over water, conflict, and cooperation continues, what is most revealing is the common understanding of water that connects development and security with concerns over the planetary impacts of human activity.[66]

In the context of water scarcity, emerging concerns over water security in IWRM evolved into a platform for linking management to development more clearly. By 1996, global assessments pegged human appropriations of freshwater at 54 percent of available runoff and projected this number would increase.[67] These updates to Gilbert White's initial world water assessment highlighted the challenge of filling out the substantial content to what "integration" really meant. Like water scarcity before it, some measure of (or at least clarity regarding) "security" was needed if it was to move beyond rhetoric to reality. In 1998, White tied IWRM into the longer history of water management from single-purpose, single-means projects, through the International Hydrologic Decade, to developing and managing water through multipurpose, multiple-means approaches.[68] This return to history, like the hydrologic histories of "water and man" in the 1970s, was not unique to White. Jerome Delli Priscoli, who was a World Bank consultant as well as a senior advisor to the U.S. Army Corps of Engineers, also appealed to history to frame the search for "integration" in water management as a natural phenomenon. Priscoli awkwardly claimed in the journal *Water Policy*— the official journal of the World Water Council—that "integration" was a social manifestation of the lifelong search for meaning after humans leave the watery comfort of the womb.[69]

Put in such natural terms, achieving water security in IWRM framed the project of human adjustment for the modern age, and, as it did, a new language of coevolution was gradually introduced to update the notion of human adjustment.[70] Ignoring the deep ethnocentrism entrained in both water management and development, IWRM was now being presented in an evolutionary guise that aligned it with social, economic, and, environmental processes. As one of the most widely cited definitions of IWRM reveals, registering culture, economics, and geography within the notion of "process" was key to a broader, global vision. This definition was drafted by the Global Water Partnership, which the UN Development Program and the World Bank initiated established in 1996 to articulate the Dublin Principles within the post-Rio context.[71] As the new millennium drew near, the Global Water Partnership defined IWRM as

> a process which promotes the coordinated development and management of water, land and related resources, in order to maximize the resultant economic and social welfare in an equitable manner without compromising the sustainability of vital ecosystems.[72]

According to the Global Water Partnership, economic support for IWRM should be administered through what was then the newly formed Global Environment Facility.[73] The Global Water Partnership's emphasis on IWRM as a "process" allayed concerns that integration was prescriptive or universal while still claiming it offered a holistic perspective amenable to global contexts. A key consideration for the Global Water Partnership was to position IWRM with respect to water security. The integration of water management and development, on this view, was part of ensuring that institutional and economic processes guiding "human society," and their interactions with local water cycles, could adjust multiple worlds to one Earth. This is what allowed IWRM to maintain the valence of rationality—integration was neither ad hoc nor prescriptively universal but a coordinator of coevolutionary processes—as participants in decision making came to see their differential positions with respect to each other alongside the common need for mutual adjustments to scarce water resources. As the Global Water Partnership's definition of IWRM gained traction globally, the integration of processes was solidified as key to achieving water security.

By registering IWRM to process, water security formed an additional stopping rule for normal water: The uniformitarianism of geologic processes and social evolution under abundance and the unity of watersheds and democratic methods under scarcity were now being reformulated as a set of processes that linked the human-water relationship to the security of both democratic forms of participatory management and ecosystem vitality. There are two key points here. First, water security emerged from a reflexive exercise. In this sense, the human-water relationship is precarious not only owing to natural variability but also owing to the force put on water systems by humans. The precarious nature of vital ecosystems can manifest at the global level in terms of climate change, nationally in reference to interstate conflict, regionally with respect to watershed indices, or locally in affects on human health. Second, the sustainable development project and its integration of multiple worlds to a single Earth comes to characterize how IWRM uses one view of water to mediate the processes linking management to development. In this twofold sense, then, to participate in IWRM processes is to take up the form of life intrinsic to normal water.

The foregrounding of IWRM in the context of climate change and, as White put it, water's "physical and social characteristics" had several advantages. Principal among them was that it linked IWRM to global environmental changes wrought by human activity in a shared understanding of geological and social processes. It also confirmed that the challenges posed by water scarcity were global, even if effects would be differential at the regional scale. These differential, situated outcomes of water scarcity created the potential for conflict. As a result, water security conditioned responses to water scarcity at the scale of interstate conflict, human development, and ecological health. Once security was seen as emerging from the challenge of scarcity, IWRM could be seen as requiring ongoing management of the human-water relationships central to so many aspects of social, economic, and biophysical processes. Of course, normal water had always been entangled with the geological, social, and technical ways that water resources affected the health and development of the "solidarity of life." What changed was that there was no longer any explicit reference to the symbolic meanings of its original cosmology or later appeals to nationalist formations of American liberalism. Process—not "the People"—was the basis for naturalization in the era of neoliberalism.

IWRM and Its Public

As IWRM became hegemonic in global development discourse, critics charged it was either too ambiguous or, when clear, favored technical precision over consideration of cultural or political difference.[74] There is merit to the critiques of IWRM. Yet at times they miss how ambiguity functioned within IWRM to subsume cultural and political difference within procedural norms. Under the rubric of "process," procedural norms aligned social, technical, and geologic claims about national and individual health in ways that linked one culture's myths about normal water to the co-production of the Earth system. The integration of management and development was a project central not only to the coordination of UN agencies but also to the increasing role that the World Economic Forum began to play in water in the mid-1990s. This was an integration of a planetary vision, on the one hand, and an increasingly globalized economy on the other. During this period, key UN agencies—including UNESCO, the Food and Agricultural Organization, the UN Development Program, the World Health Organization, UNICEF, the World Meteorological Organization, and UNCED— partnered with the World Bank and expert networks like the Global Water Partnership to create the World Water Council and convene the World Commission for Water in the 21st Century. Between 1998 and 2000 the Commission articulated the World Water Vision.[75]

The World Water Vision was spearheaded by Ismail Serageldin, the chair of the World Commission for Water in the 21st Century. At the time, Serageldin was vice president for special programs at the World Bank as well as the chair of the Global Water Partnership. The Commission first met on July 14, 1998, as a group of twenty-one world experts known for their "contributions to science and humanity."[76] Two subsequent meetings were scheduled for March and August 1999 in Cairo and Stockholm, respectively, with a planned release of the Vision the following year on World Water Day (March 22) in The Hague. At the July 14 meeting in Washington, DC, experts laid out the main dimensions of global problems—population growth, environmental constraints, institutional path dependencies, the need for demand-side management, the need for baseline data, and so forth—while also reaffirming that "every molecule of water is doing something."[77] Further, participants suggested that notions of "free markets" should be abandoned since market competition required careful government regulation and was not as "free" as proponents claimed. Why, participants asked, should governments set up rules for only these types of transactions? The lack of positive experiences with institutional reforms and water pricing suggested these ideas did not seem "to come naturally to utilities or ministries."[78]

Despite the hard lessons learned from market reforms in places like Chile, the Commission doubled down on economic reasoning by forwarding "full cost pricing" as central to IWRM in a "water secure world."[79] The idea of "full cost pricing" is that end users should be charged the full cost of getting water to them as a means to incentivizing conservation. Full cost pricing required significant reforms in the political economy of water, which the World Bank had worked on since sponsoring a workshop on the topic in November 1998.[80] The linking slogan for achieving the Vision's aim to water security was one of "making water everybody's business." The slogan was originally suggested by Anil Agarwal, director of the Center for Science and the Environment in India, and "Making Water Everybody's Business" became the subtitle for the Vision and a way to link individuals to water through wholly procedural means.[81] In this way, what was required was not a governmental intervention but a broad transition of the public itself. Indeed, a public crafted through the narrative of abundance, scarcity, and security that was beginning to come into view. It was no longer just hydropower that was the "people's business," as Lilienthal had argued. Rather, there was a global public connected by the processes that link the costs of water resources to both management and development. These views, including a narrative running from Mar del Plata, through Dublin, and on to Rio, were marshaled into a Ministerial Declaration from The Hague entitled "Water Security in the 21st Century."[82] It is worth quoting the opening statement of the Ministerial Declaration to see how this historical and conceptual union was accomplished:

> Water is vital for the life and health of people and ecosystems and a basic requirement for the development of countries, but around the world women, men and children lack access to adequate and safe water to meet their most basic needs. Water resources, and the related ecosystems that provide and sustain them, are under threat from pollution, unsustainable use, land-use changes, climate change and many other forces. The link between these threats and poverty is clear, for it is the poor who are hit first and hardest. This leads to one simple conclusion: business as usual is not an option. There is, of course, a huge diversity of needs and situations around the globe, but together we have a common goal: **to provide water security in the 21st Century**. This means ensuring that freshwater, coastal and related ecosystems are protected and improved; that sustainable development and political stability are promoted, that every person has access to enough safe water at an affordable cost to lead a healthy and

productive life and that the vulnerable are protected from the risks of water-related hazards.[83]

Together, the Commission's report, the Vision, and the Ministerial Declaration put water security at top of the agenda for agencies focused on development and water management. Conceiving of water scarcity and water security in reference to a "human society" ultimately allowed there to be a "common goal" despite the acknowledged "diversity of needs and situations around the globe." Maintaining a common program of action in light of diverse interests and actors required a common way of thinking that was shared by all and yet capacious enough to mediate difference without appearing to favor any place or people. This way of thinking was encapsulated by normal water and its project of gathering social and evolutionary contingencies into the service of liberal forms of life. As the quote from The Hague declaration makes clear, water resources are under threat. Yet this is nothing new. So it has always been for normal water, from the early conservation arguments to the coming water famines of the mid-twentieth century. In The Hague, however, the notion of "making water everybody's business" installed water resources as mediating the achievement of a common goal of water security worldwide.

Making water everybody's business was not a job for water managers alone, the reason being that water was affected by multiple sectors and across all aspects of economic and industrial activity: food, energy production, and so on. As the next chapter considers, the deep interlinkages between water and other resource sectors meant that water needed to be managed, but that management itself was only one aspect of a broader program of good water governance. As the Ministerial Declaration from The Hague put it, a main challenge of achieving water security is "to ensure good governance, so that the involvement of the public and the interests of all stakeholders are included in the management of water resources."[84] The next chapter considers the difficulty of maintaining a commitment to a single "public" in the participatory governance schematic of IWRM. Here, however, what might be highlighted is the pretense that shrouds within procedural techniques how the management of things—water resources—have their life within liberal forms of life. Mobilizing around water resources, the shared goals of an imagined "human society" were mediated by judgments of a particular political community and its practices of addressing scarcity and achieving security through the integration of management and development. When the cloak of objectivity is pulled back, however, the co-production of water scarcity and water security under IWRM reveals how the sustainable development claim that "the Earth is one but the world is not" employed the notion of "process" to consolidate multiple social worlds to a single view of the blue planet.

7

Securing the Water-Energy-Food-Climate Nexus

In short, without planetary stewardship for water resilience, it is difficult to see how the world could eradicate poverty and hunger, two of the emerging Sustainable Development Goals to replace the UN Millennium Development Goals. To succeed with these twin objectives, of global water resilience and human development, will require a mind shift in water thinking, as well as a change in our views on "the environment."

—Johan Rockström and others

In 2004, the World Bank published its assessment of water's "gloomy arithmetic."[1] But the math behind scarce water and growing demand wasn't the only thing troubling experts. Water markets had delivered more promise than punch, and privatization efforts often fumbled over the complex organizational, institutional, and social structures already in place to govern water. In Bolivia, privatization led to intense conflict, while in England and Wales privatization fostered so much distrust that water use actually increased during drought.[2] In places where economic reforms weren't attempted, enthusiasm for integrated water resources management (IWRM) was also dampening. Many questioned its assumptions about culture and gender while others saw IWRM as being too close to the World Bank's economic agenda.[3] After barely a decade, even the Bank conceded IWRM was virtually a dead letter. It now favored a "pragmatic, principled approach" to water management, especially in view of climate change.[4] The principles remained the same: those articulated in Dublin in 1992. The pragmatics, however, were shifting. Geopolitical risk calculations took on new forms as security threats loomed and an increasingly globalized economy searched for secure investments. Water infrastructure, as it had since the start of international development, fit the bill.

Water security gained widespread adoption after the meeting in The Hague (discussed last chapter) and the subsequent Johannesburg conference that marked the 10-year anniversary of Rio in 2002. Yet the development apparatus for achieving water security, IWRM, was being deeply criticized, even by former proponents.[5] Beyond the critiques of IWRM, however, global experts complained about the network of global conferences promoting IWRM and argued that since consensus on key global water concerns was established, there was little added value in coming together to repeat the message.[6] Integrated water resources management was beginning to look like an empty shell. It had a hardened exterior alloyed with sustainable development policies worldwide, but it needed something to breathe new life into it. Into this space stepped a number of parallel developments that shifted water resources management both in the United States and globally.

In a remarkable shift over the next decade, water security was used to retrofit the principles of IWRM to a new organizing concept: the water-energy-food-climate nexus. The World Economic Forum led the charge, describing water security as gossamer—a thin, delicate web—that linked planetary hydrology to risks facing food, energy, climate, and global financial systems.[7] Integrated water resources management was not up to the challenge of managing this nexus, not, however, because sustainable development's program of aligning "many worlds" to "one Earth" was misguided but because it was increasingly recognized that this alignment had already taken place. As the epigraph implies, integrating the fact that humans were already contributing to (if not causing) global environmental change required a new view of planetary stewardship.[8] As this chapter explores, managing the transition into the Anthropocene did not employ the galloping ethnocentrism of Earth-making. Rather, water management in the Anthropocene was and remains a more subtle assertion of liberal forms of life, a social world in which water resources mediate human impacts on the Earth system and the links among, and the risks to, the water-energy-food-climate nexus.

International water experts responded to the new take on human-environment integration—as announced fact rather than promised reconciliation—in an almost predictable way: by launching another water decade. Appropriately, the decade of "Water for Life" (2005–2015) matched the title of Gilbert White's final book. Co-authored with James

Wescoat in 2003, White's final book integrated water management with environmental policy and connected his long-standing concerns regarding human adjustment to the broad bases of choice needed to manage water in an era of global change.[9] Throughout the new water decade, water managers increasingly sought to deal with change by enhancing resilience—the capacity of a system to respond to disturbances while still maintaining its functions and identity. "Resilience" became the watchword for understanding how complex social and ecological systems already linked water resources with health, poverty, and financial capacity.[10] Beyond the water sector, the Millennium Development Goals adopted by the United Nations in 2000 were in full swing by 2005. The goals advocated "good governance at the international level and . . . transparency in the financial, monetary, and trading system."[11] The objective of good governance was to free up financial capacity for development and to halve by 2015 the proportion of people "unable to reach or to afford safe drinking water."[12] Governance, in short, became the way to organize the "broadest bases of choice" for sustainability. As one influential account put it, "Water governance is concerned with those political, social and economic organization and institutions (and their relationships), which are important for water development and management."[13]

In the Anthropocene, enhancing resilience strengthened water security by bolstering the links among water, food, energy, economics, and the Earth in a way that increased capacity to deal with change and surprise. The gossamer of water security needed to be both ductile and durable. By 2005, Paul Crutzen and Eugene Stoermer had already introduced the Anthropocene, and a raft of studies increasingly revealed human impacts on global water systems in ways that reinforced the hydrological narrative of "man and water" that had concretized around normal water in the late 1970s. As 2015 neared, a new set of Sustainable Development Goals began to take shape, and advocates of the water-energy-food-climate nexus positioned intersecting networks of global water expertise and global financial mavens to carry water management forward to 2030. As this chapter considers, this flurry of activity rendered water management in terms of coevolution that made water resources as normal to the Anthropocene as they had been to Earth-making.

From IWRM to Resilience

In 2005, Paul Sabatier and his colleagues published a landmark work, *Swimming Upstream*, which detailed the failures of, and prospects for, water governance in the United States.[14] *Swimming Upstream* capitalized on the slow but detectable shift away from top-down forms of water management toward increased participation from stakeholders affected by water-use decisions. Also in 2005, one of the largest-ever collaborations of scientists published the results of the Millennium Ecosystem Assessment, which consolidated a scientific picture of Earth's ecosystems and forwarded ideas of resilience and adaptive management to link environmental management, development, and governance.[15] The central idea of adaptive management is to take an experimental approach to policy and to craft institutions through which to learn from experience.[16] American water scholars, such as David Feldman, were at the fore of connecting the shift toward collaborative, participatory approaches to water governance with adaptive management under the banner of sustainable development.[17]

Neither adaptive management nor its driving concept of resilience arrived unannounced to sustainable development.[18] In the early 1970s, C. S. "Buzz" Holling pioneered the idea that ecological systems should be understood as persisting under conditions of change and not as oriented toward achieving equilibrium. Further, an ecological system's ability to tolerate disturbance while still maintaining the same functions and processes could be understood as a measure of its resilience.[19] The aim of adaptive management was to enhance the capacity of social and ecological systems to tolerate disturbances.[20] In 1986, Holling contributed a key chapter to the volume *Sustainable Development of the Biosphere*, which also included essays from other leading scientists, including Paul Crutzen.[21] There, Holling introduced the idea that systems have multiple potential states, called basins of attraction. If pushed beyond certain tipping points, ecological systems may flip. Once flipped, changes may be irreversible as ecological relationships transform, such as when a forest is cleared for agriculture and erosion sets in such that establishing a similar forest is no longer possible.[22]

In 2005, Holling's arguments led environmental philosophers like Bryan Norton to hail adaptive management as a way to recover a tradition of American pragmatism in resource conservation and as a way past policy gridlock in the United States.[23] Both Norton and Holling connected their ideas to Aldo Leopold, whose understanding of conservation had developed under the influence of WJ McGee's counterpart in the U.S. Forest Service, Gifford Pinchot. Norton considers Aldo Leopold the forerunner of adaptive management, and Holling dedicated a key paper to Leopold, noting that Leopold "clearly anticipated" the rejection of "command and control" resource management and embraced the change that characterizes complex systems.[24] In fact, and as the final chapter of this book considers, water management significantly influenced Leopold. Yet the shift toward adaptive approaches in water management did not draw on Leopold in more than cursory terms. Rather, scholars like Malin Falkenmark, Carl Folke, and Johan Rockström were the key influences linking water to resilience and then to understandings of the Earth system in the Anthropocene.[25]

In the 1980s, Malin Falkenmark led the research group that proposed one of the most widely cited metrics of water stress, and, through the 1990s, she argued that one of the greatest challenges facing the new millennium was the need to link food security, water security, and environmental security.[26] Falkenmark had previously served as the rapporteur for the UN conference in Mar del Plata, been a consultant to the World Bank, and had also been on the Technical Advisory Committee of the Global Water Partnership that provided the widely cited definition of IWRM discussed in the last chapter. In 2004, and together with Johan Rockström, Falkenmark also drew attention to how water management had typically been concerned only with the visible, "blue" water flows of things like rivers and reservoirs while neglecting the invisible, "green" water flows from evapotranspiration and land-cover change.[27] Integrated water resources management was shortsighted, in Falkenmark's view, because it did not address the land problems that arose in coevolutionary systems where human activity affected both blue and green water.[28] In 2008, Falkenmark was among those who rejected the assumption of stationarity (the idea that, while variable, the hydrological cycle fluctuates within an envelope of stability) because of anthropogenic climate change.[29]

The rejection of stationarity undermined the assumption that there was a "natural" framework of decision making—either Rational Planning or economics—that could integrate water management in the Anthropocene.[30] Anthropogenic climate change rendered Earth's water systems too variable for comprehensive management. Moreover, as scientific evidence mounted, it was evident that human activities were driving water security concerns beyond social and political conflicts and into concerns over biodiversity and ecosystem vitality.[31] In this context, IWRM was inadequate because what was needed was a water management approach that looked at complex systems as they were: the outcome of coevolutionary processes that were already integrated at multiple spatial and temporal scales.[32] As noted in the last chapter, a senior advisor to the U.S. Army Corps of Engineers, Jerome Delli Priscoli, had also seized on the idea of coevolution in an attempt to naturalize "integration" to the search for a reconnection to water outside the womb.[33] Malin Falkenmark and Carl Folke did not take that route. They argued that coevolution created solidarity among humans and non-humans as watersheds shaped, and were reshaped by, the social and ecological processes that humans and non-humans lived within and modified over time.[34] This was not quite the "solidarity of life" as McGee had conceived of it but, rather, a form of "ecohydrosolidarity" based on the coevolution of ecological, hydrological, and social systems.

For Falkenmark, a coevolutionary basis for understanding human-water relationships meant that integrated water management had to fit with social and ecological systems that were already integrated.[35] People had always used water in ways that shaped their environments, and they would continue to do so. The problem arising in the Anthropocene was that humans were affecting the conditions for coevolution through accelerated changes to the Earth system. In 2009, Falkenmark co-authored a paper, with Johan Rockström as lead author, that introduced the concept of planetary boundaries, which expanded the idea of tipping points to the Earth system as a whole.[36] To achieve sustainability, human uses of freshwater needed to be within a "safe operating space" that did not exceed the planetary boundaries within which existing relationships among Earth's life support systems had coevolved. As such, this safe operating space was closely connected to regional freshwater impacts and their cumulative significance for the global water system.[37] Critically, the notion of planetary boundaries recognizes the emergent properties of the Earth system and water's role within them. As these ideas ascended in the global water community, water security became a register for managing the risks of human activity to the Earth system and to natural resources themselves. As the Global Water Partnership argued in 2009,

> The essence of water security is that concern for the resource base itself is coupled with concern that services which exploit the resource base for human survival and well-being, as well as for agriculture and other economic enterprise, should be developed and managed in an equitable, efficient and integrated manner.[38]

The Nexus

While hydrologists and water managers pushed the concept of adaptive management in the United States and internationally, water security was also deployed in the context of growing evidence that humans are major drivers of planetary systems. Worries over planetary stewardship precipitated a consequential shift as water managers increasingly focused on the links between systems that were, in quantitative terms, already integrated. It seemed plain, even common sense, to look at the links among economies, societies, and ecology and at the nexus where water and other systems—food, energy, and climate—shaped both social worlds and the Earth system.

Like resilience and adaptive management, the idea of a nexus among water, energy, and other sectors was not entirely new. In 1983, the Tennessee Valley Authority had marked its fifty-year anniversary by celebrating its continued tutoring of "energy-starved" developing nations.[39] The same year, the United Nations University's Food-Energy Nexus Programme also employed the idea of a "nexus" in resource management.[40] Prior to this, notions of the nexus had been used in economics and to some degree in cell biology, but its most famous application among academics was Alfred North Whitehead's use of the term to link social order and individual experience to the processes through which events constitute reality.[41] Originally proposed in his Gifford Lectures, Whitehead developed a concept of the nexus alongside his rejection of ideas of "nature" that were based on a bifurcation of mind and matter.[42] One of the first applications of the nexus in water management was an energy initiative in Bangalore that used the nexus to understand the impacts of subsidies on groundwater extraction.[43] In the United States, links between water and energy came to the fore in the 1990s. In fact, what is now considered a classic work of water history, Richard White's 1995 *The Organic Machine*, reinterpreted watershed management and industrial development in the northwest United States as a set of contests over hydrologic, human, and food energy.[44]

Recall that in 1989, Peter Gleick had linked water to general circulation models of the climate. In 1994, Gleick published an article on "Water and Energy" that spelled out the interconnections among energy, risks to water security in America, and resource conservation.[45] Gleick's essay was cited extensively in 2006 by the U.S. Department of Energy in its report to Congress on the interdependencies of water and energy.[46] The 2006 report by the Department of Energy was followed up by focused work on the water impacts of unconventional fossil fuel extraction (e.g., hydraulic fracturing) in Senate hearings in 2009. At these hearings, Gleick was one of several experts who addressed the interconnections of water, energy, and climate to domestic energy production in the United States.[47]

Building on these links of water, energy, and climate, several U.S. government committees used the concept of the nexus to expand the remit of water security between 2010 and 2012.[48] The water-energy-climate nexus fit with broader concerns over domestic security in the United States, but it also worked to coordinate water management with the type of accounting and audit structures that, as we will see below, were increasingly touted at the global level as key to stabilizing international finance. The next year, the U.S. Office of National Intelligence released its assessment of international water security risks. The report focused on global watersheds deemed strategically important to U.S. interests: the Nile, Tigris-Euphrates, Mekong, Jordan, Indus, Brahmaputra, and Amu Darya.[49] It emphasized the need for effective water management and the role of American expertise in connecting water resources management to American interests. On March 22, 2012 (World Water Day), U.S. Secretary of State Hillary Rodham Clinton launched the U.S. Water Partnership. The new initiative set the stage for Clinton's speech at the September 2012 UN Roundtable on Water Security, where she reiterated how the mismanagement of water scarcity was tied to issues of international and human security.[50]

The Nexus and the Gossamer of Water Security

To put connections among water, energy, economics, climate, and security in context, it is helpful to consider how an approach to the water-energy-food-climate nexus (hereafter called "nexus") gained purchase globally. As can perhaps be anticipated, this took place on the back of what normal water had already accomplished with respect to water abundance and water scarcity. Under water security, the fact that humans are already a driving force of planetary systems comes to be seen as a fact of coevolution. Again, not quite "Earth-making," but not too far from it either: The key difference is that within the nexus, water security employs water resources—with its attendant forms of life—to transition from collecting multiple social worlds into a holistic view of the planet to a view of connecting the supply chains that link water, food, energy, and the climate to an Earth system dominated by human activity.[51] All of these factors were gathered under the umbrella of "water security." As the final section of this chapter considers, alternate views of the Earth or of social worlds were not denied. Rather, it was by securing the supply chains that deliver water, food, and energy that a planet under pressure could countenance difference among many publics. As forms of poly-centric governance proliferated under this model, they were entangled with the web of security that normal water provides.

The first year of the "Water for Life" Decade, 2005, was also the first year that the World Economic Forum published a global risk assessment. Over the next decade, the World Economic Forum's risk assessments pushed the nexus to the fore of international economic discourse in a way directly relevant to water governance. The World Economic Forum had uniquely positioned itself for this role after having set up its Global Governance Initiative in 2003 to both independently monitor progress on the Millennium Development Goals and to achieve "good governance" across "developing countries and economies in transition."[52] This governance initiative also supported its aims of aligning its members with the World Trade Organization's agricultural trade liberalization position in developing countries. By taking up the mantle of articulating the concept of the nexus, the WEF also leveraged its long-standing commitment to multi-stakeholder engagements that Geoffrey Pigman argues is part of how the WEF shapes the "social reconstruction of interests . . . through repeated discursive interactions."[53]

In 2004, the WEF published a risk assessment but later remarked that it had not been adequately "global." Subsequently, four criteria were developed to establish what qualified as a global risk: First, the risk must affect at least three regions of the world and a minimum of two continents while also affecting at least three industries. Second, the risk had to exceed U.S.$10 billion in economic impact or have a major social impact, such as extreme suffering or loss of life. Third, it had to be uncertain how the risk would manifest over the next ten years or how severe it would be. Finally, dealing with the risk had to require a multistakeholder response and coordination among the appropriate combination of international businesses, governments, civil society institutions, and bilateral/multilateral agencies.[54]

When the WEF published its first few global risk assessments, high energy prices were a central concern, as was a boom in unconventional fossil fuel extraction—notably hydraulic fracturing. The water impacts of new extractive technologies were part of the reason that countries like the United States were holding governmental hearings on water and energy. But what happened in and through the World Economic Forum's work networked a number of ideas about water, development, and energy adaptation together to assess financial risk strategies for a human-dominated planet. These converging issues could not be ignored in 2008, when food price shocks and the global financial crisis became dual poles of global risk. That year, the nexus appeared prominently in the WEF's global report, and food security was identified as the core concern because it affected, and was affected by, "population growth, changing lifestyles, climate change and the growing use of food crops for biofuels" and was connected to heat waves, energy prices, water quality, and civil unrest.[55] The upshot of these "global risks" was to securitize water yet further by connecting water risks to those of the global economy.

Initially, the WEF identified two "sub-nexus" constellations between water-food-trade and energy-climate.[56] In 2009, however, water replaced food at the center of the WEF's nexus of global risks owing to its fundamental role in connecting global risks to food and energy.[57] The central role of water in connecting these sub-nexus formations was anticipated by a WEF collaboration known as the Energy Industry Partnership, which reported in 2008 on the relationship of "thirsty energy" to capital markets and the need for energy companies to become more active in local water management in order to integrate water in the "value chain" of production.[58] A second report was released in 2009 by the World Economic Forum, entitled *The Bubble Is Close to Bursting*, which played on the "bubble" in the sub-prime mortgage crisis in the United States to argue that the geopolitical risks associated with the incorrect valuation of water were pivotal to the next two decades of international security.[59] The report on the "water bubble" was circulated at the WEF's annual meeting in Davos, Switzerland, where the UN Secretary-General, Ban Ki-moon, asked forum members to prioritize water security on the international economic agenda.[60]

Members of the World Economic Forum also formed the 2030 Water Resources Group, a public-private-civil society network that operates as an informal collaboration among the International Finance Corporation, the WEF, multilateral and bilateral agencies, private companies (e.g., PepsiCo, Coca-Cola, Nestlé) and non-governmental organizations (e.g., the World Wildlife Fund).[61] The 2030 Water Resources Group reinforced the concept of the nexus and chose the year 2030 as a key horizon to meet water challenges to scarcity, security, and finance. Choosing 2030 overlapped the Water Resources Group's working period with the horizon set for the emerging Sustainable Development Goals that were to replace the Millennium Development Goals after 2015. In 2009, the Water Resources Group published a major report recommending that finance should play an enhanced role in meeting gaps between water supply and demand in the water-energy nexus.[62] It argued that a combination of increased water prices and regular schedules for loan payments to financiers would provide incentive for financial institutions to supply capital for infrastructural and operational reforms. By tying water finance to infrastructure and operations, the potential for securitizing loans created a way to connect water to supply chains producing food or energy. If water wasn't going to be the basis for currency, and if water markets were too politically hot, then at the very least normal water would extract rents from loan payments and profit from financial products that securitized loans.

The World Economic Forum's focus on public-private-civil society networks aligned with its previous public-private water projects, which had begun in 2003 with a focus on infrastructure development in India, South Africa, and elsewhere.[63] For its part, the World Bank had also developed a strategy in 2003 to link integrated, adaptive resource management and global finance to both ecology and development economics.[64] The World Bank's senior water advisor, David Grey, argued that infrastructure was key to water security because climate change required not only enhancing access to water but also protecting vulnerable populations from extreme effects, such as floods.[65] Perhaps unsurprisingly, the 2010 WEF risk report explicitly linked systemic financial risks to institutional, political, and infrastructural resilience.[66] In 2011, when the World Economic Forum published its response to Ban Ki-moon's request regarding water security, the nexus connected global risk assessments regarding ecological and economic risks to elements of chance and surprise that made enhancing the resilience of complex systems critical.

It was hard to miss the association that the World Economic Forum made between water security and the nexus when it titled its report *Water Security: The Water-Food-Energy-Climate Nexus*. The WEF report reaffirmed previous global risk reports, such as how food price shocks in 2008 and 2010 were intractably connected to "a structural problem in how we manage water across the web of our global economy."[67] Throughout 2011, the 2030 Water Resources Group held a series of high-level conferences on "Collaborative Pathways to a Water Resilient Economy" in Brazil, South Africa, and China.[68] These meetings, and an additional one on water security in Jordan, informed a briefing report for the 2012 WEF meeting in Davos. As water security was made operational through the supply-chain links in the nexus, it became commonplace to use resilience to fit economics to water in a way that mirrored how, on the managerial side, resilience and adaptive management were advanced to address lingering problems in development programs like IWRM. In both cases, the key was to strengthen the capacity to adapt, including the capacity to adapt to the problems caused by financial instability.

How did resilience link global finance to the nexus? In part, through the groundwork laid by the WEF, which defined resilience in its first global assessment simply as "tolerance to risk."[69] In WEF reports from 2006 to 2008, resilience was elaborated to align more clearly with the ability to tolerate surprise and uncertainty, often positioned as a "downstream" capacity to absorb and respond to risks that cannot be predicted or controlled. This understanding of resilience aligned with ecology, which had long recognized the importance of uncertainty and surprise.[70] Capitalizing on this commonality, the WEF's 2011 book on water security defined resilience as "the ability of a system to reorganize under change and deliver its core function continually, despite the impact of external or internally generated risks."[71] From 2011 onward, resilience has been a mainstay in the World Economic Forum risk assessments and is frequently linked to the nexus.[72] By linking the nexus to considerations of global financial risk through resilience, the WEF solidified the importance of managing the web of interdependent connections that water facilitated across biophysical and economic systems. At the same time, the WEF emphasized the importance of "integrated and multistakeholder resource planning" in designing adaptation strategies.[73] Other organizations, such as the Food and Agricultural Organization, also began to tout a closer connection of governance, institutions, and finance as a way to address water scarcity and security.[74]

As the nexus gathered steam, it was perhaps inevitable that academics, think tanks, and policy makers would take it up. In 2011, a major conference was held in Bonn, Germany, where the nexus was advanced as a way to transition from the traditional concerns of sustainable development to a framework befitting an increasingly urbanized world.[75] The Bonn gathering was timed to inform the Rio+20 conference in 2012. Now two decades since Rio, the nexus was forwarded as central to transitions toward a green economy and to developing the 2015 Sustainable Development Goals.[76] In 2013, UN Water released a briefing on water security and the emerging global water agenda that forged another conceptual link between the nexus, the global economy, and development.[77] The perspective of UN Water was shaped by a report on water security drafted by governments from Australia, Brazil, Canada, Japan, and Sweden, which included a foreword by Gro Harlem Brundtland that linked the concept of sustainable development to the Millennium Development Goals and to the anticipated Sustainable Development Goals.[78] Through these networks of water and development experts, a common view of water security that linked planetary dynamics to global governance was coming into view. Seen in context, the World Economic Forum and the 2030 Water Resources Group had largely succeeded in welding the nexus and resilience to water security as the preferred path for financing development. By 2014, the nexus was the theme for World Water Day.[79]

With the risks to the nexus affixed to global financial risks, the World Economic Forum's 2014 report signaled that water, as part of a macro-economic, structural nexus, was in the top three risks to the resilience of the global economy.[80] By 2015, in the tenth global risk assessment, water ranked as the highest risk for potential impact on the nexus, interstate conflicts, and even "large-scale involuntary migration."[81] The next year, water moved into the top position as the most significant long-term (i.e., ten-year) risk in the WEF assessment. Affirming the importance of the nexus is now commonplace: The United Nations 2014 World Water Development Report states that "Water, energy and food are inextricably linked."[82] Likewise, the U.S. Geological Survey takes interconnection as a self-evident starting point for an Earth system perspective toward the water-energy nexus.[83] The World Economic Forum's assessment was further solidified when water experts in the Global Water System Project called for a nexus approach to expand financial, institutional, technical, and intellectual resources to achieve "water, energy and food security for everyone" within "planetary boundaries."[84] Water security was now firmly established as the way to link multiple social worlds to "one blue planet."[85]

Anthropocene Publics

"Gossamer" is a remarkably apt metaphor for understanding how it is normal water that underlies water security. In a mesh-like film, there is no unique vantage point, no characteristics that privilege any social perspective, and no privileged point of reference for understanding what makes the gossamer good. It just is good, simply because it cannot be done without unless one is willing to radically adjust or simply abandon the forms of life it supports. Yet when there is no recourse to alternate forms of subjectivity, social habits, or symbolic goods, then radical adjustments are not what William James would call a "live option." Rather, keeping the web connected is what matters. This is a self-effacing move in which the forms of life that give rise to water security retire from view while nevertheless forwarding the direct governance of water resources as the mediating register for understanding what kinds of connections are to be made between water, energy, food, the economy, and the Earth.

As with abundance and scarcity before it, there is considerable traffic among academics, water management practitioners, and policy makers to get water security off and running. Geographers like Karen Bakker called for increased research and political focus on water security.[86] Others called for connections to be made between how water managers were educated when it came to understanding water concerns at the different scales affecting food, water, and energy security.[87] The shifting riverbed of thought—where integration is a coevolutionary fact of an interconnected world—also led to calls for managers to just "get on" with the pragmatic dimensions of water management: to integrate without IWRM.[88] But doing so risks missing seeing how water management in the nexus so closely mirrors the recommendations initially proffered by WJ McGee.

Recall that McGee had already suggested making water the material basis for economics and finance by replacing the gold standard with water. Granted, this was a bit ambitious. But his other recommendations would be difficult to pick out from a lineup of policy suspects today, such as his claim that "natural growth and orderly development [are best] fostered by combining individual and institutional agency in the highest practicable degree."[89] Or, again, that such coordination should take place among "business and civic organizations, corporations, communities, municipalities, states and federal agencies."[90] These are very similar to, if not structurally indistinguishable from, contemporary calls in water governance. The difference now is that federal agencies, and states themselves, have been repositioned as different iterations of liberalism have taken shape. After the economic reforms of the 1980s and 1990s, and after economic reforms had produced (at best) mixed results, the next iteration of liberalism used normal water to forge links to global finance in which the use of capital investment and speculation were mobilized to increase adaptive capacity.[91]

An obvious difference between Earth-making and the Anthropocene is how human domination of the Earth system figures in aligning risks to planetary hydrology with those of global finance. This marks an important shift: Under the International Hydrologic Decade and into Mar del Plata, the connections between the local and the global were crafted in a way that supported "industrial societies," and, particularly in the U.S. case, capitalist forms of industrialism that supported American liberalism internationally. Drawing on the Conservation movement and the Tennessee Valley Authority, the form of international development that fed into the project of sustainable development was outfitted especially for local-global scales that were themselves produced to support an understanding of water that befit industrialism. Yet by the time a holistic, collective program came about under IWRM in the 1990s, there was already a shift away from industrial capitalism in many countries. As such, the context in which IWRM emerged was not the one it was being applied to. By the time IWRM caught its breath in the new millennium, economic relationships between humans and the planet were increasingly focused on financialized forms of capital investment. The nexus connected water to concerns regarding planetary systems, like the water cycle, and its relation to financial capital by mobilizing a whole series of non-global connections, such as the supply chains needed to reliably deliver water, food, and energy.

The uptake of the nexus in water management was premised on a series of calls for more effective water governance that began earlier in the twenty-first century.[92] Mirroring adaptive management's rejection of a "command-and-control" approach to resources, the emphasis on water governance sought to transition entire sociotechnical systems through which decisions are made. The goal, in line with the "procedural turn" in water management discussed last chapter, was to coordinate participation in water use decisions under liberal norms for reaching consensus.[93] Water experts had already envisioned how the water sector could fit adaptive management to new techniques of social learning. Through transition management, these ideas were advanced with respect to global water governance in a way that reaffirmed the link of water to energy.[94] In fact, transition management first took hold in the energy sector in the Netherlands as a way to connect shifts toward market-oriented policies with changes to political cultures in environmental governance.[95]

As the remit of water management expanded to include the social and technical structures governing how decisions were reached, there was a rejection of "panaceas"—like IWRM—that held out faith for holistic, rational models. These models were too water-centric in attempting to comprehensively align the broadest bases of choice with integrated development and management. When integration of humans and water is a fact of coevolution, what is needed is a governance model that provides as many perspectives on integration as possible. On this front, the preferred alternative was a polycentric model of decision making that would provide a more resilient institutional structure.[96] Polycentric governance does not rely on a single community to legitimate claims regarding the public good. Instead, there are multiple loci of legitimacy and, consequently, multiple publics that produce different visions of the good life in ways that provide different perspectives on resource management. Leading theorists of collective action, such as Elinor Ostrom, advocated for polycentric approaches because they allowed for collective decision making without presuming upon a single institutional model or social structure for coordinating action.[97] Polycentric approaches also moved beyond binary oppositions between state and markets to find innovative solutions to resource dilemmas.[98] The only real use for holistic frameworks like IWRM was that the common institutional features they established could be relativized to local contexts where management would proceed in an adaptive fashion.[99]

Polycentric governance was especially well suited to the fact that, in the Anthropocene, water's relationships to economies, societies, and ecological communities were often surprising.[100] For instance, anthropogenic climate warming in the latter half of the twentieth century had been expected to increase the intensity of storms and other water events (by warming the atmosphere and enabling it to hold more water vapor). But this didn't happen, in part, because other forms of human pollution, particularly aerosols, curbed the effects. Then, in the early twenty-first century, policies put in place decades earlier started to reduce aerosols in the atmosphere, and the hydrologic cycle gained the intensity originally expected.[101] The dynamics of a human-dominated planet aligned polycentric governance with a whole series of concerns, from the large water demands rapidly urbanizing human populations made on watersheds to the need to start treating wastewater as a resource—an idea previously explored in a book Richard Helmer co-edited in 1997.[102]

The corollary to polycentric governance was an Earth system imagined in terms congruent with liberal, democratic forms of governance. The dream of uniting many worlds to one Earth had not been abandoned, but it was reformulated with a different imagination of ecological and social systems underlying it. In the Anthropocene, what was of paramount concern was observing how connections were forged, mutated, and abandoned across highly complex, ever-changing social and ecological systems—and, related to this, the development of water sciences that connected the industrial age to the current milieu.[103] Yet this leads to a fairly exceptional claim, namely, that there is a common understanding of water across polycentric governance arrangements that also fits with accounts of planetary hydrology.

In the Anthropocene, there is a common view of water that connects multiple social worlds to the Earth. Indeed, although there are competing notions of water security, there is broad acceptance of the understanding that water resources are the objects of governance. As the paper that this chapter's epigraph comes from argues, the "water drama" in the Anthropocene arises from a failure to see that constant change and negotiation is key to finding commensurate views of security that enhance the prospects of human development. According to the authors, problems began when water management emphasized control of "blue water" and ignored the invisible flows of "green water" from land cover change. This water-centrism of IWRM was deemed a land problem redux—an institutional form that did not align with coevolutionary geological processes—even though it emerged out of the U.S.-led International Hydrological Decade and concerns over the land phase of the "hydrologic geocycle." A resilient approach to the Anthropocene, by contrast, would integrate understandings of the Earth system with the water needed for human development.[104] Yet all of this presumes upon normal water and in the latest instance on self-effacing when it comes to how earlier attempts to solve the "land problem" shaped later concerns of water management. As earlier chapters have shown, the co-production of world water assessments that wind their way through international scientific and water management networks issued from liberal forms of life. For instance, the histories of hydrologic engineering and cost-benefit economics that conditioned the "blue water" approach of IWRM were themselves a response to the linking of conservation and international development post–World War II. These hydrologic histories of "water and man" in the 1970s had earlier precursors in the ideas of conservation and multipurpose river basin development. So, as novel as this vision of the "water drama" in the Anthropocene sounds, it has a longer history.

The proliferation of "publics" in the Anthropocene situates water security at the confluence of claims about human impacts on Earth systems, economics, and governance.[105] The proliferation of multiple publics in polycentric forms of governance only works if there is some thing held in common—water resources—that connects them in a shared governance framework. When all connections in the nexus are mediated by water resources, water security begins to sound a lot like Henry Ford's attitude toward automobiles: You can have any color you'd like, so long as it's black. In addition, the continued crisscrossing over technical, social, planetary, and health-related concerns positions water resources as universally necessary and without substitute. The common practices that judge water a resource enables the UN Decade of "Water for Life" to function as the site in which the contradictions over water resources gain civil status. The form of life in which claims of subjective, social, or symbolic specificity are anathema is also the one that is naturalizing processes of social and ecological coevolution regardless of cultural difference. The gossamer of water security has its life within the system of hypotheses that arose as different iterations of liberal forms of life undertook the task of human adjustment and, once naturalized, adaptation.

Water Ethics for Coevolution

In 1997 UNESCO launched a program to develop ethical principles for water that paralleled its growing emphasis on participatory management and shared governance. This international discourse on "water ethics" sought to establish norms (or rules of right conduct) across the many contexts of integrated water resources management that also legitimated new forms of water governance.[106] In 2004, UNESCO published a "Water and Ethics" series that began by reiterating the long-standing commitment in water resources management to not divide society from nature in favor of a coevolutionary view.[107] Other essays in the series consider issues that mirror development categories: gender, irrigation, agriculture, groundwater, and so forth. This orientation to development sectors rather than cultural difference sparked a range of responses that

developed competing notions of "water ethics."[108] Especially problematic was how the UNESCO series uncritically adopted the hegemonic
view that water is a resource. In fact, the lead author of UNESCO's intro-
ductory essay on water and ethics, Jerome Delli Priscoli, later argued
that water management needed to become even more utilitarian.[109]

It is exceedingly difficult to imagine how water resources management could be more utilitarian, and it is even more difficult to imagine
how this would be an improvement. The extended, evolutionary version
of utilitarianism offered over a century ago by WJ McGee set the stage
for U.S. water management. The expansion of this model under the
strange colonial arguments of David Lilienthal brought liberal, utilitarian ideas to international development. This was followed by a growing
emphasis on objective, cost-benefit analysis under Gilbert White and set
much of the normative tone for sustainable development. Comparing
claims from McGee to the mantra of sustainable development makes
this plain: A century ago McGee wrote that the conservation of natural
resources required ensuring "the equal rights of present and future generations in and to the resources of the country."[110] In 1987, sustainable
development was defined as meeting "the needs of the present without compromising the ability of future generations to meet their own
needs."[111] As IWRM ascended as part of the sustainable development
agenda, the utilitarian aim of maximizing human welfare without compromising vital ecosystems became hegemonic. Yet even if we accepted
a utilitarian ethic, the manner in which the UNESCO series positions
water ethics as an issue of coevolution naturalizes the processes through
which all water values—all symbolic ends—are arrived at to the forms
of life that normal water issues from.

Normal Water and the New Development Nexus

Retrofitting IWRM through adaptive management and resilience and
aligning risks to water, energy, food, and the climate with those to global
finance positioned normal water for the new development nexus that
took shape through the Sustainable Development Goals in 2015. The
SDGs argue that people and planet are intricately woven together across
nations and need IWRM to govern the critical relationships to which
all people have a right.[112] The SDGs also reflect the work of UN Water

and the UN Development Program that, since 2006, have been linking water scarcity to social inequality.[113] But the SDGs also install normal water in formal development agreements to mediate a series of "nexuses" that connect water to the security of supply chains affecting energy and food.[114] The fact that the nexus has achieved such a prominent place in development discourse signals how interlinked crises of food, energy, climate, and poverty are understood with respect to the management of social and political transitions needed to achieve sustainability.

Following the release of the SDGs in 2015, a Global Water Partnership and Organization for Economic Co-operation and Development taskforce on water security argued that accelerating the transition to sustainability required addressing water security by linking complex hydrological systems to global finance, environmental sustainability, and the various ways that social worlds are formed in response to risk and uncertainty.[115] However, these "transition discourses" are not neutral. Reflecting on what transition discourses imply for the connections among environment, development, and new Earth stories that seek to bridge the chasm claimed between society and nature, Arturo Escobar has remarked on two possibilities.[116] One is that transitions signal new ways of making up the world, with new ontological and epistemological bases for connecting multiple crises to the remediation of inequality. The other possibility is that transition discourses will outflank options for substantive change and install new narratives of the Earth in which promises of a new world are, at best, simply new views of a world that has changed little, if at all.

The new development nexus is a retrenchment of normal water and its myth regarding the superiority of liberal forms of life as best equipped for governing the social and evolutionary possibilities made available by water. It is, in a manner refracted through multiple iterations of liberalism, another form of Earth-making: a refusal of the distinction between humans and nature and an assertion of an interconnected planet where humans are a geological force. It is also a scheme of unrepentant contingency, in which management must make adroit use of geological, social, and technical advantages to enhance the health (i.e., the resilience) of individuals, their economies, and the planet. It aims for "abundance within planetary boundaries"—a way of living on a big world and a small planet that is shaped by the force of human action.[117]

The consequence is a consolidation of ways of thinking about water in a common, monological language of water resources. Considering the history of water resources, it is unsurprising that they are uniquely outfitted to traffic across the sciences and social sciences that are concerned about water management and development in the Anthropocene. Water resources mediate the points of connection in the gossamer of water security and ensure that global supply-chain links in the nexus are all of the same kind. Through the nexus, the philosophy of water management has managed the transition from the hypothesis of Earth-making to the Anthropocene.

PART IV

Rethinking the Anthropocene

8

The Anthropocene and the Naturalization of Process

I rather believe with Faulkner, "The past is never dead, it's not even past," and this for the simple reason that the world we live in at any moment *is* the world of the past; it consists of the monuments and the relics of what has been done by men for better or worse; its facts are always what has *become* . . . . In other words, it is quite true that the past *haunts* us; it is the past's function to haunt us who are present and wish to live in the world as it really is, that is, has *become* what it is now.
—Hannah Arendt

Since normal water's earliest articulations in the writings of John Wesley Powell and WJ McGee, no quarter has been given to the idea that there is an ontological gap between humans and nature. Their view (as idiosyncratic as it was) was that agency was spread far and wide, across and throughout the contingent processes of planetary evolution. Once haphazard, evolutionary processes were now being directed by liberal societies that had evolved to the point where they could direct social, technical, and geological contingencies to care for the planet as one would an ailing parent. Later, David Lilienthal and Gilbert White entrenched this ethnocentrism to augur for a universal exit strategy from colonialism. For his part, Lilienthal advanced the colonial experience of the American south as parallel to the post-colonial era of international development. White helped to develop an approach to water management that naturalized hydrology to the history of civilizations and that affixed water resources to the emerging picture of the Earth system that took shape in the late twentieth century.

In the twenty-first century, humanity's outsized proportion of the planet's freshwater is frequently marshaled alongside calls for a new view of planetary stewardship in the Anthropocene. Following Luna

Leopold's lead, there has been no sustained attempt to understand the philosophy of water management that already exists. Instead, what he termed the "gut feeling" that linked water's value to the fate of nations and the planet has been interpreted and critiqued as part of modernity's malaise—in which a dualism of society and nature leads to a form of "nature-conquest" that drives both ecological crisis and the oppression of non-western "others" and that is explained through theories about, for instance, state rationality. This book, however, recovers the lost philosophy of water management and explains how it shapes common ways of thinking about water, ways that are no less disturbing but that are not adequately explained by applying theories of modernity to water. This chapter examines what recovering the lost philosophy of water management implies for new ideas of materiality and non-human agency that aim at society/nature dualisms instead of the history and politics that brought water from Earth-making into the Anthropocene.

Recall that Clive Hamilton considers the modern social sciences irrelevant to the Anthropocene to the extent that they are premised on an indefensible dualism separating humans from nature.[1] Indeed, the Anthropocene has prompted scholars across anthropology, geography, and economics (to name only a few disciplines) to reassess how humans are understood with respect to the Earth system.[2] One broadly endorsed approach has been to "make things public" by dethroning the idea that humans are the only agents in the cosmos and by recognizing how non-human agents and processes affect things like flood control or how large dams act as agents on the landscape.[3] There are many approaches to "making things public," but where water resources are concerned they uniformly misidentify the problem. The difficulty is not a society/nature dualism or even unique human agency. Rather, the problem is the historical attempt (and ongoing consequences) of a failed strain of social science in the United States that sought to do away with the society/nature dualism. The upshot is that, even though many contemporary accounts of materiality and non-human agency are ideologically opposed to the practices that normal water legitimates, they do not gain philosophical purchase against it.

A second problem with "making things public" arises when new philosophical avenues for the social sciences commit a fallacy I term "the naturalization of process." Below, I argue this fallacy all too frequently links human and geologic histories in arguments about what the Anthropocene implies. The motivation to link Earth and human histories through shared processes is understandable: By appealing to geological processes—deep time—to connect human and Earth histories, any dualism between humans and nature is precluded by a shared geological heritage. Further, shared geological processes can then be mobilized to show how multiple agents—whether human or not—emerge historically and in broader ecological relationships. As noted at the outset of this book, accounts of this type consider a monological view a strong point because it secures a shared ontological basis for human and non-human action. Early theorists in the Cosmos Club thought this a strong point of linking human histories to geology, too, which led them to naturalize geologic processes to their own social world—a world that now profoundly shapes how water resources crisscross social, technical, and geological claims regarding the health of people and the planet.

If theoretical critiques of society/nature dualisms miss the mark, and if burrowing into what sort of "thing" water is entangles us with common ways of thinking we wish to confront, then what is the alternative? Stefan Helmreich suggests that we can think "athwart theory" rather than getting caught up in essentialist debates about what water or other "things" are.[4] This is helpful given that, on the one hand, the forgotten philosophy of water management has often been distorted by theories of water and modernity that themselves have had material effects as the rationale for claims academics have made, such as those regarding water scarcity and security. On the other hand, thinking athwart theory is useful because, in practice, there is no essential definition of "water resources." Water resources reflect practices that change, such as when abundance was hailed as step out of European metaphysics and then later considered a result of hubris just in case the characteristics of "the People" looked too nationalistic. So, since we can't escape an entanglement with water resources, we must find new practices for thinking about the world that they helped to create. Following the epigraph from Hannah Arendt, we could say that water resources are monuments of a world past that, in a sense, haunt the Anthropocene.[5]

Thinking "athwart theory" allows for theorizing itself to be seen as a kind of practice—one that teaches ways of picturing things through a mental scheme or lens, such as when accounts of water management are pictured through dualisms of society and nature. Yet we don't reach agreements about how to see the world prior to ordering things within it. As Wittgenstein argued, our agreements rely on the judgments and the practices we use to reach them. For instance, the judgments of abundance, scarcity, and security that connect water resources to different iterations of liberal forms of life are now thoroughly engrained in the practiced, normal ways we think about (and often teach) water management. In this chapter, I consider practices that can disrupt normal ways of thinking. And, after more carefully articulating the difficulties with "making things public" and the fallacy of naturalizing process, I follow the Danish philosopher Søren Kierkegaard to interrupt theories about natural processes. Kierkegaard was principally interested in the naturalization of historical processes he spied in the work of Hegel. I am interested in those that are appearing at the end of the Holocene.[6]

Making Things Public

Making things public captures three things at once. First, there is the notion of making, and a renewed attention to how things, including concepts themselves, are crafted, negotiated, and reworked.[7] Making isn't limited to human action because humans live in a meshwork of interacting, ecological webs of life.[8] Second, there is a notion of things, often referenced to Heidegger's essay "What Is a Thing?"[9] Things are what we work with, and relate to, as part of making up our world.[10] Philosophically, things contrast with objects. In fact, objects are often only evident when they malfunction, such as when a tool breaks. For example, in the Anthropocene the idea of "nature" can be thought of as a tool of thought that has broken.[11] The aim of "making things public" is to show how accounts of the world are themselves shaped by the things we use to make up the world. But who is this "we"? Third, and finally, "making things public" opens up accounts of things and practices beyond anthropocentric assumptions about human understanding to include non-humans. The "public," on this account, must be emancipated from what Bruno Latour calls "prematurely naturalized objectified facts" that separate humans from the non-human things through which knowledge is co-produced.[12]

The problem with "prematurely naturalized objectified facts" is not just that facts don't appear from nowhere and that accepting them implies somebody there to do the accepting. It is that there is no natural order of things that make the conditions for objective or necessary knowledge possible, such as the subject Kant imagined who comes equipped to navigate a universe of mind and matter. The conditions of knowledge production are contingent, and the ways these conditions are formed cannot be dissociated from the knowledge produced within them. The worry is that, if the contingent forces that shape the production of knowledge are ignored, we will lose sight not only of the many ways in which the conditions for the production of knowledge are shaped by powerful actors but also how these conditions are shaped through the actions of more than just humans.[13] If the co-production of knowledge is ignored or maligned, we may incorrectly and prematurely assume that objective facts issue from natural conditions rather than as the result of many contingent factors.[14] Making things public, then, seeks to internalize the contingent conditions of knowledge co-production and to do so without granting humans special status.

One upshot of making things public is the rejection, or at least significant reformulation, of critical thought. Bruno Latour, for instance, thinks critical thought has "run out of steam."[15] To see why, we can recall how, at least since Descartes, the dictum of critical thought has been to doubt things as they appear to our senses. The subsequent challenge, perhaps most profoundly shaped by Kant, was to articulate the limits of reason without appealing to metaphysical sources of authority. Kant's solution was to make metaphysics a science. But this was later inverted in a project of naturalizing reason itself and, as noted earlier, it was later shaped by Cold War attempts to purge the social and natural sciences of human values in the name of objectivity.[16]

Without the firmament formerly provided by metaphysical authority, or a priori accounts of human reason, there has been a shift to immanent explanations of the human condition. There is no intrinsic reason, on this line of argument, to curtail what makes different conditions of knowledge production possible if these were also produced through immanent processes. Geological, social, and ecological processes of evolution are all fair game. So, too, are technologies like writing, telescopes, genetic sequencing, global circulation models, electricity grids, dreams, and internal combustion; even the actions of other species may affect the conditions and content of reason and what counts as reasonable.[17] Immanent explanations of the human condition reject the notion that we can use critical inquiry to establish an objective account of our earth-bound condition because there is no starting point for doubt that is not itself contingent. Instead of assuming that there exists a "view from no-where," immanent explanations instead highlight how attempts to objectively describe the Earth system inevitably catch us back up not only with non-human forces shaping the human condition but also with the technologies, practices, and social structures through which knowledge is co-produced.[18]

I share the concern over prematurely naturalized objectified facts and also think the contingent dynamics that shape the co-production of knowledge are vital to our understanding. But extending this worry to water management is misplaced if the philosophical target is a society/nature dualism that is used to prematurely naturalize facts. The problems of normal water are not this dualism but the consequences of one solution to the society/nature dualism and the policy and governance program it gave rise to. As such, Latour's rejection of critical inquiry misses the philosophical target I am interested in. So does his solution, which is to reject the distance gained by critical doubt—the distance created by separating appearance and reality—in favor of getting closer to "facts" through a realism that attends to non-human actions and to the social practices through which social worlds are made up.[19] For Latour, non-human agents shape the co-production of knowledge in the Anthropocene and the way in which social orders are imagined and enacted.[20] Moreover, the newfound abundance of agency in the Anthropocene that comes from seeing humans as one of many geological forces leads Latour to raise questions over how to secure a viable polity to the territory needed for life without appealing to God, nature, or uncontestable facts.[21] In short, Latour faces a "land problem" that is co-produced by the project of making things public.

Approaches to the Anthropocene that operate without appeals to transcendental forms of reason must find another basis upon which to conjoin different kinds of contingency across Earth and human histories. One option is to just state the Anthropocene's historical implications as fact, as Timothy Morton does when he claims, "All humans . . . are now aware that they have entered a new phase of history in which nonhumans are no longer excluded or merely decorative features of their social, psychic, and philosophical space."[22] Morton is simply wrong on this point—many people are unaware (sometimes blissfully so) of any new phase of history or the implications Morton claims for it. Another is to treat the Anthropocene as a series of "metabolic rifts," where human transformation of the Earth produces waste products that are so heavily reconfigured that their component parts do not reenter their former cycles, which leads to a cascading effect of environmental degradation.[23] This is no doubt happening, but it does not adequately capture the water case or how a certain cultural understanding of water is woven into the account of Earth system itself.

A more promising approach to rethinking the intersections of human and geological history is to see where points of contact can be found, and where tensions will remain, in the very effort to tell these sorts of histories. This has been one aim of Dipesh Chakrabarty and his attempt to rethink history in order to sort out how the human species "stumbled into" the Anthropocene.[24] Jason Moore and Andreas Malm independently argue that a focus on the human "species" obscures how a cultural subset of people is primarily responsible for the massive planetary impacts of human activity.[25] Chakrabarty, however, holds that parsing out a subset of humans, such as those in capitalist societies, generates its own rifts between different imaginations of the "planetary" through which the Earth system is understood and the "global" accounts of capitalism offered by the social sciences.[26] As I have argued throughout this book, however, there was no stumbling. When it comes to water—itself a model for bigger agendas—there was a clear effort to position humans at the helm of planetary evolution and to direct contingency into the service of liberal forms of life. That water resources now crisscross planetary understandings of the Earth system and risks to the global economy in the Anthropocene is no accident.

In contrast to Chakrabarty, my claim is that an earlier convergence of different forms of contingency co-produced the understanding of water that now traffics between accounts of planetary hydrology and water's fit with social and economic institutions: Water resources truck between the "planetary" and the "global," often in ways that capitalize on the slippages between the two to support liberal forms of life. Water resources were, and remain, a site for colliding human and geologic processes. It was through normal water that a single planetary story came into view and, through a series of human adjustments to this idea and the governance and policy programs it gave rise to, that this planetary story gained global reach. In what follows, I argue that we render the Anthropocene anthropologically opaque when we reference it to "things" that we should "make public" because, in so doing, we lose sight of how the naturalization of contingent processes—not the premature naturalization of objectified facts—has already linked geologic and human histories. The naturalization of process was not done under the auspices of state rationality or society/nature dualisms. Rather, contingent processes were naturalized in the hopes of uniting the social and natural sciences and of aligning state management institutions with liberal views of life as precarious adjustment. Indeed, water resources mediate the contingent geological, social, and technological processes that are enfolded into concrete policies and management practices proposed to ameliorate humanity's "water drama" in the Anthropocene.

Normal water is entangled with the details of U.S. experiences with (and interpretations of) colonialism, post-colonial development, and sustainability. Normal water is also full of encounters with competing expertise, agendas, and the resistance of other social and political actors. Of course, academically, the philosophy of water management failed in a most unremarkable way: It was forgotten. Yet its ethnocentric and colonial outlook persists in key institutions and provides a model for uniting conservation with international development and, more recently, global economic and financial institutions. This philosophy is also built into accounts of humanity's impact on Earth's water systems in the Anthropocene. When the mercurial origins of normal water are considered, however, the reasons for its uptake are not convincing. Despite these intellectual failings, water resources mediate all sorts of domestic and international agreements and weave through reconciliations that have been made to a world of water resources. If we followed the epigraph from Arendt, then we could hold that water resources are monuments of a world past, the facts about which have now become. These facts reflect the premature naturalization of geological processes, and they haunt the Anthropocene.

The Naturalization of Process

Normal water naturalizes Earth processes to liberal forms of life across different kinds of contingencies: geological, social, technical, and those required for the health of liberal individuals and the planet. In its naturalization of process, normal water collided Earth and world such that the chance outcome of geological action was that liberal societies were best suited to guide and care for planetary evolution. Since normal water took shape in the late nineteenth century, it not been recanted. If anything, normal water has been fortified alongside evolving iterations of liberalism and co-productions of knowledge about planetary hydrology. What has escaped notice, however, is that any premature naturalization of objective facts pales in comparison to the devastating impact that arose from the premature naturalization of processes that linked geology and liberal forms of life. This section considers what the naturalization of process implies for environmental politics in the Anthropocene.

Earth, World, and Process

Hannah Arendt has argued that the priority given to process is a peculiar modern conceit and, at that, one frequently wielded to evacuate politics from considerations of how social difference affects the human condition.[27] In *The Human Condition*, Arendt distinguishes labor, work, and action as three types of activities that condition humans as earthbound creatures. "Labor" refers to those activities required for subsistence, while "work" refers to the artifacts humans produce to construct their worlds. Work produces things that would not have otherwise come about. In distinguishing work from labor, Arendt also draws a distinction between the earth and the world. That is, between the geoid upon which we live and the social world we share with others. Both mutually condition human experience, but the distinction plays an important role in a third area: action. For Arendt, action is the condition of our plural existence and corresponds "to the fact that men, not Man, live on the earth and inhabit the world."[28] Action is a social fact about existence that Arendt draws on to identify how multiple, competing worlds may arise through the actions of different groups as labor and work shape a shared earth under differential conditions in which humans are more, and often less, free.

Arendt's analysis of the modern era is that, through process, action is linked in a seemingly natural way to political claims about human freedom. Beginning with etymology, Arendt notes that "nature" in Latin (*nasci*) or Greek (*phyien*) comes with the notion that "natural processes . . . come into being without the help of man, and those things are natural which are not 'made' but grow by themselves into whatever they become."[29] Which is to say, many Earth processes are independent of humans. The modern era, for Arendt, is marked by the effort to make new forms of "nature" appear by unchaining existing processes and repurposing them to make up the world in a particular way.[30] Arendt notes, drawing on Werner Heisenberg, that as this transformation of Earth processes into the world of human action becomes normalized, the conditions enabled by technology come to appear as a natural development in which the human organism is transplanted into the "environment of man."[31] For Arendt,

> It is quite probable that the continuous process pursuant to the channeling of nature's never-ending processes into the human world, though it may very well destroy the world *qua* world as human artifice, will as reliably and limitlessly provide the species man-kind with the necessities of life as nature herself did before men erected their artificial home on earth and set up a barrier between nature and themselves.[32]

Arendt's identification of how processes are naturalized to a particular world—a world that at its outer limit undermines itself, qua world, by collapsing the possibility for drawing a distinction between human artifice and Earth processes—recommends a way forward in interpreting the Anthropocene. The Anthropocene would, on this view, mark the point at which the Earth/world distinction is no longer tenable. This is a deeply political conceptualization. It depends on whose world is no longer tenable and which world is no longer understood as human artifice but as having been collapsed to the processes that characterize both its history and that of the Earth.[33] But referencing the Anthropocene to the social world in which the collapse of an Earth/world distinction has meaning also sites the Anthropocene in the political actions through which geological processes come to be seen as connecting both human and geologic histories. Note that this does not characterize human history writ large. Instead, it implicates a particular world as identifiable, and responsible, for unchaining the processes of nature to make the human environment and for being able to give an account of the Earth on these terms.

Arendt's proposal helps to explain the late nineteenth-century theories of Earth-making and the reversal that saw humans as co-producing the earth itself, such as in the "technogeography" of Otis Mason. As Arendt notes, such views require that one take the point of view of the universe because Earth must be seen as the sort of thing where natural processes could lead to the evolution of beings capable of making it up in directed fashion. But arriving at this view of the Earth, and of humans as part of geological processes, must also be a geological outcome if this view is not to fall back upon metaphysis. That is, a geological view of humans must be pure cosmological chance—the processes that led to this view must not be metaphysically unique—much like the early members of Washington's Cosmos Club hoped for in their "liberal positivism." Arendt, however, considers the attempt to take up the "view of the universe" a modern conceit that ignores how taking the point of view of the universe has actually come about through a cosmology and accompanying technologies that emerged out of one world of action. As Arendt writes,

> If . . . we return once more to the discovery of the Archimedean point and apply it, as Kafka warned us not to do, to man himself and to what he is doing on earth, it at once becomes manifest that all his activities, watched from a sufficiently removed vantage point in the universe, would appear not as activities of any kind but as processes, so that, as a scientist recently put it, modern motorization would appear like a process of biological mutation in which human bodies gradually begin to be covered by shells of steel.[34]

The early Earth-makers might not have had a problem with Arendt's slag on the progress of metal shells for motoring about. They were happy to reconcile human development in a stage theory of progress that improved upon haphazard evolution and that culminated in America's nascent scientific society. Yet if we consider the foregoing arguments of this book, the following argument comes into view: The naturalization of process was initially sought to collapse the Earth/world distinction in a way that would support liberal forms of life by making contingency an inherent aspect of the Earth's most vital agent—water—that, through evolutionary chance, could now be rendered a resource. Geologically infused social sciences in the United States confirmed this link of geological and human histories. Ongoing commitment to the project of normal water naturalized contingent process by teaching judgments of abundance, scarcity, and security alongside different iterations of liberalism and into the emerging scientific networks of twentieth-century hydrology until a common way of thinking about water gained planetary scope and global reach. Uniting human and Earth histories was a premature naturalization of process that resulted from one cosmological view and consequent practices that taught judgments without reference to alternate forms of life.

Once the naturalization of processes is identified, "making things public" seems an even less desirable project. This because "making things public" is often mobilized by ideas of contingent process that condition both human and non-human evolution as a route to rejecting human exceptionalism. I am not against the use of process per se. But contingent processes should not be naturalized anymore than "objective facts" should, and the ease with which theories of process naturalize disparate contingencies in water management should be confronted. For instance, Erik Swyngedouw claims that water is a hybrid of social and natural relations, a "'thing' that fuses together physical, biological, social, political, economic, and cultural processes."[35] But water resources were not premised on a society/nature divide, so they cannot now be a hybrid of it. Neither does water fuse different kinds of processes together in any natural fashion. Rather, it was through the politics of normal water that contingent processes were combined and sustained through practices that now permeate conservation, development, integrated water resources management, global water governance, and accounts of water in the Anthropocene.

Once we reject the naturalization of process, it is also evident that human privilege is not intrinsically connected to the predicament of the Anthropocene. Many forms of life have this feature, including virtually all of those adhering to axial religions and a great many besides.[36] So accounts that conflate ontological democracy with the rejection of human privilege smuggle in precisely what is at stake: It is not "human privilege" per se that is problematic but the privileging of forms of life that manage certain things, like water resources, without reference to notions of subjectivity, social relationships, or symbolic goods that could expose the premature naturalization of process. As if to reinforce this point, the philosophy of water management eventually struck upon the notion of the nexus—precisely the same term that Alfred North Whitehead used to speak about the refusal to bifurcate society and nature.[37] The fact that this discourse on the water-energy-food-climate nexus exists, and that governments, funding agencies, and global financial networks now take it into account as part of conceiving of human impacts on the planet, should alert us to the practices through which this bifurcation was refused time and again as normal water evolved alongside liberal forms of life. Disrupting the naturalization of process, and the social pretenses that positioned liberal forms of life as uniquely equipped to manage geological contingencies, is the political task of the Anthropocene.

Irony and Social Pretense

In his examination of the Anthropocene and U.S. environmental politics, Jedediah Purdy argues we should not succumb to dystopian views of neoliberal inequality but instead seek to galvanize new democratic possibilities.[38] His solution embraces post-humanism—and with it the idea that in theory all forms of life have equal value—and seeks to recover a tradition of wrestling with the value and meaning of the natural world in a geological time when nature is no longer. Purdy's strategy, however, does not connect the Anthropocene to concrete institutions but instead to competing "environmental imaginations" in the United States. For instance, Purdy repeats the standard account of Progressive Era policies in the United States as a debate between Gifford Pinchot's view of conservation and John Muir's notion of preservation, which both vied for influence in the imagination of environmental politics the early twentieth century. But conservation politics need to be positioned, as this book has done, in the perceived need for forms of management that do not appeal to social or natural law and instead seek a contingent, geological basis for uniting human and Earth histories. This idea of radical contingency is the more telling moment of conservation. Indeed, its influence resonates today in how the human drama of water in the Anthropocene is pictured through normal water and the project of gathering social and evolutionary possibilities into a planetary account. This picture bristles with inequality and needs to be seen, not as normal, but unfamiliar.

Irony is a way to disrupt normal water without appealing to "things" or theory. Although one could theorize about irony, that would not capture the spirit or intent of what it asks us to do, which consists in reflecting on our normal, practiced ways of making up the world and the difficulty of being in that world. Irony is experienced as an internal disruption of social pretense. This makes irony particularly apt for disrupting liberalism's remarkable ability to outflank, dispossess, and close off other ways of living. It can also shake up the pretense that water resources are able to conjoin all manner of contingencies in ways that just happen to fit with liberal forms of governing the Earth system. Typically, remarks on irony center on individuals like Socrates, Kierkegaard, or Nietzsche, who sought to disrupt (some might say, antagonize) the social worlds of their contemporaries. After considering how irony disrupts the notion that all histories can be naturalized to process, I return to what this means for normal water in preparation for the next chapter, which considers another ironist, Aldo Leopold, who sought to disrupt conservation and watershed management in the United States.

The Concept of Irony

Søren Kierkegaard employed irony to counter and then exit critical thought. Writing under the pseudonym Johannes Climacus, Kierkegaard argued that critical thought, especially since Hegel, had made it all too easy to be human. One merely had to look at where one was born, under what structures of authority one lived, and where one's duties to the state or the church lay in order to confirm one's identity. Of additional concern to Kierkegaard was that this kind of historicism made it too easy to be Christian, since the pretenses of these social worlds could also confirm personal faith.[39] For Kierkegaard or, rather, the young Johannes Climacus, who tried to live by the critical dictum "to doubt," things were much more difficult. In a striking parody of modern philosophical thought, Kierkegaard followed Socrates' example of irony, whose life in ancient Greece never ceased from disrupting the notions of citizenship and the good life held by his fellow Athenians.[40]

Like Socrates, Kierkegaard did not think one was human by birth. Rather, "to become human or to learn what it means to be human does not come that easily."[41] For the mature Kierkegaard—his view changed considerably after he wrote his master's thesis, *The Concept of Irony*[42]— irony is much more than turns of phrase, linguistic expressions, or indirect forms of speech. Irony unsettles how one lives within a particular social world and the categories of thought and practice that world provides. For instance, consider poor Climacus: He wants to be a modern philosopher and knows he should begin by doubting things as they appear to him. Yet he cannot figure out where to start doubting and, every time he begins, finds that he simply cannot doubt everything. In this, he doesn't have it as easy as Descartes, whose daily meditations on doubt happily trust his memory of the day before without hesitation.[43] So, even when it comes to being a modern, doubting philosopher, irony has its place to play in unsettling the ease with which practical identities are formed.

Jonathan Lear has offered a provocative account Kierkegaard's concept of irony and, in particular, the role of social pretense in forming practical identities.[44] "Social pretense" is not a derogatory term but one that picks out the human capacity to take up particular and often plural identities. We may have multiple practical identities at once, as parents, siblings, long-distance lovers, or rock 'n' roll history aficionados. What irony focuses on, however, is how social pretenses rely on habits adopted and learned within a particular form of life, the stopping rules of which are shared with others. Social pretenses for how to be a teacher or a student, for instance, are set in broader spheres of education policy, classroom architecture, and so on. Anthropologists and other social scientists have, of course, long studied the social and institutional conditions affecting practical identities. What is peculiar about irony is that it seeks to make the familiar aspects of social pretenses and social spaces unfamiliar—not even the philosopher knows where to start doubting. As Lear writes, irony disrupts our world and the ease with which we inhabit it by unsettling our ability "to locate familiar things in familiar places."[45] In short: Something normal becomes otherwise.

One dimension of current ecological theory is that it aims to disrupt the social pretenses that privilege humans. This disruption is supposed to come about by showing how many other life forms have capacities once thought uniquely human (e.g., language, social structures, emotion, etc.). Irony asks us to consider something different. Indeed, and unfortunately, we can encounter many strange, wonderful, and utterly foreign forms of life (and biological life forms) without our practical identities being affected, as the experience and study of colonization frequently shows. Kierkegaard's remarks on irony share this concern: Assent to social pretense can override the articles of experience. For example, the critique of environmentalism by Ramachandra Guha draws out precisely how the social pretenses of wealthy, predominantly western individuals and organizations support a vision of environmentalism that is out of step with the realities faced by millions of the world's poor.[46] Are mainstream environmentalists not serious about changing the planet? No, they are often quite committed, yet this commitment may never disrupt the social pretenses through which they assume their practical identities as ecologically conscientious citizens.

Kierkegaard employed irony to disrupt the ease of being human (and the ease of being Christian, in specific) that in his day accorded Hegelian historicism with accounts of cosmological order. Conveniently for a discussion of the Anthropocene, Kierkegaard used a geologic example to make his point. Yet instead of using geology to naturalize contingent processes, as did members of the Cosmos Club, Kierkegaard countered Hegel by using geology as a moment of ironic disruption. As he wrote,

> To travel to South America, to descend into subterranean caves to excavate the remains of extinct animal types and antediluvian fossils—in this there is nothing ironic, for the animals extant there now do not pretend to be the same animals.[47]

By unpacking this statement, we can see how Kierkegaard helps to confront the naturalization of process. Indeed, a subtle, yet thoroughgoing, point we can take from Kierkegaard is that our experience of ourselves qua humans is not natural. Our subjective understandings are entangled with the social worlds we inhabit. As Lear points out, the issue in Kierkegaard's geological example is not whether other animals have social lives (forms of rationality, patterns of hierarchy, etc.).[48] Rather, it is that a squirrel or a beaver does not take up a practical identity in reference to its ancestors. By contrast, human histories are sited with respect to social pretenses regarding how practical identities inhabited today are referenced to those of our ancestors. Hydrology was naturalized, for instance, to histories of water and man. Yet irony disrupts the view that practical identities are the natural sedimentation of human history. In this way, Kierkegaard strikes in a different mode at theories that naturalize contingent historical processes, such Hegel's dialectical historicism or the evolutionary progressivism of McGee and Powell—or those who prop up the "civilizing mission" today.

One of Kierkegaard's points is that critical thought fails because it universalizes doubt in order to traverse between former and contemporary ways of being human, that is, between the actual lives of our ancestors and their appearance to us, who assume the practical identity of being their descendants and partakers in their traditions. Doubt requires us to shed appeals to authority (which is the target of Kierkegaard's Christian angst) and instead links tradition and reason together through historical process, as in Hegel's historicism. Kierkegaard considered this too far removed from our actual experience. In fact, he thought Hegel was like somebody "who builds an enormous castle and himself lives alongside it in a shed."[49] This is because, despite the impressive conceptual apparatus (the castle), there is no way to live according to it because the articles of experience are already evacuated to the dialectics of historical process. This is reminiscent of Powell's view that Hegel "reified the void" through his occult postulate of a gap between appearance and reality. Of course, Powell was fine with enrolling both appearance and reality in processes of geological uniformitarianism, which elided the fact that social pretenses also exist in "scientific societies" like the one he envisioned.

For Kierkegaard, the best a Hegelian system could do was to provide a conversation on, and opportunities to reflect upon, different social pretenses. This constraint is also reminiscent of the arguments of Powell and McGee that confronted the master-slave dialectic in Hegel for how it construed British-American relations in reference to the "colonizer" rather than as something geologically novel. Returning to Kierkegaard, Hegel's historicism held no hope for disrupting social pretense because it subsumed human and natural history within the dialectics of process. In doing so, modern philosophy prematurely naturalized process as part of the pretense that made the dictum of critical thought—to doubt—the method by which to reconcile appearance and reality. Yet there was no way to be certain of whether this was ever achieved because one could always doubt more. The outcome was that "modern philosophy must ... be assumed to be always in the process of becoming, otherwise there would always be something more modern in relation to which it would be older."[50] For contemporary work in the Anthropocene, philosophies of "becoming" that wind their way into political theories and anthropological works are suitable only to the extent that they do not mobilize "becoming" by naturalizing process.

Irony and Normal Water

Normal water is not a theory. It names a set of judgments that were used to stop the search for further justification of one picture of the world. That picture brought human and planetary evolution together under the aegis of process. The aim was to secure social and evolutionary possibilities in service to forms of life that accorded with the U.S. state and "the People" that formed its Constitution. Where this project traveled, it indexed human adjustment to "resources" as a way to forward the social pretense that liberal forms of life were best suited to deal with the array of geological, social, and technical contingencies that affected individual and planetary health. Indeed, it even became possible to make up the past with a narrative of modern hydrology such that the health and development of states and individuals could fit with these processes anywhere on Earth and at any time. In this world picture, people everywhere had always managed water, are doing so today, and will be doing so tomorrow. But this picture paints over the unique claims of subjects, different social groups, and alternate symbolic goods others may hold as intrinsic ends.

One way to disrupt this project in a way that is not outflanked by the liberal logic of "doing without" is to make a move in line with the epigraph from Arendt, that is, to hold that the world in which we live is not *the* world. It is, rather, a world that has become through an orientation to the monuments of times past. Water resources—perhaps natural resources, more broadly—haunt the present as remnants of a premature naturalization of process. These monuments installed temporal and spatial assumptions into a project that routinely deployed water management in national and international projects of conservation and development. To unsettle normal water, a first step is the diagnosis of the practices through which a common way of thinking about water has led to the naturalization, and reproduction of, certain forms of violence.

This chapter considered why "making things public" will not exorcise the things haunting the Anthropocene. What is required is a view that avoids the pitfall of making human privilege intrinsic to the Anthropocene and that can arrest the naturalization of process. Irony is one path to shaking up the pretenses that make social worlds seem entirely normal and in which we are altogether confident about how to find our way about. Many Anthropocene theorists draw on ecology in order to "make things public" and challenge human exceptionalism. But this often leaves untouched the deep ethnocentrism of normal water and the naturalization of process that weds multiple kinds of contingency to liberal forms of life. There are, of course, many ways that ecology bursts through quotidian, normal ways of making up the world. Many of them influenced Luna Leopold's father, Aldo. The elder Leopold disrupted a number of the social pretenses of conservation in an effort to motivate a deeper care for ecological communities. And he started out by rethinking water management.

9

Thinking Ecologically in an Age of Geology

We have got to slippery ice where there is no friction and so in a certain sense the conditions are ideal, but also, just because of that, we are unable to walk. We want to walk: so we need friction. Back to the rough ground!
—Ludwig Wittgenstein

And so they live and have their being—these cranes—not in the constricted present, but in the wider reaches of evolutionary time. Their annual return is the ticking of the geologic clock.
—Aldo Leopold

In the late nineteenth century, the man who refused to punctuate his initials in order to conserve ink—old "no points" WJ McGee[1]—touted the philosophy of water management as a New Organon. McGee thought this philosophy was a step beyond modern science because it connected a scientific society to Earth-making and, thereby, to the contingent conditions of progress. Conveniently, this scientific society was composed of "the People" of the United States. In a remarkable turn of fortune, the struggle of "the People" against colonialism had chanced upon new habits of thought that made it possible to study and to guide evolutionary processes. Thinking geologically was central to the whole shebang. It was through geology that water resources were positioned as the key agent of planetary progress. By extending geological thinking to the social sciences, water and the rest of evolution's abundance could be harnessed for the greatest good of liberal society. Of course, as McGee admitted, if this philosophy was wrong it could be a colossal blunder.

After a century of applying and tuning the philosophy of water management, common sense has it that water is a resource. More than that, water is a scarce resource made all the more difficult to manage by wanton assumptions of abundance and by failures to appreciate its deep implications for security. So well practiced is this way of thinking that conceptions of water through alternate forms of subjectivity, social relations, or symbolic goods have been flattened—ontologically, if not under the smooth surfaces created by displacing millions of people for mammoth engineering works. So well trodden is this intellectual path that the conditions are set for doing what the early Cosmos Club members hoped for but did not achieve: connecting people and planet in empirical terms. Today, with the Anthropocene in view, the conditions are in a certain sense ideal. We now have the conceptual tools at hand to think about water—as a resource—across multiple social and scientific disciplines and in widely diverse contexts that must now adjust and adapt to the fact that humans are a geological force. This is a profound cultural accomplishment. But the glassy essence of this intellectual tradition has come at a cost to other ways of thinking and forms of life in which water's relations are different.

When conditions become too ideal, we can lose the friction we need to walk. As Wittgenstein advised those who would collapse philosophy into science, we need to get back to the rough ground.[2] Wittgenstein's advice holds a lesson for normal water, which has collapsed management practices to a single planetary story. Some, such as Peter Brown, have argued that the notion of "natural resources" should be rejected as a power grab made by "nature's one philosophizing species."[3] Putting things in species terms packs rhetorical punch, but it comes at the expense of seeing how water resources persist as the haunting monuments of men—not Man. Water resources are part of a social world designed to position liberal societies at the helm of evolution and to conserve an ailing mother Earth. As they were lugged around as the anthropological counterpart to one geologic era, the Holocene, they supported a project in which appropriating ever more water was part of entering another, the Anthropocene. In short, it's difficult to walk because these common ways of thinking make it hard to imagine water not being a resource.

The great conceit of normal water is that liberal societies can, in principle, manage water without reference to anything other. Not even nature is needed. All that is needed is a deep embrace of contingency and a belief that liberal societies are best equipped to deal with chance. With that in hand, a whole series of strange claims can be rationalized,

like treating the U.S. experience as the model for post-colonial development, or for the shackles of colonialism to be broken by uniting watershed management to regional development, or for the spread of these
ideas through many non-global means (conferences, working groups,
meetings with state officials, books, finance, and more) to become the
basis for global water governance, or, finally, for so bold a claim as the
Brundtland Report made—that the Earth is one but the world is not—to
be widely endorsed by governments and organizations around the world
without a second thought as to how water resources linked conservation and development to the environment within one social world. Of
course, normal water also had one postscript effect: It established cultural cover for collapsing different understandings of water to a single
story in the Anthropocene. Water resources have become a kind of total
geological fact.

The failure to arrest normal water was and remains linked with a
fallacy that naturalizes processes so as to align projects of human adjustment with contingent geologic dynamics. This fallacy enables an
ethnocentric view of contingency to link, in a scripted moment of
chance, Earth system evolution and the institutions of liberal societies
that led to both conservation and to a form of development premised
on it. This chapter challenges normal water from two vantage points.
The first unsettles it domestically, through an alternate understanding
of U.S. conservation from Aldo Leopold, whose work has inspired not
only his son Luna but many ecologists, lawyers, and water lovers.[4] The
second draws lessons from alternate water ethics that have persisted,
often in the face of overwhelming pressure for water to be managed
through the New Organon—which, for many, has been nothing short
of a colossal blunder. No vantage point has the final word on the matter,
and significant challenges remain. Yet there are ways to get back to the
rough ground and to form new stopping rules—new narratives—for the
deep, weird, and wonderful relations made possible by water.

Leopold and the Land Problem

Aldo Leopold was an American, born in 1887. He graduated from the
Yale School of Forestry in 1909, which had been founded by a gener-
ous donation from the Pinchot family whose son, Gifford Pinchot, was

McGee's compatriot in conservation. After Yale, Leopold joined the U.S. Forest Service and worked in the southwest, in District 3 (New Mexico and Arizona), until 1923. Early in his career, Leopold held fast to the utilitarian ethic that Pinchot had learned from McGee regarding the greatest good for the greatest number for the longest time.[5] Then, in 1920, Leopold underwent a significant change in perspective toward what he later described to Pinchot as an "ecological mode of thinking."[6] In 1923, Leopold published a "watershed handbook" for District 3 to combat the severe erosion problems caused by conventional conservation techniques. In 1924, Leopold transferred to Madison, Wisconsin, where he conducted a number of game surveys.[7]

The Great Depression of the 1930s left Leopold so unimpressed by New Deal conservation proposals that he declined an offer to become head forester of the Tennessee Valley Authority.[8] Instead, Leopold took up a position at the University of Wisconsin where he later became the first professor of game management in the United States. After his conversion to an ecological mode of thinking, Leopold drafted a number of essays that critiqued the notion of "land" underpinning American conservation. Many of these were motivated out of his concern for water.[9] Through his ecological mode of thinking, Leopold sought to return conservation to the rough ground. As the epigraph from Leopold suggests, ecology challenges the "geological thinking" of early conservation. Indeed, in an ecological mode of thought the actions of innumerable agents, such as cranes, are the ticking of the geologic clock.[10] Ecological actions make for a very different geologic clock than those presumed by linear views of progress, or even by McGee's elliptical view of planetary time, because ecological processes are emergent. For Leopold, the geological clock ticks spatially, through ecological actions that cannot be naturalized into the march of evolutionary progress.

Leopold sought to disrupt American conservation and watershed management. In this sense, he was something of an ironist inasmuch as he unsettled both the solution to the "land problem" in early notions of conservation and the myth upon which it was based. As becomes evident, however, Leopold's focus on addressing his contemporaries leaves important issues untouched, and this has left him open to valid criticism. The view I offer differs from that of Julianne Lutz Newton, who has identified geologic evolution and ecological diversity as two elements of Leopold's thinking.[11] To make this case, Newton conceives of ecological diversity in temporal terms, as a time slice of life "at a given moment."[12] I advance a view that follows Leopold's sentiment that ecological agents, like cranes, do not have their life in the "constricted present." So I follow others who hold that geology and ecology brook no easy distinctions in a broader view of life on Earth.[13] To think ecologically, it is not sufficient to look at a time slice of evolution because spatial variation and ecological patterns operate at numerous scales that are not accurately compared at any single moment. These spatial variations and ecological patterns are not always "scalable," either, to one another or to what humans may make of them.[14] The same holds true for land.

Land Disrupted

Recall that Otis Mason and WJ McGee addressed the "land problem" by linking the institution of property to the "technogeography" through which humans and other geological agents had shaped both the Earth and social evolution in a way that gave rise to the United States, which must now consciously adjust its institutions to the findings of geology and anthropology. McGee pushed further, holding that water, as a planetary agent like no other, must be secured as the material and moral basis of value to truly confront the "land problem" at its colonial roots. These ideas enrobed the management of private property and of public rights in a cosmology that linked individual freedom to the interdependent conditions that made the pursuit of freedom possible. The task of state managers, in this view, was to pursue a "liberal positivism" that ensured that the conditions for maximizing individual freedom were maintained. This included mobilizing the state's administrative machinery to achieve conservation's moral vision of evolutionary utilitarianism.

In Leopold's view, the solution to the "land problem" in American conservation was defective because it conceived of property as a relationship of expedience, where owners could dispatch with land as Odysseus had done with his slaves. For his part, Leopold held that conservationists maintained this problematic premise when they naturalized geologic evolution without regard for how ecological communities are shaped by deep spatial interconnections. Leopold thought conservation had inherited an inadequate ethical attitude that aimed to "integrate the individual to society," such as in laissez-faire notions that began with autonomous and free persons who entered a social contract with one another. As this book showed, John Wesley Powell, WJ McGee, and others sought to reverse this ethical attitude by conceiving of individuals as interdependent and social. Leopold, however, considered the geological "accretions" of early conservationists just as problematic in their attempts to "integrate social organization to the individual."[15] Leopold held that neither this democratic reversal (i.e., "liberal positivism") nor the view it had reversed had an ethical relation to land. Rather, both valued land instrumentally for its use in integrating the individual to society or for integrating social integration—which for McGee meant the entire "solidarity of life"—to the individual.

What seemed manifestly wrongheaded to Leopold was any view of property that assumed that land could be dispatched through the expediency accorded to private property. Even though conservationists had acknowledged that it took a geologically long time for the Earth to evolve the conditions for liberal society, they were mistaken to naturalize that claim to legitimate individual actions that treated property as essentially free from that fact. McGee, of course, had wanted to avoid this mistake by tying the exercise of freedom, such as that in private market exchanges, to the social nature of water and the interdependent persons who freely exchanged property. But that had simply not come to pass—perhaps mercifully so, given his ethnocentric formula. In any case, the notion of private property in American conservation remained one of expediency, where the institutions that legitimated individual entitlements allowed people the liberty to discharge their rights as they saw fit. When carried into national resource planning, the notion of expedience in decisions regarding land and water management resulted in contradictions that Leopold argued no "sober citizen" would tolerate if they knew what such "amateur tamperings" into the shared environmental heritage of Americans implied.[16]

In his essay, "Lakes and Their Relations to Terrestrial Life Patterns," Leopold argued conservation was beset by three contradictions. The first was the presumed independence, in ecological terms, of bureaucracies like the U.S. Forest Service, the Bureau of Reclamation, and the U.S. Army Corps of Engineers. This independence became especially stark after the Inland Waterways Commission was disbanded in 1920.

The second was the notion that mechanistic replacements for natural processes improved the existing state of affairs because mechanistic processes are directed, while natural processes are haphazard. Finally, Leopold argued that conservation was often focused solely on human considerations and ignored the response of ecological communities to human action. These three contradictions meant that Americans too wise to tolerate "tinkerings with their political constitution" were unknowingly accepting "radical amendments" to the constitution of the ecological community.[17] Leopold did not hold back in singling out the failure of conservation to understand how these radical amendments rippled through ecological systems as collective and complex adjustments were made to human actions. He also didn't think conservationists had anything like the complete knowledge, or even the right tools, they needed to manage the ways in which ecological systems adjust to human disturbances. As he wrote,

> The conservationist knows them as facts, but previous attempts to explain those facts have been unsatisfactory, because our ecology was too rudimentary to cope with them. Attempts to guide these adjustments (conservation) have been largely unsuccessful for the same reason.[18]

Critics of Leopold often target his reliance on science to forge a link between conservation and politics. Ursula Heise, for instance, describes Leopold as "distinctively modern" and argues that he is committed to a gradual Enlightenment in which political and ethical consideration expands beyond the human community through scientific theories of ecological evolution and the language of modern rights.[19] Because the expansion of moral consideration and political rights to women and non-western peoples were hard fought political victories and not the outcome of Enlightenment reason, this critique argues, cloaking this "progression" in ecological garb means that Leopold fails to confront its essentially patriarchal logic. Further, when this expanded moral sphere is applied to "nature" or "wilderness," ecology itself provides cover for putatively progressive norms that actually reinforce dominant power relations.

This is a powerful criticism, and to a degree Leopold is rightly charged with it. Like Henry David Thoreau, Leopold mourned lost ecological contexts. He described trips to his farm in Sand County, Wisconsin, as "refuge from too much modernity."[20] And he warned of the spiritual dangers of thinking that food comes from a grocer or heat from a furnace. Yet we can find a more nuanced set of claims in Leopold than those reducing his ideas to an American tradition that indexes a virtuous landscape to social stability.[21] Indeed, there is a way to read Leopold as an ironist for whom ecology is not a grand theory but rather a register to disrupt the social pretenses of his contemporaries. Reading Leopold as an ironist helps to clarify the exhortations he made to his colleagues to take experimental approaches to environmental management and to go out in the world and try things.[22] It also squares with his own attempts to salvage his ecologically "bankrupt" farm in Sand County.[23] Finally, and as with other ironists, reading Leopold in this way helps situate his many exhortations to care for the community.

Leopold, Community, and Conservation

A distinction between extension and expansion helps to explain how Leopold troubled the Enlightenment idea that a sphere of moral or political consideration gradually expands its canvas. As he argued, the "extension of ethics, so far studied only by philosophers, is actually a process in ecological evolution."[24] In Leopold's view, an ecological extension of ethics disrupts the idea that geological "accretions" of social progress resulted in a form of conservation that supported claims that the United States was exceptional. This is particularly the case for issues of political and ethical judgment, which Leopold held should be referenced to a community that was not constituted by humans alone. For Leopold, ethical judgments were not the outcome of an expanding canvas of Enlightenment rationality but were, rather, a communal "instinct in-the-making" that taught individuals to make judgments under conditions too complex for them to rationally discern what they ought to do.[25]

Leopold's ecological orientation to ethics was extensive. He held that how ethical judgments are reached changes as the result of changing ecological relationships. Although his distinction of ethical extension from an ethical expansion was not without problems, as critics like Heise remind us, Leopold employed it to trouble the social pretenses of his contemporaries and to prompt an ethic of care. According to Leopold, adjusting to the ecological community is a first, critical step in ethics. Like other conservationists, Leopold prioritized the interdependence of life as central to the long-term viability of the American Republic.[26] Unlike the "social subject" of earlier conservationists, however, Leopold did not hold that recognition of interdependence implied progress. This is evident in his critique of expediency as a guide to solving the "land problem" and is also part of his arguments against conservation education and economic valuation techniques that do not teach care for the community as such. As Leopold asks throughout *A Sand County Almanac*: How we are to value the community if we are not taught to care for it? Like other ironists, Leopold points out the difficulties of learning to care for the ecological community as a member of it, mirroring to some extent the way Socrates raised the difficulty of examining one's life as part of caring for, and partaking in, the Athenian Republic.[27]

Like McGee and the relational system of classification developed by others in the Cosmos Club, Leopold began by reclassifying land. Leopold, however, rejected the inference that conservation was necessary because, in the haphazard reaches of time, evolution chanced upon the conditions for liberal society to prosper in the United States. Instead, Leopold reclassified "land" as more than simply the soil to include "waters, plants and animals."[28] The ecological community, for Leopold, is everything assembled within the category of "land." In Leopold's view, community goods arise from the ways an ecological assemblage evolves through a complex and diverse set of processes and functions that involve both cooperative and competitive interactions. The goodness of the community is due to what the parts have done. As he wrote in *Round River*:

> If the land mechanism as a whole is good, then every part is good, whether we understand it or not. If the biota, in the course of aeons, has built something we like but do not understand, then who but a fool would discard seemingly useless parts? To keep every cog and wheel is the first precaution of intelligent tinkering.[29]

For Leopold, it is completely fine to manage ecological systems—to tinker—so long as the first principle is to keep every "cog and wheel" of the ecological community. This is an important step away from traditional conservation because it requires major adjustments. Contra traditional conservation, where "Earth-making" improved upon evolutionary chance by bringing it into the service of self-direction, Leopold holds that human adjustments are not only temporal but spatial as well—ecological adjustments operate "at right angles to evolution."[30] Leopold thought the nascent science of ecology was a mode of thinking that attempted this feat of thinking on "a plane perpendicular to Darwin."[31] An ecological mode of thinking augments the "deep time" required by geological evolution to accommodate the "deep space" required by the distribution of difference that provides for the abundance of ecological diversity.[32]

Spatial ecological relationships disrupt the idea that liberal societies can or should funnel geological abundance into their service. In an ecological mode of thought, the land is not a problem but rather a set of spatial relationships—as evidenced by the annual trips of the cranes in "Marshland Elegy." The movements of the ecological community are the ticking of the geologic clock. As such, Leopold's view of the "land" is not projected against immutable nature. In fact, his view of land confronts the naturalization of evolutionary processes to a specific social world, which troubles conservation's solution to the "land problem." How Leopold sets about disrupting conservation's view of the land merits closer consideration because he focuses specifically on practices of judgment. By looking closely at one example, we can see how his attempt to disrupt the social world of his contemporaries was connected to water.

In his 1943 essay, "What Is a Weed?" Leopold chastises the instrumental way in which horsemint, prairie goldenrod, and wild rose (among other plants) are judged as so much agricultural interference in an Iowa field guide.[33] The instrumental assumptions of the class "weed" prompt Leopold to write, "One is moved to ask whether, in Iowa, nothing useless has the right to grow along brooks. Indeed why not abolish the brook, which wastes many acres of otherwise useful farmland."[34] What is interesting is that Leopold, like a good ironist, does not contest the standard view. Instead, he extends it (to watery brooks) in a way that reveals a more general problem with conservation and its practices of judgment. For instance, conservationists of the day also debated whether hawks or owls were bad or good. In either case, Leopold argues, "We should have been better off to assert, in the first place, that good and bad are attributes of numbers, not of species; that hawks and owls are members of the native fauna, and as such are entitled to share the land with us."[35] Leopold's view turns on questions of numbers and degree, not kind. Indeed, flowers, watery brooks, and birds of prey can all be "weeds" insofar as traditional conservation is concerned because they all evolved haphazardly. This leads Leopold to an incisive criticism regarding how we teach judgments regarding land in the conclusion of the essay:

> It seems to me that both agriculture and conservation are in the process of inner conflict. Each has an ecological school of land-use, and what I may call an "iron-heel" school. If it be a fact that the former is the truer, then both have a common problem of constructing an ecological land-practice. Thus and not otherwise, will one cease to contradict the other. Thus, and not otherwise, will either prosper in the long run.[36]

In "What Is a Weed?" Leopold employs the language of truth testing found in American pragmatism—the long run—to disrupt notions of the community within the "iron-heel" schools of agriculture and conservation.[37] What matters presently, however, is that Leopold's notion of the community is not "the People" McGee identified, nor is it aligned with an evolutionary utilitarianism to solve the "land problem." Instead, an ecological mode of thinking disrupts judgments about weeds, hawks, and water by making the community unfamiliar. Conservation's failure to take an ecological view stokes Leopold's foment about the faulty premises of classification systems that ignore the reciprocal links between systems of classification, management practices, and ecological adjustments—that is, premises that fail to confront the myth in which the properties of the "land" provide a natural expedient for property.

Myths Adjusted

Leopold was not content to disrupt American conservation. He was also concerned with how his society was exhausting the land by virtue of its own myths. He worried about how previous civilizations in what is now the southwest United States had come and gone without causing the land to expire while his own culture was busy dismantling the evolutionary heritage of the region.[38] He did not think earlier cultures were morally superior or that they were non-anthropocentric. In fact, Leopold thought earlier peoples likely believed they were cosmologically unique. The significant difference between those cultures and his own, however, was that discrepancies between their forms of life and their environments did not degrade ecological systems on a geologic scale. Leopold's aim, in this context, was to show that ecology disrupts certain myths of his own culture.

In his 1923 essay, "Conservation in the Southwest," Leopold argued that the mark of a decent society is that it respects life and inhabits the world without defiling it. That, like cultures before it, a decent society leaves the "earth alive, undamaged."[39] Respecting the Earth required orienting society to the long-term health of the ecological community, which itself has a geological component. Leopold articulates his perspective toward the geological health of the ecological community in his essay, "Thinking like a Mountain." There, he recounts his realization that the indiscriminate culling of wolves would leave mountain slopes open to over-grazing by ungulates, both wild and domestic. The erosion from this changing ecology would be geologically disastrous, with "rivers washing the future into the sea."[40] By contrast, taking the long-term view meant referencing the project of adjustment to cultural myths about land in order to relearn how to make judgments.[41] For Leopold, part of the adjustment U.S. society needed to make was to concede it was not uniquely positioned to judge what is worth conserving.

When it comes to water management, Leopold's view stands in stark contrast to Lilienthal's division of the administration of authority from the standards of conservation in the Tennessee Valley Authority. In fact, it was around the time Leopold wrote his technical manual on watershed management that he wrote the "Standards of Conservation." In the latter, Leopold notes that the "machinery of administration" that standardizes how conservationists spend their time (e.g., writing reports or doing fieldwork) is distinct from the "standard of conservation" that dictates what they should spend their time trying to achieve ecologically.[42] Connecting the two required settling conflicts that arise between the weird and contingent objects of conservation and the conceptual maps of administrative standards. As Leopold wrote,

> It can be safely said that when it comes to actual work on the ground, the objects of conservation are never axiomatic or obvious, but always

complex and usually conflicting. The adjustment of these conflicts not only calls for the highest order of skill but involves decisions so weighty in their consequence, and so needful of permanence and correlation, that only the highest authority should make them.[43]

Unfortunately, we can only speculate on what Leopold meant by the "highest authority" because this essay is unfinished and ends abruptly mid-sentence. If we read the above quote in terms of Plato's *Republic*, we could get the sense that Leopold advocates for ecophilosopher kings—authorities who reason through the conflict between the standards of conservation and the machinery of its administration. That's one option. Another would note that for Leopold the objects of conservation are weird, never "axiomatic or obvious." Leopold thought that we lose sight of this weirdness when we ignore the reciprocal relationships between the standards of conservation and administrative machinations, such as those covered in this book regarding Lilienthal's unity of watershed management and democratic methods. In fact, in the text immediately preceding the quote above, Leopold is concerned with what a "watershed" is. Leopold places "watershed" in quotation marks to highlight the conflicting views regarding which standards of conservation fit with which systems of administration. In the case vexing Leopold, the conflict was between policies aimed at fire suppression through cattle grazing versus those aimed at protecting siltation in waterways by limiting ranching impacts. How do we know what "watershed" protection is in this or other instances of conservation? Leopold's answer is that we can't know a priori because any answer pitches us back against complex objects of conservation. Leopold's answer is disruptive because it suggests that the question cannot be answered *within* the myth of conservation and its claims about the normal objects—natural resources—that support American progress.

Leopold reverses the onus for judgments about the aims and ends of conservation by arguing that they can be faulty in two ways. One way is if these judgments classify things (like weeds) once and for all. This is too presumptive given ecological complexity. A second is if these judgments do not recognize how any system of administration affects what we consider to be concrete options. Elsewhere, Leopold chides managers for not seeing that the looping effect of classification systems and ecologi-

cal adjustment means that they are often blind to the effects of conservation until it is too late, writing: "We do not understand or foresee these
readjustments; we are unconscious of them unless the end effect is bad."[44]

Reciprocally adjusting to the ways that the land adjusts to human actions requires a new myth, one that is not monological. To hear other
voices, Leopold makes a threefold argument. First, he warns that we are
"beset on all sides with the pitfalls of language," for example, in arguments over whether the earth is alive or dead.[45] Leopold was familiar
with Henri Bergson's vitalism, yet he drew on the Russian philosopher
P. D. Ouspensky and his way of addressing dualisms of mind and matter both in Kant and in Ernst Mach's neutral monism.[46] Ouspensky ultimately held to a version of organicism, yet Leopold came to see that
both the "live earth" philosophy of vitalists and organicists and the "dead
earth" view of mechanistic philosophies admit interdependence.[47] If we
see Earth as alive, then its "enormously slow, intricate, and interrelated
functions" suggest that it is "vastly less alive than ourselves in degree,
but vastly greater than ourselves in time and space."[48] By contrast, if we
see Earth as dead, then we must admit that its operations pre-existed
any human uses for it. Either way, Leopold's claim regarding ecological
interdependence holds.

Leopold then turned to two elements he saw as fundamental to adjusting either view to an adequate relation of human perceptions to conservation. To the mechanistic philosophers, he asks: Was Earth made for man?
To vitalist notions that humans are the pinnacle of evolution, he asks:
Which culture is the pinnacle?[49] To the mechanists, Leopold answers that
no, Earth was not made for humans, and yet mechanistic philosophies inevitably construe it that way when they presume that humans are the most
intelligent "tinkerers." To the vitalists he argued that, regardless of what
other cultures thought about their unique place in the cosmos, no other
cultures irreparably damaged Earth in the long view of geologic time. By
showing that both options admitted interdependence and yet did not follow through on its ecological implications, Leopold sought to dethrone
the cosmology of conservation and used ecology to do so. For Leopold,
ecology was a science that disrupted conservation myths by returning us
to an appreciation of the weird objects of conservation, including water.

On April 14, 1935, the day after the term "Dust Bowl" was coined by a
Denver reporter, Leopold delivered a speech entitled "Land Pathology"

at the University of Wisconsin.[50] The essay offers a helpful transition from Leopold's critique of conservation to the broader concerns of this book. In it, Leopold argues that, while we can't put the relationship of "society and land into a test tube," we have evidence of the "accelerating velocity of destructive interactions" of industrialization.[51] The U.S. experience, Leopold argued, was "unmistakable and probably unprecedented" because the geological changes it wrought happened rapidly enough to correlate them with human action.[52] He presciently argued that a human signature could be identified from natural climate change. For Leopold, an ecological mode of thinking required repositioning the social and physical sciences, indeed universities themselves, toward "hastening the needed adjustment between society as now equipped, and land use as now practiced."[53] There are limitations to Leopold's views: he was in many ways a product of American environmental thought. But he wasn't trapped by all of it. The continuing resonance of his work is reminiscent of other ironists who sought to unsettle the social worlds of their contemporaries and to inspire in them renewed commitments to care for themselves and their communities.

Water, Ethics, and the Anthropocene

When UNESCO published its "Water and Ethics" series in 2004, its opening essay distanced itself from Aldo Leopold and affirmed the coevolutionary relationship of humans and society.[54] Normal water had come full circle and was now able to assemble water in a single planetary story that united its moral and material order. Yet ecology is no longer the rudimentary science that Leopold used to critique conservation, and his insights continue to resonate with ecologists who see the attempt to control ecological systems as pathological.[55] Leopold's "land ethic" has also inspired global water experts, such as Sandra Postel, to call for a water ethic that would establish an alternate normative basis for decision making.[56] Within the United States, experts have long called for a renewed focus on equity that respects the diversity of place-based responses to hydrological variability.[57] Elsewhere, it is increasingly evident that respecting place-based norms to water is vital for respecting cultural differences.[58] The growing appreciation of human impacts on Earth's water systems, however, has not yet confronted the cultural ethos of normal water. In the Anthropocene, the narrative of water's abundance, scarcity, and security continues to codify a set of practices that stop the search for further justifications of the common, yet problematic, notion that water is a resource. As a result, even though there is broad agreement among experts that we can't holistically integrate water systems based on Rational Planning and that the collective human impact on global water systems is severe, we are still far from having the "reverence for rivers" that Luna Leopold called for in 1977. Between these poles, some misplaced confidence remains—namely, the myth that liberal forms of life are uniquely equipped to manage the social and evolutionary possibilities made available by water.

Within the philosophy of water management certain contradictions gained civil status, such as debates over the human right to water and the role of public versus private models of delivering on that right. Other potential contradictions did not gain civil status. Many are not even conceivable when water resources are the medium for common ways of thinking. The implications of articulating claims to water in the language of liberalism are not lost on those who seek the human right to water as part of a larger project of securing water in support of other political and social orders. But these implications are lost when academic explanations of these contests do not appreciate how alternate understandings of social, legal, and personal relations to water articulate with different moral and political goods.[59]

By unearthing the philosophy of water management it becomes evident why some water challenges are recognized and prioritized and why others are not. The latter include those that arise within alternate forms of life or, alternately, for alternate forms of life that do not take liberalism as a reference point. As such, adhering to the myth of normal water foreshortens consideration of numerous other options for enhancing diversity and respecting difference. This is particularly the case because, as we saw, normal water retires its own ethnocentrism from view. Yet water resources are not socially weightless: They are the outcomes of a certain way of teaching judgments that proceeded, and continues to proceed, on unequal terrain shot through with the power relations and inequalities that arose within liberalism and that persist in the things that are naturalized to it.

Rather than perpetuating normal water, or continuing to think of water as only a resource, we might follow Aldo Leopold and hold that the objects of conservation are complex and uncertain. Human-water relationships are never so obvious that "water resources" are able to naturalize geologic time and ecological space to a single public or to multiple publics that are all cut of the same cloth. Yet it is also insufficient to make the dualism dividing society from nature the target of thinking about the challenges of the Anthropocene. Using the society/nature dualism in theories about water and modernity clouds an appreciation for how the naturalization of process yielded a philosophy of water management in which water resources have are already been made public. This naturalization project got off the ground by thinking "geologically" and in many ways anticipated the contemporary focus of social scientists on what the Anthropocene implies.

The real myth is that we have adjusted to so fraudulent an idea that water is a resource.[60] To try to understand this phenomenon, this book has sought to uncover a lost philosophy. To the extent that the philosophy of water management goes unseen, humans appear to have stumbled into a strange geological era that is somehow full of dark ecologies and uncanny experiences and is not, as this book has argued, the product of an ongoing social and political project. Aldo Leopold's work attempts a kind of internal disruption to conservation and the links of administrative machinery to ecological aims that were also characteristic of attempts at multipurpose river basin development and, later, integrated water resources management. Yet Leopold's definition of culture as "a state of awareness of the land's collective functioning" is inadequate.[61] Cultures and their geographic relationships are much more than this, a fact recognized long ago by Franz Boas. As an increasing number of anthropologists and other scholars are now doing, it is critical to treat the water-sharing practices of other communities and the alternate ways of thinking, acting, and valuing they imply on their own terms.[62] The judgments of other water-sharing norms are also key to confronting the patriarchal logic of water management, which often treats "gender" as a category to be managed alongside "culture" and has yet to confront the intrinsic inequality that besets settler-colonial norms of U.S. conservation and forms of development and governance premised upon its solution to the "land problem."[63]

Several theorists, including Bruno Latour, have tacitly picked up on the importance of relations to land in the Anthropocene.[64] I say "tacitly" because these arguments have yet to make room for substantially different understandings of land and of political space—territory—associated with relations to *that kind of land*. If we are to confront how conservation and development collapsed "many worlds" to "one Earth," it is imperative that the challenges presented by the Anthropocene make it possible for alternate understandings of territory to flourish. Respecting different relationships to land is central to confronting the dispossession of many peoples and groups in the name of progress.[65] Dispossession is not always dramatic or totalizing; it often proceeds in mundane ways,[66] through bureaucracies, regulations, or procedures of good governance that chip away at (and complicate) the spaces available for alternate forms of social coordination or individual choice. So while an "ecological mode of thinking" can be helpful for disrupting the myth of normal water internally, any space created must be left open for the forms of life oppressed by normal water. Alternate forms of life are not radically other. They are themselves: heterogeneous, diverse and plural.[67]

It is wholly mundane to think of water as a resource. Yet this way of thinking about water is also a roadblock to thinking differently and to respecting understandings of water across multiple forms of life. This is not because liberal forms of life are bad. It is because normal water naturalized the conditions of possibility writ large and in a way that codified practices that appropriated wholly unequal proportions of water. For instance, despite the fact that adjusting to water resources has profoundly affected Earth's life support systems, global water governance does not substantively depart from the philosophy that gave rise to the problems it seeks to solve. Quite the opposite, the speed of governance has accelerated to keep up with the proliferation of publics required for placeless modes of governance that seek to do without reference to differences regarding subjectivity, social relations, or symbolic goods. Without the unique demands put on water by different forms of life, the conditions became ideal for thinking geologically. To walk we need friction, yet it is difficult to grip the idea that water is not a resource anymore than it is anything else. The rough ground appears as soon as you walk off the path so well worn it has the semblance of truth. Water ethics is a project of learning how different judgments about water codify alternate practices for reaching agreements that do not naturalize one story about how the "land problem" may be solved through geology.

Conclusion

Water in the Anthropocene

Across the social sciences the Anthropocene is being mobilized to confront society/nature dualisms and to reject the idea that agency is unique to humans. As I have argued in this book, similar calls went out in the late nineteenth century by WJ McGee, John Wesley Powell, and others who sought to align the social sciences in the United States with geology. Water's agency was the crux for linking a geological account of agency to biological life, the rise of civilization, and a version of self-knowledge that positioned the liberal institutions of the United States at the helm of evolutionary abundance. As a resource, water was subsequently managed to support conservation and international development and to back a version of American exceptionalism in which the United States was an evolutionary model of post-colonial progress. Indeed, normal water—the project of gathering water's social and evolutionary possibilities into the service of liberal forms of life—has proven remarkably robust. It has survived the "liberal positivism" of Powell and McGee, the universalization of "American liberalism" under David Lilienthal, and the self-effacing iteration of liberalism that arose in the late twentieth century. In the new millennium, normal water has carried on into the water-energy-food-climate nexus. Throughout, the philosophy of water management gathered different kinds of geological, technical, and social contingencies into common judgments regarding the health of people and the planet. As rules codified where to stop looking for justifications of the links between water resources and liberal forms of life, a narrative took shape regarding water abundance, scarcity, and security.

The narrative of normal water was initially registered in the language of human adjustment. Once human domination of the Earth system became an accepted fact, the language of coevolution naturalized human-water relations such that the political project of human adjustment could be repackaged into notions of adaptation. As the narrative of normal water was developed, it was the precariousness of social existence, not a theory of rationality, that provided the rationale for ensuring that control over water's many contingent relationships aligned with liberal forms of life. Normal water has been so successful at combining claims about culture, economics, and geography that thinking about water as a resource does not even appear to be a philosophical choice despite the fact that it is propped up by a host of ideas—from lost approaches to anthropology to constantly revising geographic, economic, and political approaches to environmental management and development. This naturalization presents at least two challenges for thinking about water in the Anthropocene.

The first challenge is that many disciplines in the social and natural sciences treat water as a resource and frequently tie water management problems to a society/nature dualism. Given the historical role that water's agency has played in water management from Earth-making to the Anthropocene covered in this book, however, this dualism is not the only, or perhaps even the primary, issue when it comes to understanding how the idea that water is a resource structures thinking about water management in problematic ways. A related challenge is the ongoing attempt to link interpretations of society/nature dualisms to "policy relevant" research that reinforces understandings of water through propositions of water scarcity or security.[1] Academic units at universities around the world now focus on water scarcity or water security. This focus is not problematic per se. Rather, what needs to be disrupted is the pretense that these propositions reflect the state of affairs that link dire water needs to local, regional, or global hydrology. Far from it: These propositions reflect judgments about how to organize social and political relationships to water. When these judgments are taught as the basis for understanding water challenges globally, the propositions of abundance, scarcity, and security have the colonial effect of requiring that, regardless of cultural differences, claims to water be articulated using an understanding of water that privileges liberal forms of life.

Numerous academic disciplines have reflexively confronted their own relationships to the physical and symbolic violence of colonialism. Anthropologists have reflected critically on their historic role in opening and fostering colonial relationships with other cultures. Geographers have foresworn their previous cartographic and geopolitical efforts that represented the Earth as ripe for imperial conquest. Already, discourse on the Anthropocene has led to calls for more careful disciplinary considerations of its implications.[2] I suggest something similar: Social scientists should refuse the notion that water resources are a neutral category that academics, water managers, and policy makers can use to orient water use decisions. Refusing to think of water as only a resource is especially relevant considering how the propositions of water abundance, water scarcity, and water security are employed to teach judgments about how to govern water resources in the Anthropocene. These propositions are routinely used to reinforce structures of thought that gather multiple social worlds into a single planetary story regarding risks to people, the planet, and the economy. As a corollary, these propositions teach judgments that stop the search for further justifications for the philosophy of water management and, in so doing, foster unequal practices that favor one cultural understanding of water over others.

The challenge of inequality leads to a second concern regarding how the water practices of alternate forms of life can be respected morally and materially. A clear obstacle to addressing inequality is the radical contingency that normal water claims and interprets at the expense of other ways of thinking about water. In many social and legal orders, such as those of indigenous peoples in Canada and New Zealand, there is a great deal left to chance but no corollary rejection of ultimate sources of authority.[3] As such, respecting alternate sources of authority and the social and legal relations they establish is central to meeting obligations that states have to indigenous peoples with respect to water, such as those found in (or implied by) many treaty agreements. One way to encourage equality is to relativize the stopping rules that end the search for justifications regarding different water management practices. As is clearly evident from this book, stopping rules evolve: Abundance was initially a wonderful idea about evolutionary progress, but was then later repurposed when it became part of the explanatory rationale for scarcity. Others, like the stopping rule that nature once provided, are happily being jettisoned by academics of many stripes who embrace the Anthropocene and its implications for understanding human relations to the Earth system. The challenge of seeking equality is, of course, that powerful actors have a habit of outflanking the opposition or, if that does not work, oppressing it.

This book has focused on how liberal forms of life have outflanked and oppressed alternate practices of water management as abundance, scarcity, and security came to mirror the iterations of liberal logics that "do without" unique notions of subjectivity, social relations, and symbolic goods. While political theorists often argue that the justification for liberalism is found in reasoned agreements among individuals who do not intrinsically favor any particular view of the world,[4] liberalism is nevertheless practiced through judgment. In the case of water, the symbolic power of liberal forms of life resides in the now widely accepted judgment that managing water resources across social, technical, and geological systems is critical to the health of people and the planet. The efficacy of normal water resides in the claim that agreements can be reached without reference to the practices used for actually doing so in specific places, places that are replete with the subjectivities, social relations, and symbolic ends of those who dwell within them.

The Anthropocene is a novel concept, but it is not a neutral one. The problem of water management in the Anthropocene is not that commonsense judgments about water are based on ungrounded propositions—there is a century's worth of fortification of normal water across the social and physical sciences—but that they codify an ungrounded way of acting.[5] The judgments of normal water were taught as part of a broader system of hypotheses that gave a unique geological place to liberal forms of life. These judgments were then heavily reinforced by international efforts, including scientific collaborations that retold the history of "water and man" in a manner that fit global hydrology to an emerging picture of the Earth system. But this picture needn't hold us hostage. Water is a necessary and contingent feature of all forms of social life, and it supports social and evolutionary possibilities on a spectrum that is captured only in small fractions by any one of them. Water remains ever restless in this new geological era, and the choice to continue in the commonsense view that it is only a resource is a choice against equality in the Anthropocene.

NOTES

INTRODUCTION

1 Reisner, *Cadillac Desert*.
2 Egan, *The Worst Hard Time*. Textbooks on hydrology are peppered with references to Luna Leopold—my first textbook on river dynamics cited him at least a dozen times. See Knighton, *Fluvial Forms*.
3 Luna Leopold, "A Reverence for Rivers," 429.
4 Luna Leopold, "Ethos, Equity, " 2.
5 AghaKouchak et al., "Water and Climate."
6 Postel et al., "Human Appropriation"; and Gleick and Palaniappan, "Peak Water Limits."
7 Tyler, "Impacts."
8 Clarke et al., "Projected Deglaciation."
9 Milly et al., "Stationarity Is Dead."
10 Rockström, Steffen, et al., "A Safe Operating Space"; and Steffen, Richardson, et al., "Planetary Boundaries."
11 Rockström, Falkenmark, et al., "The Unfolding Water Drama."
12 Jaramillo and Destouni, "Local Flow Regulation."
13 Orlove and Caton, "Water Sustainability"; Mauss, *The Gift*.
14 Bakker, "The 'Commons.'"
15 Losurdo, *Liberalism*.
16 Wittgenstein, *Philosophical Investigations*, §125.
17 Hacking, *The Taming of Chance*.
18 Ripl, "Water."
19 See Waters et al., "The Anthropocene."
20 Crutzen and Stoermer, "The Anthropocene."
21 Steffen, Persson, et al., "The Anthropocene"; and Hibbard et al., "Decadal Interactions."
22 Zalasiewicz et al., "When Did the Anthropocene Begin?"
23 Lewis and Maslin, "Defining the Anthropocene." Another view begins with carbon shifts associated with the agricultural revolution; see Ruddiman, "The Anthropocene."
24 Steffen, Persson, et al., "The Anthropocene."
25 Chakrabarty, "The Climate of History."
26 Ellis, Golkewijk, et al., "Anthropogenic Transformation."

27 Hobbs et al., *Novel Ecosystems*.

28 Ellis, "Ecology in an Anthropogenic Biosphere."

29 Ellis, Fuller, et al., "Dating the Anthropocene."

30 Clark, *Inhuman Nature*.

31 Hamilton et al., *The Anthropocene*.

32 Morton, *Hyperobjects*.

33 Merchant, *The Death of Nature*; Plumwood, *Feminism and the Mastery of Nature*; Spivak, "Can the Subaltern Speak?"; and Guha, *Environmentalism*.

34 Hamilton and Grinevald, "Was the Anthropocene Anticipated?"

35 See Steffen, Grinevald, et al., "The Anthropocene."

36 Marsh, *The Earth as Modified*.

37 Bergson, *Creative Evolution*.

38 Teilhard de Chardin, *The Phenomenon of Man*.

39 Vernadsky, "The Biosphere and the Noösphere," and *The Biosphere*.

40 Hamilton and Grinevald, "Was the Anthropocene Anticipated?" 66.

41 Lovelock, *Gaia*.

42 Moore, *Capitalism*; Malm, *Fossil Capital*; Haraway, "Anthropocene"; and Bonneuil and Fressoz, *The Shock of the Anthropocene*.

43 Shaler, *Man and the Earth*; and Sherlock, *Man as a Geological Agent*.

44 Lövbrand et al., "Earth System Governmentality"; and Biermann, *Earth System Governance*.

45 Conca, *Governing Water*; Alatout, "From Water Abundance to Water Scarcity"; Chartres and Samyuktha, *Out of Water*; Pachova et al., *International Water Security*; and Ioris, "The Political Nexus."

46 Latour and Weibel, *Making Things Public*.

47 Wittgenstein, *On Certainty*, §97.

48 See Trottier, "Water Crises"; and Strang, *The Meaning of Water*.

49 Beauvoir, *The Ethics of Ambiguity*.

50 Reuss, "Coping with Uncertainty."

51 Melosi, *The Sanitary City*; Benidickson, *The Culture of Flushing*; and Gandy, *The Fabric of Space*.

52 D'Souza, *Drowned and Dammed*; Hoag, *Developing the Rivers*; and Fasseur, *The Politics of Colonial Exploitation*.

53 Mukerji, *Impossible Engineering*; and Blackbourn, *The Conquest of Nature*.

54 Swyngedouw, *Liquid Power*; and Pritchard, *Confluence*.

55 Sneddon, *Concrete Revolution*; and Pietz, *The Yellow River*.

CHAPTER 1. FIRST WATER, THEN THE WORLD

1 Wittfogel, *Oriental Despotism*.

2 Fagan, *Elixir*; Fishman, *The Big Thirst*; and Solomon, *Water*.

3 WJ McGee, "The Foundation of Science," 174.

4 Blackbourn, *The Conquest of Nature*; and Cronon, *Nature's Metropolis*.

5 Lutz, "Empire Is in the Details."

6 James Scott, *Seeing like a State*.

7 See Solomon, *Water*; Fagan, *Elixir*; Chartres and Samyuktha, *Out of Water*; and Postel, *Last Oasis*.

8 See Ball, *Life's Matrix*.

9 Witzel, "Water in Mythology"; and Strang, *Gardening the World*.

10 See Björkman, *Pipe Politics*; Illich, *H₂O and the Waters of Forgetfulness*; and Matthews and Schmidt, "False Promises."

11 Gaard, "Women, Water, Energy."

12 Goodman, *Ways of Worldmaking*, 6.

13 James Scott, "High Modernist Social Engineering."

14 Hamlin, "'Waters' or 'Water'?"; and Gregory, "(Post)Colonialism."

15 Pinchot, *Breaking New Ground*, 325.

16 Bakker, *Privatizing Water*, 40.

17 See Reuss, "Seeing like an Engineer"; Espeland, *The Struggle for Water*; and Ingram, "The Political Economy."

18 Elsewhere Bakker emphasizes the specificities of water as key to understanding political, technical, and "natural" relations. See Bakker, "Water."

19 Swyngedouw, *Liquid Power*, and *Social Power*.

20 Latour, *We Have Never Been Modern*.

21 Ibid.

22 Swyngedouw, *Liquid Power*.

23 Linton, *What Is Water?*

24 Schmidt, "Historicising the Hydrosocial Cycle."

25 Bourdieu, *Pascalian Meditations*.

26 Nilsson and Petterson, "The Structural Origin."

27 VandeWall, "Why Water Is Not H₂O"; Chang, *Is Water H₂O?*; and Brakel, *Philosophy of Chemistry*.

28 See Bacon, *Novum Organum*.

29 Kant, *Critique of Pure Reason*.

30 Gaston, *The Concept of World*, 15.

31 Kant, *Perpetual Peace*, and *Lectures on Anthropology*; and Elden and Mendieta, *Reading Kant's Geography*.

32 See Bennett, *Vibrant Matter*; Coole and Frost, *New Materialisms*; and Haraway, *When Species Meet*.

33 Meehan, "Tool-Power."

34 Morton, *Ecology without Nature*.

35 Ibid.

36 Morton, *Hyperobjects*.

37 Ibid. Also see Morton, *The Ecological Thought*.

38 Morton, *Hyperobjects*.

39 It is also unclear how Morton employs "world" as he engages Husserl, Heidegger, or Derrida, who all had variations on the concept. See Gaston, *The Concept of World*.

40 See Morton, *Ecology without Nature*.

41 Mill, *On Liberty, Three Essays on Religion*, and *Principles of Political Economy*.
42 Mach, *The Analysis of Sensations*.
43 Banks, "Neutral Monism Reconsidered."
44 Frederick Turner, *The Significance of the Frontier*.
45 Wittgenstein, *Philosophical Investigations*.
46 Hacking, *Historical Ontology*, 17.
47 Wittgensetin, *Philosophical Investigations*, §75.
48 Wittgenstein, *On Certainty*, §§137–150.
49 Ibid., §140.
50 Ibid., §105.
51 Monk, *Ludwig Wittgenstein*.
52 See Frazer, *The Golden Bough*.
53 Tully, *Strange Multiplicity*, 113, 310.
54 Wittgenstein, *Philosophical Investigations*, §104.
55 Ibid., §115.
56 Wittgenstin, *On Certainty*, §139.
57 Wittgenstein, *The Blue and the Brown Books*.
58 Coole and Frost, *New Materialisms*, 8.
59 Arendt, *Lectures*.
60 Bourdieu, *Distinction*, and *Pascalian Meditations*.
61 Weber, "Politics as a Vocation."
62 Bourdieu, *Language and Symbolic Power*.
63 See Singer, *Entitlement*.
64 McNay, *The Misguided Search*.
65 Tully, *Strange Multiplicity*; and Skinner, *The Foundations*.
66 See Hacking, *Historical Ontology*.
67 Wittgenstein, *Philosophical Investigations*, §217.
68 Ibid., §241.
69 Ibid., §125.

CHAPTER 2. LAISSEZ-FAIRE METAPHYSICS
1 Stocking, *Victorian Anthropology*.
2 See Worster, *A River Running West*; and Aton, *Powell*.
3 Worster, *A River Running West*, 551.
4 deBuys, *Seeing Things Whole*, 21.
5 Logan, review of Powell's "Truth and Error"; and Lester Ward, "Truth and Error."
6 John Wesley Powell, unpublished letter to *Science* magazine, June 7, 1887, National Anthropological Archives, Smithsonian Institution, Washington, DC, "Biographical Notes on Major John Wesley Powell," 13 pp., MS 4024-h.
7 Bergson, *The Two Sources*, 100.
8 Lacey, "The World of the Bureaus."
9 The Cosmos Club website is at www.cosmosclub.org. The quote from Stegner, *Beyond the Hundredth Meridian*.

10 Lacey, "The Mysteries."

11 Lester Ward, *Glimpses*, 5:109.

12 Spencer, *Social Statistics*, and *The Man versus the State*.

13 Peirce, "The Architecture"; James, "Remarks"; and Dewey, *Outlines of a Critical Theory of Ethics*.

14 Hofstadter, *Social Darwinism*, 20.

15 Marsh, *The Earth as Modified*.

16 Lacey, "The Mysteries," 426.

17 Otis Mason, "The Land Problem."

18 Otis Mason, "Technogeography," and "Influence."

19 See Otis Mason, "The Land Problem."

20 Powell, *Lands of the Arid Region*.

21 See Merchant, "Fish First!"

22 Rudwick, *Bursting the Limits*.

23 Lyell, *Principles of Geology*.

24 Powell, *Exploration of the Colorado River*, 153. Emphasis in original.

25 WJ McGee, "What Is a Glacier?," "On the Cause of the Glacial Period," "Shale and Davis' 'Glaciers,'" "On Local Subsidence," and "Glacial Canyons."

26 See Davies, *The Earth in Decay*.

27 See Lacey, "The Mysteries."

28 WJ McGee, "The Classification of Geographic Forms," 27.

29 WJ McGee, "Geology for 1887 and 1888," 259.

30 WJ McGee, "The Field of Geology," 196.

31 Powell, "Darwin's Contributions."

32 Thomas Huxley, "Science and Pseudo-science."

33 See WJ McGee, "Man's Place in Nature"; and Thomas Huxley, *Man's Place in Nature*.

34 WJ McGee, unpublished draft essay on John Wesley Powell, n.d., National Anthropological Archives, Smithsonian Institution, Washington, DC, Bureau of American Ethnology Series, "Letter Books: Letters Sent by WJ McGee," box 58, 156.

35 Gilb, *Frederick Webb Hodge*; and Worster, *A River Running West*.

36 WJ McGee, "Letter to Franklin W Hooper, August 1, 1895," National Anthropological Archives, Smithsonian Institution, Washington, DC, Bureau of American Ethnology Series, "Letter Books: Letters Sent by WJ McGee," box 58.

37 Samuel Hays, "The Mythology of Conservation," 41.

38 WJ McGee, "The Foundation of Science," 172.

39 Ibid., 175.

40 WJ McGee's picture metaphor may be a reference to Humboldt's famous *Naturegemälde* image of nature as a unified whole. See Wulf, *The Invention of Nature*.

41 Powell, *Truth and Error*, 3.

42 Ibid., 407.

43 Ibid., 109.

44 Ibid., 14.
45 Peirce, "Man's Glassy Essence."
46 Lester Ward, *Glimpses*, 1:xxxiii.
47 Lester Ward, "Status of the Mind Problem."
48 James, "Does Consciousness Exist?"
49 Lester Ward, "Status of the Mind Problem."
50 Lester Ward, *Glimpses*; and Worster, *A River Running West*, 552.
51 Lester Ward, "Mind as a Social Factor."
52 Bergson, *Creative Evolution*.
53 Powell, "Darwin's Contributions."
54 See Peirce, "Deduction, Induction, and Hypothesis."
55 Pyne, *Grove Karl Gilbert*.
56 Gilbert, "Inculcation of Scientific Method," 286.
57 Ibid., 287.
58 Peirce, "Pragmatism," 231.
59 Pyne, *Grove Karl Gilbert*, 192.
60 Gilbert, "The Origin of Hypotheses."
61 Pyne, "Methodologies for Geology."
62 Chamberlin, "The Method."
63 WJ McGee, "Letter to Dr. F. M. Colby, March 8, 1903," National Anthropological Archives, Smithsonian Institution, Washington, DC, Bureau of American Ethnology Series, "Letter Books: Letters Sent by W J McGee," box 58.
64 WJ McGee, "The Earth the Home of Man," 2.
65 Ibid., 3.
66 Ibid., 5.
67 See Spencer, *The Principles of Psychology*.
68 Pearce, "From 'Circumstances' to 'Environment.'"
69 James, "Remarks."
70 WJ McGee, "The Earth the Home of Man."
71 Ibid., 17.
72 Ibid.
73 See Schweitzer, *The Philosophy of Civilization*.
74 WJ McGee, "The Earth the Home of Man," 18.
75 Ibid., 28.
76 Merchant, *Reinventing Eden*.
77 Mill, *On Liberty*.
78 Spencer, *Social Statistics*, 78.
79 Powell, *Truth and Error*, 423.
80 Powell, "The Course of Human Progress"; and WJ McGee, "The Trend of Human Progress."
81 Lacey, "The World of the Bureaus."
82 Ibid., 137.
83 Ibid.

84 Lévi-Strauss, "Anthropology."

85 Powell, "The Course of Human Progress."

86 Powell, *Introduction to the Study of Indian Languages.*

87 Powell, *Truth and Error.* See also WJ McGee, "The Beginnings of Mathematics."

88 See Dewey, *Psychology.*

89 Mill, *A System of Logic.*

90 Peirce, "The Order of Nature."

91 Menand, *The Metaphysical Club.*

92 Brasch, "Einstein's Appreciation."

93 Baker, "The Pragmatic Roots."

94 Peirce, "The Law of Mind."

95 Brent, *Charles Sanders Peirce.*

96 Eisele, "The Charles S. Peirce–Simon Newcomb Correspondence."

97 Lamb, "The Story."

98 Wiener, *Charles S. Peirce*, 275–321.

99 Peirce, "The Century's Great Men."

100 See Brent, *Charles Sanders Peirce.*

101 Peirce, "Uniformity," 227.

102 Ibid., 226.

103 Peirce, "Synechism, Fallibilism, and Evolution," 358.

104 Peirce, "Some Consequences of Four Incapacities," 247.

105 Menand, *The Metaphysical Club*; and Lacey, "The World of the Bureaus."

106 Powell, "The Lessons of Folklore."

107 Powell, *Truth and Error*, 117–120.

108 Powell, "Sociology."

109 James, "Remarks," 17.

110 Hegel, *Phenomenology of Mind.*

111 Ibid., 239; and Coulthard, *Red Skin, White Masks.*

112 Hegel, *The Philosophy of History.*

113 On abundance generally, see Schleifer, *Modernism and Time.*

CHAPTER 3. MANAGING WATER FOR "THE PEOPLE"

1 Emma McGee, *Life of WJ McGee.*

2 Hazel Fontana and Bernard Fontana, *Trails to Tiburon.*

3 Cross, "W. J. McGee"; and Lacey, "The Mysteries."

4 During archival research at the Smithsonian, a box suggesting more personal materials on McGee could not be located.

5 Worster, *Nature's Economy.*

6 Merchant, *Reinventing Eden*, 103.

7 Merchant, "Fish First!"

8 WJ McGee, "The Superstructure of Science," 171.

9 Lacey, "The Mysteries."

10 Oravec, "Presidential Public Policy."

11 Wescoat, "'Watersheds' in Regional Planning."

12 WJ McGee, "The Growth of the United States."

13 Tyrrell, *Crisis of the Wasteful Nation*, 117.

14 Lacey, "The World of the Bureaus."

15 Powell, "Competition as a Factor," 309.

16 WJ McGee, "The Relation of Institutions," 705.

17 WJ McGee, "Fifty Years of American Science," 320.

18 WJ McGee, "Cardinal Principles of Science."

19 Ibid., 9.

20 Ward also held that "society is a relation" and that neither relations nor their scientific explanations required metaphysics. See Lester Ward, "Contemporary Sociology."

21 WJ McGee, "Man's Place in Nature."

22 WJ McGee, National Anthropological Archives, Smithsonian Institution, Washington, DC, Records of the Bureau of American Ethnology, series 1, "Correspondence Letterbooks," box 58, 78.

23 Ibid., 79.

24 Ibid., 78.

25 Mill, *Principles of Political Economy*.

26 Boas, "The Mind of Primitive Man."

27 Boas, "Speech on March 5, 1913."

28 See Worster, *A River Running West*.

29 Pisani, "Water Planning."

30 See Tyrrell, *Crisis of the Wasteful Nation*.

31 Rousseau, *Politics and the Arts*, 126.

32 WJ McGee, "Our Great River," 8580.

33 See Cross, "W. J. McGee."

34 Pinchot, "Speech on March 5, 2013," 21.

35 Wescoat, "'Watersheds' in Regional Planning."

36 Pinchot, *Breaking New Ground*, 359.

37 Inland Waterways Commission, *Preliminary Report*.

38 Blanchard et al., *Proceedings*.

39 WJ McGee, "Outlines of Hydrology."

40 Ibid., 200.

41 Ibid., 195.

42 Darrigol, *Worlds of Flow*.

43 WJ McGee, "The Flood Plains of Rivers."

44 Bray, "Joseph Nicolas Nicollet." Nicollet's surveys also erased many indigenous places from the map. See Picha, "Joseph N. Nicollet."

45 WJ McGee, "Outlines of Hydrology," 206.

46 Ibid., 210; emphasis in original.

47 WJ McGee, "Water as a Resource."

48 WJ McGee, "Principles of Water-Power Development."

49 Darton, "Memoir of W J McGee." Darton was referring to WJ McGee, *The Potable Waters of the Eastern United States.*

50 Locke, *Two Treatises of Government.*

51 WJ McGee, "Principles of Water-Power Development," 817.

52 *Lochner v. New York*, 198 US 45 (1905).

53 WJ McGee, "Principles of Water-Power Development," 819.

54 WJ McGee, "Desert Thirst as Disease."

55 WJ McGee, "Principles of Water-Power Development," 823.

56 Barber, "Irving Fisher of Yale."

57 Irving Fisher, *Memorial.*

58 WJ McGee, "Principles of Water-Power Development," 825.

59 Pinchot, *Breaking New Ground.*

60 See Stoll, *Inherit the Holy Mountain.*

61 Worster, "Watershed Democracy."

62 Casanowicz, "Proceedings," 82.

63 WJ McGee, "The Conservation of Natural Resources," 100.

64 Lacey, "Federalism and National Planning."

65 Lacey, "The World of the Bureaus."

66 Powell, "Outlines of Sociology."

67 McGee, "The Five-Fold Functions of Government."

68 WJ McGee, "The Cult of Conservation."

69 See *The McGee Memorial Meeting*, 28.

70 See WJ McGee, "Our Great River."

71 *Winters v. United States*, 207 US 564 (1908).

72 WJ McGee, "Principles of Water-Power Development," 818.

73 Taylor, *Modern Social Imaginaries.*

74 WJ McGee, "The Five-Fold Functions of Government," 277.

75 WJ McGee, "National Growth and National Character."

76 WJ McGee, "Movement of Water in Semi-arid Regions."

77 Singer, "Original Acquisition of Property."

78 WJ McGee, "Our Inland Waterways."

79 World Commission on Environment and Development, *Our Common Future.*

CHAPTER 4. AMERICA'S POST-COLONIAL MODEL OF DEVELOPMENT

1 See Worster, "Watershed Democracy."

2 Ross, "Man over Nature."

3 Hays, *Conservation*; and Wengert, "The Ideological Basis."

4 Hubbard, *Origins of the TVA.*

5 Wengert, "Antecedents of TVA."

6 Lilienthal, *TVA: Democracy on the March*, xi.

7 Ibid., xxi.

8 Dewey, *Freedom and Culture*, 176.

9 See Hubbard, *Origins of the TVA*; Pritchett, *The Tennessee Valley Authority*; Hargrove, *Prisoners of Myth*; and Selznick, *TVA*.

10 James Scott, "High Modernist Social Engineering."

11 See Colignon, *Power Plays*.

12 Schlesinger, *The Coming of the New Deal*.

13 Monk, *Robert Oppenheimer*.

14 Pointed out by Ekbladh, *The Great American Mission*. See David Lilienthal, *Big Business*.

15 Neuse, *David E. Lilienthal*.

16 Willkie later wrote a best seller; see Willkie, *One World*.

17 Lilienthal, *The Journals of David E. Lilienthal: The TVA Years*.

18 Morgan, *The Making of the TVA*.

19 For an excellent history, see Ekbladh, *The Great American Mission*.

20 Tennessee Valley Authority, *TVA*, 5.

21 See Lilienthal, *TVA: Democracy on the March*, 56.

22 Ibid., 75; emphasis in original.

23 Ibid., 76.

24 Richard White, *The Organic Machine*.

25 Lilienthal, *TVA: Democracy on the March*, 198; emphasis in original.

26 Ibid., 93; emphasis in original. See Lilienthal, *The TVA: An Experiment*.

27 Lilienthal, *TVA: Democracy on the March*, 150–152, 189–190.

28 Dewey, *Freedom and Culture*, 175; emphasis in original. Quoted in Lilienthal, *TVA: Democracy on the March*, 194.

29 Dewey, *Liberalism and Social Action*.

30 Pappas, *John Dewey's Ethics*. See also Dewey, *Experience and Nature*.

31 Dewey, *The Public and Its Problems*, 140.

32 See Colignon, *Power Plays*.

33 See McCraw, *Morgan vs. Lilienthal*.

34 See Ekbladh, "Meeting the Challenge."

35 See Lilienthal, "Electricity."

36 Lilienthal, *TVA: Democracy on the March*, 203–204; emphases in original.

37 Goldschmidt, "The Development of the US South."

38 Lilienthal, *TVA: Democracy on the March*, 150.

39 Hargrove, "David Lilienthal."

40 See Tennessee Valley Authority, *Nature's Constant Gift*.

41 See Gilbert White, *Strategies*.

42 Schlesinger, *The Vital Center*.

43 Collins, *Uncle Sam's Billion Dollar Baby*.

44 Clapp, *TVA and Its Critics*.

45 Clapp, "Lessons of the TVA." See also Finer, *T.V.A.*

46 See also Clapp, "The Tennessee Valley Is Paying Off."

47 Clapp, "Interview."

48 Tennessee Valley Public Power Association, *National Defense and TVA.*; copy courtesy of the Harvard Graduate School of Design Loeb Library.

49 Gary, *The Nervous Liberals.*

50 Hamblin, *Arming Mother Nature.*

51 Harding, *Objectivity*; and Reisch, *How the Cold War Transformed the Philosophy of Science.*

52 Norton, *Sustainability.*

53 See Mead, *Cultural Patterns and Technical Change.*

54 See Gilman, *Mandarins of the Future.*

55 See Mandler, *Return from the Natives.*

56 See Christopher Fisher, "The Illusion of Progress."

57 Feldman, *Water Resources Management.*

58 See Ekbladh, "Meeting the Challenge."

59 Truman, "Truman's Inaugural Address."

60 See Ekbladh, *The Great American Mission.*

61 Ibid. See also Pietz, *The Yellow River.*

62 UNESCO, *The Scientific Conference on Resource Conservation*, 1.

63 See Ekbladh, "Meeting the Challenge."

64 Ibid. See also Julian Huxley, "Plans for Tomorrow."

65 Asher et al., *The United Nations*, 195.

66 James Scott, "High Modernist Social Engineering."

67 Schlesinger, *The Vital Center*, 233.

68 Ekbladh, "Mr. TVA."

69 Ekbladh, *The Great American Mission.*

70 U.S. President's Water Resources Policy Commission, *A Water Policy for the American People*, 6.

71 Ibid., 7, 8.

72 Hayek, *The Road to Serfdom.*

73 Hayek, "The Use of Knowledge in Society."

74 U.S. President's Water Resources Policy Commission, *A Water Policy for the American People*, 8.

75 Mitchell, *Carbon Democracy.*

76 Ibid., 132.

77 Mitchell, "Economentality."

78 Neil Smith, *American Empire.*

79 Hayek, "A Commodity Reserve Currency."

80 See also Barber, "Irving Fisher of Yale."

81 Rostow, *The Stages of Economic Growth.*

82 Sachs, *Planet Dialectics.*

83 Edward Mason and Robert Asher, *The World Bank since Bretton Woods.*

84 Salman, *The World Bank Policy*; and Cavers and Nelson, *Electric Power Regulation.*

85 See Sneddon, *Concrete Revolution.*

86 Lilienthal, "Another 'Korea' in the Making?"

87 Edward Mason and Robert Asher, *The World Bank since Bretton Woods*, 612.

88 Akhter, "The Hydropolitical Cold War."

89 Haines, "(Inter)Nationalist Rivers?"

90 Salman, *The World Bank Policy for Projects on International Waterways*.

91 Ekbladh, "Mr. TVA."

92 Edward Mason and Robert Asher, *The World Bank since Bretton Woods*.

93 Bochenski and Diamond, "TVA's in the Middle East."

94 Mitchell, *Rule of Experts*.

95 U.S. Senate Committee on Appropriations, *Financing of Aswan High Dam*.

96 Ibid. See, generally, Beckert, *Empire of Cotton*.

97 See Teisch, *Engineering Nature*; and Sneddon, *Concrete Revolution*.

98 Goodwin, "The Valley Authority Idea." Also see Klingensmith, *"One Valley and a Thousand."*

99 Klingensmith, *"One Valley and a Thousand."*

100 Christopher Fisher, "Moral Purpose."

101 Lowdermilk, *Palestine*; and *Jewish Telegraphic Agency*, "TVA Head."

102 Alatout, "From Water Abundance to Water Scarcity," and "Bringing Abundance into Environmental Politics."

103 Ekbladh, "Mr. TVA."

104 Ekbladh, *The Great American Mission*.

105 Biggs, "Reclamation Nations"; and Sneddon, *Concrete Revolution*.

106 See Reisner, *Cadillac Desert*.

107 Sneddon, *Concrete Revolution*.

108 UN Economic Commission for Asia and the Far East, *Development of Water Resources*, 42.

109 Goldschmidt, "The Development of the U.S. South," 228.

110 Gardner, "From the Colorado to the Mekong."

111 Johnson, "Pattern for Peace in Southeast Asia," 151–152.

112 *New York Times*, "David E. Lilienthal Is Dead at 81."

CHAPTER 5. THE SPACE OF SCARCITY

1 Gilbert White, *Resources and Needs*, 5.

2 Harding, *Objectivity*, 2015.

3 Dewey, *Liberalism and Social Action*, 52–60.

4 Dewey, "Ethical Principles underlying Education," 69.

5 Boas, "The Study of Geography."

6 See Wescoat, "The 'Practical Range of Choice.'"

7 Thomas, *Man's Role*.

8 Wittfogel, *Oriental Despotism*.

9 Glacken, *Traces on the Rhodian Shore*.

10 Thomas, *Man's Role*.

11 Neil Smith, *American Empire*.

12 Sauer, "The Agency of Man," 68.
13 Hinshaw, *Living within Nature's Extremes.*
14 WJ McGee, "The Science of Humanity," 430.
15 Dewey, "Evolution and Ethics."
16 Ibid.
17 The best overview of their interactions is by Wescoat, "Common Themes."
18 Ibid.
19 Barrows, "Geography as Human Ecology."
20 Dewey, "Evolution and Ethics," 339.
21 Santayana, "Dewey's Naturalistic Metaphysics."
22 Dewey, "Half-Hearted Naturalism."
23 See also Pappas, *John Dewey's Ethics.*
24 Wescoat, "Common Themes"; and Hinshaw, *Living within Nature's Extremes.*
25 Gilbert White, *Human Adjustment to Floods.*
26 James, *The Varieties of Religious Experience.*
27 James, "Great Men, Great Thoughts."
28 See Clawson, *New Deal Planning.*
29 Reuss, *Water Resources People and Issues.*
30 Clawson, *New Deal Planning.*
31 Person, *Little Waters.*
32 Luna Leopold and Thomas Maddock, *The Flood Control Controversy.*
33 Porter, *Trust in Numbers.*
34 Gilbert White, *Human Adjustment to Floods.*
35 U.S. President's Water Resources Policy Commission, *A Water Policy for the American People*, 18.
36 Reuss, *Water Resources People and Issues.* See also Maass, *Muddy Waters.*
37 See Feldman, *Water Resources Management.*
38 Frank Moss, *The Water Crisis.*
39 Meigs, "Water Problems in the United States."
40 Wright, *The Coming Water Famine.*
41 U.S. Federal Council for Science and Technology Ad Hoc Panel on Hydrology, *Scientific Hydrology.*
42 Reuss, *Water Resources People and Issues*, 52. See Maass and Hufschmidt, "Report on the Harvard Program."
43 Gilbert White, "Broader Bases for Choice."
44 Chamberlin, "The Method."
45 Gilbert White, "Contributions of Geographical Analysis."
46 Reuss, *Water Resources People and Issues*, 35.
47 Hinshaw, *Living within Nature's Extremes*, 101.
48 Ekbladh, *The Great American Mission.*
49 See United Nations, *Proceedings.*
50 Asher et al., *The United Nations.*
51 United Nations, *Integrated River Basin Development.*

52 Ibid., 3.
53 Gilbert White, "Vietnam."
54 Hinshaw, *Living within Nature's Extremes*.
55 See Wheeler, "Co-operation for Development."
56 Korzoun et al., *Atlas of World Water Balance*.
57 UNESCO, *Three Centuries of Scientific Hydrology*.
58 Ad Hoc Committee, *An Outline of International Programs in Hydrology*.
59 Nace and Panel on Hydrology (USA), "A Plan for International Cooperation," 10.
60 Nace, "The International Hydrological Decade," 419.
61 Ibid., 413.
62 Nace, "Water Resources."
63 Nace, *Water and Man*.
64 Contra Linton, *What Is Water?*
65 Biswas, *History of Hydrology*.
66 Ibid., 319.
67 Norman Smith, *Man and Water*.
68 Stamm, "Bureau of Reclamation."
69 Fitzsimmons and Salama, *Man and Water*.
70 Gilbert White, "Role of Geography," 106.
71 Carson, *Silent Spring*.
72 Gilbert White et al., *Drawers of Water*.
73 Nace, "The Hydrological Cycle," 21.
74 Ibid.
75 Tuan, *The Hydrologic Cycle*.
76 Davies, *The Earth in Decay*.
77 Reisch, *How the Cold War Transformed the Philosophy of Science*.
78 See Szasz, *Ecopopulism*.
79 Hinshaw, *Living within Nature's Extremes*.
80 Environmental Science and Public Policy Archives, Harvard University, Cambridge, MA, Peter Thacher Papers, vol. 2, box 12 [106].
81 Gilbert White, *Strategies*.
82 UN General Assembly, "3513 (XXX) United Nations Water Conference."
83 See Lazarus, *The Making of Environmental Law*. Technically, the Clean Water Act amended the Federal Water Pollution Control Act of 1948.
84 Institution of Civil Engineers, *Engineering Hydrology Today*.
85 Satterthwaite, *Barbara Ward*. See also Barbara Ward, *The Home of Man*, and *Progress for a Small Planet*.
86 See Stein, *Water*.
87 See Beer et al., *Clean Water for All*.
88 Gilbert White, *Water for All*.
89 Gilbert White, *Resources and Needs*. See also Biswas, *United Nations Water Conference*.
90 Biswas, *United Nations Water Conference*; and Sabin, *The Bet*.

91 For the "Policy Options" report, see Biswas, *United Nations Water Conference*. The World Bank report appears as Warford, "Pricing as a Means."

92 Harold Brown, *Rationality*.

93 See the UN Water Conference, *Report of the United Nations Water Conference*.

94 Ibid.

95 See Marshall Moss and Gary Tasker, "The Role of Stochastic Hydrology"; Marshall Moss, "Space, Time"; and Odum, *Fundamentals of Ecology*.

96 UN Water Conference, *Report of the United Nations Water Conference*, 97.

97 Biswas, *United Nations Water Conference*, xii.

98 See Tsing, "On Nonscalability."

99 Lilienthal, *The Journals of David E. Lilienthal: The Venturesome Years*.

100 Ibid.

101 Foltz, "Iran's Water Crisis."

102 See Akhil Gupta, *Post-colonial Developments*; Agrawal, *Environmentality*; Li, *The Will to Improve*; and Chakrabarty, *Provincializing Europe*.

103 See Nikolas Rose, "The Death of the Social?"; and Polanyi, *The Great Transformation*.

104 Conca, *Governing Water*, 73.

CHAPTER 6. THE GLOBALIZATION OF NORMAL WATER

1 International Water Resources Association, "Sustainable Development and Water," 184; emphasis in original.

2 Falkenmark et al., "Macro-Scale Water Scarcity."

3 Compare Ohlsson, "Water Conflicts"; Rijsberman, "Water Scarcity"; and Savenije, "Water Scarcity Indicators."

4 See Lindblom, "A Century of Planning."

5 See for critiques of water scarcity, see Bakker, *An Uncooperative Commodity*; Mehta, *The Politics and Poetics of Water*; and Barnes, *Cultivating the Nile*.

6 Schmidt, "Water Management and the Procedural Turn."

7 Sandel, *Democracy's Discontent*; Habermas, *Between Facts and Norms*; and Rawls, *Justice as Fairness*.

8 See Norton, *Sustainability*.

9 Blatter and Ingram, *Reflections on Water*.

10 UNEP, *The UN-Water Status Report*.

11 "Protection of the Quality and Supply of Freshwater Resources," January 28, 1991, UN Report A/CONF.151/PC/13, Environmental Science and Public Policy Archives, Harvard University, Cambridge, MA, Peter Thacher Papers, vol. 1, box 47[441].

12 Falkenmark, "The Greatest Water Problem."

13 UN General Assembly, "Resolution A/RES/44/228."

14 Conca, *Governing Water*.

15 Harvey, *A Brief History of Neoliberalism*, and "The Nature of Environment."

16 Wendy Brown, *Undoing the Demos*.

17 See Boelens et al., *Out of the Mainstream*, esp. Achterhuis et al., "Water Property Relations."

18 See Povinelli, *Economies of Abandonment*.
19 World Commission on Environment and Development, *Our Common Future*.
20 Thacher, "Master Plan for the Watery Planet."
21 Holdgate et al., *The World Environment*.
22 White, "Comparative Analysis of Complex River Development."
23 Priscoli, "The Development of Transnational Regimes," 30.
24 Kneese and Bower, *Managing Water Quality*.
25 Environmental Science and Public Policy Archives, Harvard University, Cambridge, MA, Peter Thacher Papers, vol. 1, box 94[900].
26 Environmental Science and Public Policy Archives, Harvard University, Cambridge, MA, Peter Thacher Papers, vol. 1, box 95[904], esp. "Natural Resource Accounts: French Experience and the Case of Water Resources."
27 Kysar, *Regulating from Nowhere*.
28 Environmental Science and Public Policy Archives, Harvard University, Cambridge, MA, Peter Thacher Papers, vol. 1, box 96[922].
29 Gilbert White, "Paths to Risk Analysis."
30 Dublin Statement.
31 See Helmer, "Water Quality Monitoring."
32 Environmental Science and Public Policy Archives, Harvard University, Cambridge, MA, Maurice Strong Papers, box 461[4372].
33 Environmental Science and Public Policy Archives, Harvard University, Cambridge, MA, Maurice Strong Papers, box 640[5693].
34 Environmental Science and Public Policy Archives, Harvard University, Cambridge, MA, Maurice Strong Papers, box 640[5966].
35 Sagoff, *Price, Principle*, 14.
36 Dublin Statement.
37 Sax, "The Public Trust Doctrine"; Ingram and Oggins, "The Public Trust Doctrine"; and Wilkinson, "The Headwaters."
38 Maass and Anderson, . . . *And the Desert Shall Rejoice*.
39 Ingram et al., "Guidelines."
40 Ostrom, *Governing the Commons*.
41 Carol Rose, "Energy and Efficiency"; and Freyfogle, "Water Rights."
42 Durant and Holmes, "Thou Shalt Not Covet Thy Neighbor's Water."
43 Natural Research Council, *Water Transfers in the West*, x.
44 Schorr, *The Colorado Doctrine*.
45 Sax, "Understanding Transfers."
46 Wilkinson, "Indian Water Rights," 220; and Anderson and Leal, *Free Market Environmentalism*. See Rodriguez, *Acequia*.
47 See Stone, *Should Trees Have Standing?*
48 Bauer, *Siren Song*.
49 Ibid. See Bauer, "Results of Chilean Water Markets"; Briscoe et al., "Managing Water"; Easter et al., "Formal and Informal Markets"; Thobani, "Formal Water Markets"; and Baer, "Private Water."

50 After failing to fund the Aswan High Dam, for instance, the United States became a principal donor of water development aid to Egypt to adjust political and economic institutions in American interests. See Barnes, *Cultivating the Nile*.

51 See the Dublin Statement.

52 Environmental Science and Public Policy Archives, Harvard University, Cambridge, MA, Peter Thacher Papers, vol. 1, box 49[452].

53 Cook et al., "The Persistence of 'Normal' Catchment Management."

54 Environmental Science and Public Policy Archives, Harvard University, Cambridge, MA, Peter Thacher Papers, vol. 2, box 42[375].

55 UN Conference on Environment and Development, *Agenda 21*.

56 World Bank, *Water Resources Management*.

57 World Bank, *From Scarcity to Security*.

58 Gleick, "Climate Change."

59 Hulme et al., "Unstable Climates." See also Behringer, *A Cultural History of Climate*.

60 L'vovich and White, "Use and Transformation of Terrestrial Water Systems." See, generally, B. L. Turner et al., *The Earth as Transformed by Human Action*.

61 Gleick, *Water in Crisis*.

62 Ibid., ii.

63 See also Gleick, "Environment, Resources," and "Water and Conflict."

64 Wolf, "Conflict and Cooperation."

65 Meredith Giordano and Aaron Wolf, "Sharing Waters."

66 LeRoy, "Troubled Waters"; and Falkenmark and Lundqvist, "Towards Water Security."

67 Postel et al., "Human Appropriation."

68 White, "Reflections on the 50-Year International Search."

69 Priscoli, "Water and Civilization."

70 Ibid.

71 Rogers et al., *Water as a Social and Economic Good*; and Solanes and Gonzalez-Villarreal, *The Dublin Principles*.

72 Global Water Partnership Technical Advisory Committee, *Integrated Water Resources Management*, 22.

73 The Global Environment Facility is a partnership among the World Bank, the UN Development Program, and the UN Environment Program. See the World Bank, *Funding for the Global Environment*; and Reed, *The Global Environmental Facility*.

74 Biswas, "Integrated Water Resources Management"; Jeffrey and Gearey, "Integrated Water Resources Management"; Heathcote, *Integrated Watershed Management*; and Ingram, "Beyond Universal Remedies."

75 William Cosgrove and Frank Rijsberman, *World Water Vision*. See also Environmental Science and Public Policy Archives, Harvard University, Cambridge, MA, Maurice Strong Papers, box 659[6116].

76 Environmental Science and Public Policy Archives, Harvard University, Cambridge, MA, Maurice Strong Papers, box 656[6095].

77 Environmental Science and Public Policy Archives, Harvard University, Cambridge, MA, Maurice Strong Papers, box 656[6095].

78 Ibid.

79 World Water Council, "A Water Secure World."

80 Published as Dinar, *The Political Economy of Water Pricing Reforms*.

81 Environmental Science and Public Policy Archives, Harvard University, Cambridge, MA, Maurice Strong Papers, box 659[6116]. See also Agarwal et al., *Making Water Everybody's Business*.

82 The Hague, Ministerial Declaration.

83 Ibid., 1; emphasis in original.

84 Ibid.

CHAPTER 7. SECURING THE WATER-ENERGY-FOOD-CLIMATE NEXUS

1 World Bank, *Water Resources Sector Strategy*.

2 Bakker, *An Uncooperative Commodity*; and Olivera, *Cochabamba!*

3 See Meinzen-Dick and Nkonya, "Understanding Legal Pluralism."

4 World Bank, *Water Resources Sector Strategy*, 3.

5 Biswas, "Integrated Water Resources Management."

6 Gleick and Lane, "Large International Water Meetings"; and Biswas, "From Mar del Plata to Kyoto."

7 World Economic Forum, *Water Security*.

8 Rockström, Falkenmark, et al., "The Unfolding Water Drama."

9 Wescoat and White, *Water for Life*.

10 See Sachs and McArthur, "The Millennium Project."

11 United Nations, *Resolution 55/2*, 4.

12 Ibid., 5.

13 Rogers and Hall, *Effective Water Governance*, 16.

14 Sabatier et al., *Swimming Upstream*.

15 Millennium Ecosystem Assessment, *Ecosystems and Human Well-Being*.

16 Lee, *Compass and Gyroscope*.

17 Feldman, *Water Policy*.

18 See also Folke et al., "Resilience Thinking"; Walker et al., "Resilience, Adaptability"; and Gunderson and Holling, *Panarchy*.

19 Holling, "Resilience and Stability." See also Folke, "Resilience."

20 Holling, *Adaptive Environmental Assessment and Management*.

21 Crutzen and Graedel, "The Role of Atmospheric Chemistry."

22 Holling, "The Resilience of Terrestrial Ecosystems." Holling also proposed an adaptive cycle to align changing ecological systems with experimental policies.

23 Norton, *Sustainability*.

24 Holling and Meffe, "Command and Control," 335.

25 Falkenmark and Rockström, *Balancing Water*; and Folke, "Freshwater for Resilience."

26 See Falkenmark et al., "Macro-Scale Water Scarcity"; and Falkenmark, "The Greatest Water Problem."

27 Falkenmark and Rockström, *Balancing Water*.
28 Falkenmark and Folke, "Ecohydrosolidarity."
29 Milly et al., "Stationarity Is Dead."
30 Schmidt, "Integrating Water Management."
31 Ripl, "Water"; Vörösmarty, Lettenmaier, et al., "Humans Transforming the Global Water System"; and Vörösmarty, McIntyre, et al., "Global Threats."
32 Folke, "Freshwater for Resilience."
33 See Priscoli, "Water and Civilization."
34 Falkenmark and Folke, "The Ethics of Socio-ecohydrological Catchment Management."
35 Falkenmark, "Towards Integrated Catchment Management."
36 Rockström, Steffen, et al., "A Safe Operating Space."
37 See Meybeck, "Global Analysis"; and Vörösmarty, Lettenmaier, et al., "Humans Transforming the Global Water System."
38 Global Water Partnership, *Global Water Security*, 1.
39 McLeod, "TVA Tutors Foreign Utility Engineers."
40 Christopher Scott et al., "The Water-Energy-Food Nexus."
41 Whitehead, *Process and Reality*.
42 I am using "mind and matter" as a shorthand for Whitehead's criticisms of the Lockean distinction between primary and secondary qualities, his arguments against the notions of absolute space and time, and his dissatisfaction with aspects of Einstein's view. See Whitehead, *The Concept of Nature*.
43 Christopher Scott et al., "The Water-Energy-Food Nexus"; and Sant and Dixit, "Beneficiaries of IPS Subsidy."
44 White, *The Organic Machine*.
45 Gleick, "Water and Energy."
46 U.S. Department of Energy, *Energy Demands on Water Resources*.
47 Committee on Energy and Natural Resources, *Energy-Water Nexus*.
48 U.S. Government Accountability Office, *Energy-Water Nexus, Energy-Water Nexus: Coordinated Federal Approach*, and *Energy-Water Nexus: Information on the Quantity, Quality, and Management*.
49 Office of the Director of National Intelligence, *Global Water Security*.
50 Clinton, "Clinton at U.N. Roundtable."
51 See also Howells and Rogner, "Water-Energy Nexus."
52 Pigman, *The World Economic Forum*, 4.
53 Ibid.
54 World Economic Forum, *Global Risks, 2006*.
55 World Economic Forum, *Global Risks, 2008*, 6.
56 Allan, Keulertz, and Woertz, "The Water-Food-Energy Nexus."
57 World Economic Forum, *Global Risks, 2009*.
58 World Economic Forum, *Thirsty Energy*.
59 World Economic Forum, *The Bubble Is Close to Bursting*.
60 UN Water, *Water in a Changing World*.

61 For more information, see the website of the 2030 Water Resources Group, www.2030wrg.org.

62 2030 Water Resources Group, *Charting Our Future*.

63 World Economic Forum, *Realizing the Potential*.

64 World Bank, *Public Communication Programs*.

65 Grey and Sadoff, "Sink or Swim?"

66 World Economic Forum, *Global Risks, 2010*.

67 World Economic Forum, *Water Security*, 1.

68 2030 Water Resources Group, *The Water Resources Group*.

69 World Economic Forum, *Global Risks to the Business Environment, 2005*, 5.

70 Folke, "Resilience."

71 World Economic Forum, *Water Security*, 42.

72 World Economic Forum, *Global Risks, 2011*.

73 Ibid., 31.

74 Food and Agricultural Organization, *Coping with Water Scarcity*. See also Lundqvist et al., *Water, Food Security and Human Dignity*.

75 Hoff, *Understanding the Nexus*.

76 Ringler et al., "The Nexus."

77 UN Water, *Water Security*.

78 Bigas et al., *The Global Water Crisis*.

79 Srinivasan, "International World Water Day, 2014."

80 World Economic Forum, *Global Risks, 2014*.

81 World Economic Forum, *Global Risks, 2015*, 21.

82 UN Water, *World Water Development Report, 2014*, 54.

83 Healy et al., *The Water-Energy Nexus*.

84 Global Water System Project, *Call to Action*, 1.

85 Grey et al., "Water Security."

86 Bakker, "Water Security."

87 Hussey and Pittock, "The Energy-Water Nexus"; Schubert and Gupta, "Comparing Global Coordination Mechanisms"; Lankford et al., *Water Security*; and Briscoe, "Practice and Teaching."

88 Mark Giordano and Tushaar Shah, "From IWRM back to Integrated Water Resources Management."

89 WJ McGee, "Principles of Water-Power Development," 818.

90 Ibid.

91 Bayliss, "The Financialization of Water"; March and Purcell, "The Muddy Waters"; Cooper, "Turbulent Worlds"; Ballestero, "The Ethics of a Formula"; and Goldman, "How 'Water for All!' Policy Became Hegemonic."

92 Rogers and Hall, *Effective Water Governance*.

93 Priscoli, "What Is Public Participation?"

94 Pahl-Wostl, "Transitions towards Adaptive Management"; and Pahl-Wostl et al., "Social Learning."

95 Loorbach, "Transition Management."

96 Ostrom, "A Diagnostic Approach"; and Meinzen-Dick, "Beyond Panaceas."

97 Ostrom maintained, problematically in my view, that rationality is consonant across groups. Although she held that the institutions in which claims were articulated affected rational calculations, there was nevertheless a rational subject at the basis of her modified game-theoretic arguments. See Ostrom, *Understanding Institutional Diversity.*

98 Ostrom, "Beyond Markets and States."

99 Meinzen-Dick, "Beyond Panaceas."

100 Joyeeta Gupta et al., "'Glocal' Water Governance."

101 Wu et al., "Anthropogenic Impact."

102 McDonald et al., "Water on an Urban Planet"; and Hespanhol, "Wastewater as a Resource."

103 Savenije et al., "Evolving Water Science."

104 Rockström, Falkenmark, et al., "The Unfolding Water Drama."

105 See Grafton et al., *Water.*

106 Selborne, "The Ethics of Freshwater."

107 Priscoli et al., *Water and Ethics.*

108 Chamberlain, *Troubled Waters*; Whiteley et al., *Water, Place and Equity*; Peter Brown and Jeremy Schmidt, *Water Ethics*; and Schmidt and Peppard, "Water Ethics."

109 Priscoli, "Evolution of Public Involvement."

110 WJ McGee, "The Conservation of Natural Resources," 100.

111 World Commission on Environment and Development, *Our Common Future*, 8.

112 UN General Assembly, *Transforming Our World.*

113 UN Development Program, *Beyond Scarcity*; and UN Water, *Water in a Changing World.* See also Mehta and Movik, *Flows and Practices.*

114 United Nations, *Global Sustainable Development Report, 2015 Edition.*

115 Sadoff et al., *Securing Water.*

116 Escobar, *Encountering Development.*

117 Rockström and Klum, *Big World, Small Planet.*

CHAPTER 8. THE ANTHROPOCENE AND THE NATURALIZATION OF PROCESS

1 Hamilton et al., *The Anthropocene.*

2 For example, see Tsing, *The Mushroom at the End of the World*; Yusoff, "Anthropogenesis"; and Peter Brown and Peter Timmerman, *Ecological Economics for the Anthropocene.*

3 Whatmore and Landström, "Flood Apprentices"; Sneddon, *Concrete Revolution*; and Latour and Weibel, *Making Things Public.*

4 Helmreich, *Alien Ocean.*

5 Arendt, *Responsibility and Judgment*, 270.

6 Kierkegaard, *Johannes Climacus*, and *Concluding Unscientific Postscript.* The American pragmatist Richard Rorty uses irony to build solidarity within liberal

forms of life (see Rorty, *Contingency, Irony, and Solidarity*). I have two objections
to his account. First, he argues that the "final vocabularies" of religion and metaphysics are different descriptions and re-descriptions of the world. Yet, ultimately,
Rorty treats liberalism itself as a final vocabulary. This is related to a second
problem, in which Rorty gives John Stuart Mill the "last word" on liberalism. It is
inconsistent for Rorty to eschew theory in favor of irony, on the one hand, while
letting liberalism stand outside of its historical relationships after Mill, on the
other (see Parekh, "Superior People"; and Losurdo, *Liberalism*).

7 See Stengers, "A Constructivist Reading."
8 Ingold, "Toward an Ecology of Materials."
9 Heidegger, *Poetry, Language, Thought.*
10 Latour, "Why Has Critique Run out of Steam?"
11 See Morton, *Hyperobjects.*
12 Latour, *Politics of Nature*, 227.
13 Jasanoff, *States of Knowledge.*
14 Latour, "Politics of Nature."
15 Latour, "Why Has Critique Run out of Steam?"
16 See, Harding, *Objectivity*; and Reisch, *How the Cold War Transformed the Philosophy of Science.*
17 Bennett, *Vibrant Matter*; Coole and Frost, *New Materialisms*; Haraway, *When Species Meet*; and Kohn, *How Forests Think.*
18 Lövbrand et al., "Earth System Governmentality"; Carruth and Marzec, "Environmental Visualization"; and DeLoughrey, "Satellite Planetarity."
19 Latour, "Why Has Critique Run out of Steam?"
20 Latour, "Agency at the Time of the Anthropocene."
21 Latour, "Telling Friends from Foes."
22 Morton, *Hyperobjects*, 22.
23 Wark, *Molecular Red.*
24 Chakrabarty, "The Climate of History."
25 Moore, *Capitalism*; and Malm, *Fossil Capital.*
26 Chakrabarty, "Climate and Capital."
27 Arendt, *The Promise of Politics*, 2005. A caveat is in order here. There are really
two moments of naturalization: one that inscribes social practices into things, and
a second where these judgments condition subsequent practices. See Bourdieu,
Pascalian Meditations.
28 Arendt, *The Human Condition*, 7.
29 Ibid., 150.
30 Ibid., 231.
31 Ibid.
32 Ibid., 153.
33 This fits somewhat with treatments of geology as a semiotic science; see Szerszynski, "The End."
34 Arendt, *The Human Condition*, 323.

35 Swyngedouw, *Liquid Power*, 19.

36 Armstrong, *The Great Transformation*.

37 Whitehead, *The Concept of Nature*.

38 Purdy, *After Nature*.

39 Kierkegaard, *Concluding Unscientific Postscript*.

40 See Goldstein, *Plato at the Googleplex*.

41 Kierkegaard, *Søren Kierkegaard's Journals and Papers*, 278.

42 Kierkegaard, *The Concept of Irony*.

43 See Descartes, *Meditations*.

44 Lear, *A Case for Irony*.

45 Ibid., 15.

46 Guha, *Environmentalism*.

47 Kierkegaard, *Søren Kierkegaard's Journals and Papers*, 277.

48 Lear, *A Case for Irony*, 9–16.

49 Kierkegaard, *Søren Kierkegaard's Journals and Papers*, §3308: "Most systematizers in relation to their systems are like a man who builds an enormous castle and himself lives alongside it in a shed; they themselves do not live in the enormous systematic building."

50 Kierkegaard, *Johannes Climacus*, 38.

CHAPTER 9. THINKING ECOLOGICALLY IN AN AGE OF GEOLOGY

1 Tyrrell, *Crisis of the Wasteful Nation*.

2 Wittgenstein, *Philosophical Investigations*, §46.

3 Peter Brown, "Are There Any Natural Resources?" 12.

4 See Postel, *Last Oasis*; Holling and Meffe, "Command and Control"; and Wilkinson, "Aldo Leopold."

5 Aldo Leopold, "The Wilderness and Its Place in Forest Reclamation."

6 Aldo Leopold, *A Sand County Almanac and Other Writings*, 815.

7 For biographical details, see Meine, *Aldo Leopold*.

8 Ibid.

9 See Aldo Leopold, *The River of the Mother of God*.

10 Aldo Leopold, *A Sand County Almanac: With Essays*, 103.

11 Newton, *Aldo Leopold's Odyssey*.

12 Ibid., 318.

13 See Margulis and Sagan, *What Is Life?*

14 Tsing, *The Mushroom at the End of the World*; and Sayre, "Ecological and Geographical Scale."

15 Aldo Leopold, *A Sand County Almanac: With Essays*, 238.

16 Aldo Leopold, "Lakes in Relation to Terrestrial Life Patterns," 17.

17 Ibid.

18 Quoted from Newton, *Aldo Leopold's Odyssey*, 329.

19 Heise, *Sense of Place*, 36.

20 Aldo Leopold, *A Sand County Almanac: With Essays*, xviii.

21 See Cannavò, "Ecological Citizenship."

22 See Norton, *Sustainability.*

23 Cronon, "The Trouble with Wilderness."

24 Aldo Leopold, *A Sand County Almanac: With Essays,* 238.

25 Ibid., 239.

26 Newton, *Aldo Leopold's Odyssey.*

27 Callicott, "Aldo Leopold's Metaphor."

28 Aldo Leopold, *A Sand County Almanac: With Essays,* 239. Initially, Leopold's view was influenced by organic views of ecology, but his later thought is referenced to the concept of community. See Aldo Leopold, *The River of the Mother of God.*

29 Aldo Leopold, *A Sand County Almanac: With Essays,* 190.

30 Ibid., 189.

31 Ibid.

32 On "deep time," see Martin Rudwick, *Bursting the Limits.*

33 Aldo Leopold, "What Is a Weed?"

34 Ibid., 307.

35 Ibid., 309.

36 Ibid.

37 There is a debate over whether Leopold was a pragmatist between J. Baird Callicott (and others) and Bryan Norton in volumes 18 and 20 of the journal *Environmental Values.* Their full views are in Callicott, *Thinking Like a Planet.* Also see Norton, *Sustainability.*

38 Aldo Leopold, *A Sand County Almanac: With Essays,* 242–243.

39 Aldo Leopold, "Some Fundamentals of Conservation in the Southwest," 96.

40 Aldo Leopold, *A Sand County Almanac: With Essays on Conservation,* 140.

41 Flader, "Building Conservation on the Land"; and Cannavò, "Ecological Citizenship."

42 Aldo Leopold, "Standards of Conservation."

43 Ibid., 83.

44 Aldo Leopold, *A Sand County Almanac: with Essays on Conservation,* 196.

45 Aldo Leopold, "Some Fundamentals of Conservation in the Southwest," 94.

46 Ouspensky, *Tertium Organum.*

47 Meine, *Aldo Leopold.*

48 Ibid., 95.

49 Ibid.

50 Ibid.

51 Aldo Leopold, *A Sand County Almanac and Other Writings,* 355.

52 Ibid., 356.

53 Ibid., 358.

54 See Priscoli et al., *Water and Ethics.*

55 Holling and Meffe, "Command and Control."

56 Postel, *Last Oasis.*

57 Ingram et al., "Replacing Confusion with Equity."

58 Whiteley et al., *Water, Place and Equity*.

59 See Schmidt and Mitchell, "Property and the Right to Water."

60 There is also a vocal contingent that argues we have not been anthropocentric enough in our understandings of the Earth. If we cared more about ourselves, this argument claims, we'd care more about the planet. Yet this argument ultimately collapses into ethnocentrism because we must envision some version of humanity in order to be anthropocentric.

61 Aldo Leopold, *A Sand County Almanac and Other Writings*, 482.

62 See Rademacher, *Reigning the River*; Barnes, *Cultivating the Nile*; Björkman, *Pipe Politics*; Sarah Allan, *The Way of Water*; Boelens et al., *Out of the Mainstream*; and Rodriguez, *Acequia*.

63 Gaard, "Women, Water, Energy"; Merchant, *Reinventing Eden*; and Phare, *Denying the Source*. See also *Feminist Review*, special issue, "Water," with an editorial by Andrijasevic and Khalili, "Water." See, generally, Simpson, *Mohawk Interruptus*.

64 Latour, "Telling Friends from Foes."

65 Coulthard, *Red Skin, White Masks*.

66 Li, *Land's End*.

67 See Simpson, *Mohawk Interruptus*.

CONCLUSION

1 For example, see Briscoe, "Water Security."

2 Castree, "Geographers"; and Irvine, "Deep Time."

3 See Strang, "The Taniwha and the Crown"; and Phare, *Denying the Source*.

4 See Habermas, *Between Facts and Norms*; and Rawls, *Justice as Fairness*.

5 This is a paraphrase of Wittgenstein, *On Certainty*, §110.

BIBLIOGRAPHY

2030 Water Resources Group. *Charting Our Water Future: Economic Frameworks to Inform Decision Making.* [Washington, DC: 2030 Water Resources Group], 2009.

2030 Water Resources Group. *The Water Resources Group: Background, Impact and the Way Forward.* Briefing report prepared for the World Economic Forum annual meeting 2012 in Davos-Klosters, Switzerland. [Washington, DC: 2030 Water Resources Group], 2012.

Achterhuis, Hans, Rutgerd Boelens, and Margreet Zwarteveen. "Water Property Relations and Modern Policy Regimes: Neoliberal Utopia and the Disempowerment of Collective Action." In *Out of the Mainstream: Water Rights, Politics and Identity*, edited by Boelens, Rutgerd, D. Getches, and A. Guerva-Gill, 27–56. London: Earthscan, 2010.

Ad Hoc Committee on International Programs in Atmospheric Sciences and Hydrology. *An Outline of International Programs in Hydrology.* Washington, DC: National Academy of Sciences, National Research Council, 1963.

Agarwal, Anil, Sunita Narain, and Indira Khurana, eds. *Making Water Everybody's Business: Practice and Policy of Water Harvesting.* New Delhi: Centre for Science and Environment, 2001.

AghaKouchak, Amir, David Feldman, Martin Hoerling, et al. "Water and Climate: Recognize Anthropogenic Drought." *Nature* 524, no. 7566 (August 26, 2015): 409–411.

Agrawal, Arun. *Environmentality: Technologies of Government and the Making of Subjects.* Durham, NC: Duke University Press, 2005.

Akhter, Majed. "The Hydropolitical Cold War: The Indus Waters Treaty and State Formation in Pakistan." *Political Geography* 46 (2015): 65–75.

Alatout, Samer. "From Water Abundance to Water Scarcity (1936–1959): A 'Fluid' History of Jewish Subjectivity in Historic Palestine and Israel." In *Reapproaching Borders: New Perspectives on the Study of Israel-Palestine*, edited by S. Sufian and M. Levian, 199–219. Lanham, MD: Rowman & Litttlefield, 2007.

Alatout, Samer. "Bringing Abundance into Environmental Politics: Constructing a Zionist Network of Water Abundance, Immigration, and Colonization." *Social Studies of Science* 39 (2009): 363–394.

Allan, Sarah. *The Way of Water and Sprouts of Virtue.* Albany: State University of New York Press, 1997.

Allan, Tony, Martin Keulertz, and Eckart Woertz. "The Water-Food-Energy Nexus: An Introduction to Nexus Concepts and Some Conceptual and Operational Problems." *International Journal of Water Resources Development* 31, no. 3 (2015): 301–311.

Anderson, Terry, and Donald Leal. *Free Market Environmentalism*. Boulder, CO: Westview, 1991.

Andrijasevic, Rutvica, and Laleh Khalili. "Water." *Feminist Review* 103 (2013): 1–4.

Arendt, Hannah. *The Human Condition*. Chicago: University of Chicago Press, 1958.

Arendt, Hannah. *Lectures on Kant's Political Philosophy*. Chicago: University of Chicago Press, 1982.

Arendt, Hannah. *Responsibility and Judgment*. New York: Schocken Books, 2003.

Arendt, Hannah. *The Promise of Politics*. New York: Schocken Books, 2005.

Armstrong, Karen. *The Great Transformation: The Beginning of Our Religious Traditions*. New York: Knopf, 2006.

Asher, Robert, Walter Kotsching, and William Brown. *The United Nations and Economic and Social Co-operation*. Washington, DC: Brookings Institute, 1957.

Aton, James. *Powell: His Life and Legacy*. Salt Lake City: University of Utah Press, 2010.

Bacon, Francis. *Novum Organum*. New York: American Home Library Co., 1902.

Baer, Madeline. "Private Water, Public Good: Water Privatization and State Capacity in Chile." *Studies in Comparative International Development* 49, no. 2 (2014): 141–167.

Baker, Victor. "The Pragmatic Roots of American Quaternary Geology and Geomorphology." *Geomorphology* 16 (1996): 197–215.

Bakker, Karen. *An Uncooperative Commodity: Privatizing Water in England and Wales*. New York: Oxford University Press, 2004.

Bakker, Karen. "The 'Commons' versus the 'Commodity': Alter-globalization, Anti-privatization and the Human Right to Water in the Global South." *Antipode* 39, no. 3 (2007): 431–455.

Bakker, Karen. *Privatizing Water: Governance Failure and the World's Urban Water Crisis*. Ithaca, NY: Cornell University Press, 2010.

Bakker, Karen. "Water: Political, Biopolitical, Material." *Social Studies of Science* 42, no. 4 (2012): 616–623.

Bakker, Karen. "Water Security: Research Challenges and Opportunities." *Science* 337, no. 6097 (2012): 914–915.

Ball, Philip. *Life's Matrix: A Biography of Water*. Berkeley: University of California Press, 2001.

Ballestero, Andrea. "The Ethics of a Formula: Calculating a Financial-Humanitarian Price for Water." *American Ethnologist* 42, no. 2 (2015): 262–278.

Banks, Erik. "Neutral Monism Reconsidered." *Philosophical Psychology* 23, no. 2 (2010): 173–187.

Barber, William. "Irving Fisher of Yale." *American Journal of Economics and Sociology* 64, no. 1 (2005): 43–55.

Barnes, Jessica. *Cultivating the Nile: Everyday Politics of Water in Egypt*. Durham, NC: Duke University Press, 2014.

Barrows, Harlan. "Geography as Human Ecology." *Annals of the Association of American Geographers* 13, no. 1 (1923): 1–14.

Bauer, Carl. "Results of Chilean Water Markets: Empirical Research since 1990." *Water Resources Research* 40, no. 9 (2004): W09S06.

Bauer, Carl. *Siren Song: Chilean Water Law as a Model for International Reform*. Washington, DC: Resources for the Future, 2004.

Bayliss, Kate. "The Financialization of Water." *Review of Radical Political Economics* 46, no. 3 (2014): 292–307.

Beauvoir, Simone de. *The Ethics of Ambiguity*. New York: Citadel Press, 1948.

Beckert, Sven. *Empire of Cotton: A New History of Global Capitalism*. New York: Knopf, 2014.

Beer, Henrick, Russell Peterson, Sartaj Aziz, et al. *Clean Water for All: A Seminar at Habitat United Nations Conference on Human Settlements*. Washington, DC, and London: International Institute for Environment and Development, 1977.

Behringer, Wolfgang. *A Cultural History of Climate*. Translated by Patrick Camillar. Cambridge: Polity Press, 2010.

Benidickson, Jamie. *The Culture of Flushing: A Social and Legal History of Sewage*. Vancouver: UBC Press, 2007.

Bennett, Jane. *Vibrant Matter: A Political Ecology of Things*. Durham, NC: Duke University Press, 2010.

Bergson, Henri. *Creative Evolution*. Translated by A. Mitchell. New York: Holt, 1911.

Bergson, Henri. *The Two Sources of Morality and Religion*. Translated by Ashley R. Audra and Cloudesely Brereton. London: Macmillan & Co., 1935.

Biermann, Frank. *Earth System Governance: World Politics in the Anthropocene*. Cambridge, MA: MIT Press, 2014.

Bigas, Harriet, Tim Morris, Bob Sandford, and Zafar Adeel, eds. *The Global Water Crisis: Addressing an Urgent Security Issue*. Hamilton, ON: United Nations University–Institute for Water Environment and Health, 2012.

Biggs, David. "Reclamation Nations: The U.S. Bureau of Reclamation's Role in Water Management and Nation-Building in the Mekong Valley, 1945–1975." *Comparative Technology Transfer and Society* 4 (2006): 225–246.

Biswas, Asit. *History of Hydrology*. Amsterdam: North-Holland, 1970.

Biswas, Asit., ed. *United Nations Water Conference: Summary and Main Documents*. Oxford: Pergamon, 1978.

Biswas, Asit. "From Mar Del Plata to Kyoto: A Review of Global Water Policy Dialogues." *Global Environmental Change* 14 (2004): 81–88.

Biswas, Asit. "Integrated Water Resources Management: A Reassessment." *Water International* 29 (2004): 248–256.

Björkman, Lisa. 2015. *Pipe Politics, Contested Waters: Embedded Infrastructures of Millennial Mumbai*. Durham, NC: Duke University Press.

Blackbourn, David. *The Conquest of Nature: Water, Landscape, and the Making of Modern Germany*. New York: Norton, 2006.

Blanchard, Newton, John Fort, John Cutler, et al., eds. *Proceedings of a Conference of Governors in the White House, Washington, D.C., May 13–15, 1908*. Washington, DC: Government Printing Office, 1909.

Blatter, Joachim, and Helen Ingram, eds. *Reflections on Water: New Approaches to Transboundary Conflict and Cooperation*. Cambridge, MA: MIT Press, 2001.

Boas, Franz. "The Study of Geography." *Science* 9, no. 210 (1887): 137–141.

Boas, Franz. "The Mind of Primitive Man." *Science* 13 (1901): 281–289.

Boas, Franz. "Speech on March 5, 1913." In *The McGee Memorial Meeting of the Washington Academy of Sciences: Held at the Carnegie Institution, Washington, D.C., December 5, 1913*, 10–15. Baltimore: Williams & Wilkins, 1916.

Bochenski, Feliks, and William Diamond. "TVA's in the Middle East." *Middle East Journal* 4, no. 1 (1950): 52–82.

Boelens, Rutgerd, D. Getches, and A. Guerva-Gill, eds. *Out of the Mainstream: Water Rights, Politics and Identity*. London: Earthscan, 2010.

Bonneuil, Christophe, and Jean-Baptiste Fressoz. *The Shock of the Anthropocene: The Earth, History and Us*. Translated by David Fernbach. London: Verso, 2016.

Bourdieu, Pierre. *Distinction: A Social Critique of the Judgment of Taste*. Translated by Richard Nice. Cambridge, MA: Harvard University Press, 1983.

Bourdieu, Pierre. *Language and Symbolic Power*. Translated by Gino Raymond and Matthew Adamson. Cambridge: Polity Press, 1991.

Bourdieu, Pierre. *Pascalian Meditations*. Translated by Richard Nice. Cambridge: Polity Press, 2000.

Brakel, Jaap van. *Philosophy of Chemistry: Between the Manifest and the Scientific Image*. Leuven: Leuven University Press, 2000.

Brasch, Frederick. "Einstein's Appreciation of Simon Newcomb." *Science* 69, no. 1783 (1929): 248–249.

Bray, Martha. "Joseph Nicolas Nicollet, Geologist." *Proceedings of the American Philosophical Society* 114, no. 1 (1970): 37–59.

Brent, Joseph. *Charles Sanders Peirce: A Life*. Bloomington: Indiana University Press, 1998.

Briscoe, John. "Practice and Teaching of American Water Management in a Changing World." *Journal of Water Resources Planning and Management* (July/August 2010): 409–411.

Briscoe, John. "Water Security in a Changing World." *Daedalus* 144, no. 3 (2015): 27–34.

Briscoe, John, Pablo Anguita Salas, and Pena T. Humberto. "Managing Water as an Economic Resource: Reflections on the Chilean Experience." *Environment Department Papers, the World Bank* 62 (1998): 1–16.

Brown, Harold. *Rationality*. New York: Routledge, 1988.

Brown, Peter. "Are There Any Natural Resources?" *Politics and the Life Sciences* 23, no. 1 (2004): 12–20.

Brown, Peter, and Jeremy Schmidt, eds. *Water Ethics: Foundational Readings for Students and Professionals*. Washington, DC: Island Press, 2010.

Brown, Peter G., and Peter Timmerman, eds. *Ecological Economics for the Anthropocene: An Emerging Paradigm*. New York: Columbia University Press, 2015.

Brown, Wendy. *Undoing the Demos: Neoliberalism's Stealth Revolution*. New York: Zone Books, 2015.

Buchler, Justus, ed. *Philosophical Writings of Peirce*. New York: Dover, 1955.

Callicott, Baird. "Aldo Leopold's Metaphor." In *Ecosystem Health: New Goals for Environmental Management*, edited by Robert Costanza, Bryan Norton, and Benjamin Haskell, 42–56. Washington, DC: Island Press, 1992.

Callicott, Baird. *Thinking Like a Planet: The Land Ethic and the Earth Ethic*. New York: Oxford University Press, 2013.

Cannavò, Peter. "Ecological Citizenship, Time, and Corruption: Aldo Leopold's Green Republicanism." *Environmental Politics* 21, no. 6 (2012): 864–881.

Carruth, Allison, and Robert Marzec. "Environmental Visualization in the Anthropocene: Technologies, Aesthetics, Ethics." *Public Culture* 26, no. 2 (2014): 205–211.

Carson, Rachel. *Silent Spring*. New York: Houghton Mifflin, 1962.

Casanowicz, I. M. "Proceedings of the Anthropological Society of Washington." *American Anthropologist* 12, no. 1 (1910): 75–90.

Castree, Noel. "Geographers and the Discourse of an Earth Transformed: Influencing the Intellectual Weather or Changing the Intellectual Climate?" *Geographical Research* 53, no. 3 (2015): 244–254.

Cavers, David, and James Nelson. *Electric Power Regulation in Latin America*. Baltimore: Johns Hopkins University Press, 1959.

Chakrabarty, Dipesh. *Provincializing Europe: Post-colonial Thought and Historical Difference*. Princeton, NJ: Princeton University Press, 2008.

Chakrabarty, Dipesh. "The Climate of History: Four Theses." *Critical Inquiry* 35, no. 2 (2009): 197–222.

Chakrabarty, Dipesh. "Climate and Capital: On Conjoined Histories." *Critical Inquiry* 41, no. 1 (2014): 1–23.

Chamberlain, Gary. *Troubled Waters: Religion, Ethics, and the Global Water Crisis*. Lanham, MD: Rowman & Littlefield, 2008.

Chamberlin, Thomas. "The Method of Multiple Working Hypotheses." *Science*, n.s., 15, no. 366 (1890): 92–96.

Chang, Hasok. *Is Water H_2O? Evidence, Pluralism and Realism*. Dordrecht: Springer, 2012.

Chartres, Colin, and Varma Samyuktha. *Out of Water: From Abundance to Scarcity and How to Solve the World's Water Problems*. Upper Saddle River, NJ: FT Press, 2011.

Clapp, Gordon. "The Tennessee Valley Is Paying Off." Paper presented at the annual meeting of the Huntsville Chamber of Commerce, Huntsville, AL, January 20, 1948.

Clapp, Gordon. "Lessons of the TVA." Paper presented at the National Emergency Conference on Resources, Washington, DC, May 12–14, 1949.

Clapp, Gordon. "Interview." *Longines Chronoscope*. New York: Columbia Broadcasting System (CBS), 1953.

Clapp, Gordon. *TVA and Its Critics*. New York: League for Industrial Democracy, 1955.

Clark, Nigel. *Inhuman Nature: Sociable Life on a Dynamic Planet*. London: Sage, 2011.

Clarke, Garry, Alexander Jarosch, Faron Anslow, et al. "Projected Deglaciation of Western Canada in the Twenty-First Century." *Nature Geoscience* 8, no. 5 (2015): 372–377.

Clawson, Marion. *New Deal Planning: The National Resources Planning Board*. Baltimore: Johns Hopkins University Press, 1981.

Clinton, Hillary Rodham. "Clinton at U.N. Roundtable on Water Security." September 25, 2012. *IIP Digital*, U.S. Department of State. http://iipdigital.usembassy.gov.

Colignon, Richard. *Power Plays: Critical Events in the Institutionalization of the Tennessee Valley Authority*. Albany: State University of New York Press, 1997.

Collins, Frederick. *Uncle Sam's Billion Dollar Baby: A Taxpayer Looks at the TVA*. New York: Putnam's, 1945.

Committee on Energy and Natural Resources. *Energy-Water Nexus: Hearing before the Committee on Energy and Natural Resources, United States Senate, One Hundred Eleventh Congress, First Session, to Receive Testimony on Issues Related to S. 531, a Bill to Provide for the Conduct of an In-Depth Analysis of the Impact of Energy Development and Production on the Water Resources of the United States, and for Other Purposes, March 10, 2009*. Washington, DC: Government Printing Office, 2009.

Conca, Ken. *Governing Water: Contentious Transnational Politics and Global Institution Building*. Cambridge, MA: MIT Press, 2006.

Cook, Brian, Mike Kesby, Ioan Fazey, and Chris Spray. "The Persistence of 'Normal' Catchment Management despite the Participatory Turn: Exploring the Power Effects of Competing Frames of Reference." *Social Studies of Science* 43, no. 5 (2013): 754–779.

Coole, Diana, and Samantha Frost, eds. *New Materialisms: Ontology, Agency, and Politics*. Durham, NC: Duke University Press, 2010.

Cooper, Melinda. "Turbulent Worlds: Financial Markets and Environmental Crisis." *Theory, Culture and Society* 27, nos. 2–3 (2010): 167–190.

Cosgrove, William, and Frank Rijsberman. *World Water Vision: Making Water Everybody's Business*. London: Earthscan, 2000.

Coulthard, Glen Sean. *Red Skin, White Masks: Rejecting the Colonial Politics of Recognition*. Minneapolis: University of Minnesota Press, 2014.

Cronon, William. *Nature's Metropolis: Chicago and the Great West*. New York: Norton, 1991.

Cronon, William. "The Trouble with Wilderness; or, Getting Back to the Wrong Nature." *Environmental History* 1, no. 1 (1996): 7–28.

Cross, Whitney. "W. J. McGee and the Idea of Conservation." *Historian* 15, no. 2 (1953): 148–162.

Crutzen, Paul, and T. E. Graedel. "The Role of Atmospheric Chemistry in Environment-Development Interactions." In *Sustainable Development of the Biosphere*, edited by William Clark, and R. E. Munn, 213–250. Cambridge: Cambridge University Press, 1986.

Crutzen, Paul, and E. F. Stoermer. "The Anthropocene." *Global Change Newsletter* 41 (2000): 17–18.

Darrigol, Olivier. *Worlds of Flow: A History of Hydrodynamics from the Bernoullis to Prandtl*. New York: Oxford University Press, 2005.

Darton, N. H. "Memoir of W J McGee." *Annals of the Association of American Geographers* 3 (1913): 103–110.

Davies, Gordon. *The Earth in Decay: A History of British Geomorphology, 1578–1878*. London: MacDonald Technical & Scientific, 1969.

deBuys, William, ed. *Seeing Things Whole: The Essential John Wesley Powell*. Washington, DC: Island Press, 2004.

DeLoughrey, Elizabeth. "Satellite Planetarity and the Ends of the Earth." *Public Culture* 26, no. 2 (2014): 257–280.

Descartes, René. *Meditations on First Philosophy*. Translated by D. A. Cress. Indianapolis: Hackett, 1993.

Dewey, John. *Psychology*. New York: Harper & Bros., 1887.

Dewey, John. *Outlines of a Critical Theory of Ethics*. Ann Arbor, MI: Register Publishing Co., 1891.

Dewey, John. "Evolution and Ethics." *The Monist* 8, no. 3 (1898): 321–341.

Dewey, John. "Half-Hearted Naturalism." *Journal of Philosophy* 24, no. 3 (1927): 57–64.

Dewey, John. *The Public and Its Problems*. London: Allen & Unwin, 1927.

Dewey, John. *Freedom and Culture*. New York: Putnam's, 1939.

Dewey, John. *Experience and Nature*, 2nd ed. New York: Dover, 1958.

Dewey, John. *Liberalism and Social Action*. Amherst, NY: Prometheus Books, 2000.

Dewey, John. "Ethical Principles underlying Education," In *John Dewey: The Early Works, 1882–1898*, vol. 5, edited by Jo Ann Boydston, 54–83. Carbondale: Southern Illinois University Press, 2008.

Dinar, Ariel, ed. *The Political Economy of Water Pricing Reforms*. New York: Oxford University Press, 2000.

D'Souza, Rohan. *Drowned and Dammed: Colonial Capitalism and Flood Control in Eastern India*. New Delhi: Oxford University Press, 2006.

"The Dublin Statement on Water and Sustainable Development" (Dublin Statement). International Conference on Water and the Environment, Dublin, January 31, 1992. Posted at the World Meteorological Organization website, n.d., www.wmo.int. Accessed June 22, 2016.

Durant, Robert, and Michelle Holmes. "Thou Shalt Not Covet Thy Neighbor's Water: The Rio Grande Regulatory Experience." *Public Administration Review* 45, no. 6 (1985): 821–831.

Easter, William, Mark Rosegrant, and Ariel Dinar. "Formal and Informal Markets for Water: Institutions, Performance, and Constraints." *World Bank Research Observer* 14, no. 1 (1999): 99–116.

Ekbladh, David. "'Mr. TVA': Grass-Roots Development, David Lilienthal, and the Rise and Fall of the Tennessee Valley Authority as a Symbol for U.S. Overseas Development, 1933–1973." *Diplomatic History* 26, no. 3 (2002): 335–374.

Ekbladh, David. *The Great American Mission: Modernization and the Construction of an American World Order*. Princeton, NJ: Princeton University Press, 2010.

Ekbladh, David. "Meeting the Challenge from Totalitarianism: The Tennessee Valley Authority as a Global Model for Liberal Development." *International History Review* 32, no. 1 (2010): 47–67.

Egan, Timothy. *The Worst Hard Time: The Untold Story of Those Who Survived the Great American Dust Bowl.* New York: Houghton Mifflin, 2006.

Eisele, Carolyn. "The Charles S. Peirce–Simon Newcomb Correspondence." *Proceedings of the American Philosophical Society* 101, no. 5 (1957): 409–433.

Elden, Stuart, and Eduardo Mendieta, eds. *Reading Kant's Geography.* Albany: State University of New York Press, 2011.

Ellis, Erle. "Ecology in an Anthropogenic Biosphere." *Ecological Monographs* 85, no. 3 (2015): 287–331.

Ellis, Erle C., Dorian Q. Fuller, Jed O. Kaplan, and Wayne G. Lutters. "Dating the Anthropocene: Towards an Empirical Global History of Human Transformation of the Terrestrial Biosphere." *Elementa* 1, no. 000018 (2013): 1–6.

Ellis, Erle, K. Golkewijk, S. Siebert, et al. "Anthropogenic Transformation of the Biomes, 1700–2000." *Global Ecology and Biogeography* 19 (2010): 589–606.

Escobar, Arturo. *Encountering Development: The Making and Unmaking of the Third World.* Princeton, NJ: Princeton University Press, 2012.

Espeland, Wendy. *The Struggle for Water: Politics, Rationality, and Identity in the American Southwest.* Chicago: University of Chicago Press, 1998.

Fagan, Brian. *Elixir: A History of Water and Humankind.* New York: Bloomsbury, 2011.

Falkenmark, Malin. "The Greatest Water Problem: The Inability to Link Environmental Security, Water Security and Food Security." *International Journal of Water Resources Development* 17, no. 4 (2001): 539–554.

Falkenmark, Malin. "Towards Integrated Catchment Management: Opening the Paradigm Locks between Hydrology, Ecology and Policy-Making." *International Journal of Water Resources Development* 20, no. 3 (2004): 275–281.

Falkenmark, Malin, and Carl Folke. "Ecohydrosolidarity: A New Ethics for Stewardship of Value-Adding Rainfall." In *Water Ethics: Foundational Readings for Students and Professionals,* edited by Peter Brown and Jeremy Schmidt, 247–264. Washington, DC: Island Press, 2010.

Falkenmark, Malin, and Carl Folke. "The Ethics of Socio-ecohydrological Catchment Management: Toward Hydrosolidarity." *Hydrology and Earth System Sciences* 6, no. 1 (2002): 1–10.

Falkenmark, Malin, and J. Lundqvist. "Towards Water Security: Political Determination and Human Adaptation Crucial." *Natural Resources Forum* 21, no. 1 (1998): 37–51.

Falkenmark, Malin, J. Lundqvist, and C. Widstrand. "Macro-Scale Water Scarcity Requires Micro-Scale Approaches: Aspects of Vulnerability in Semi-Arid Development." *Natural Resources Forum* 13 (1989): 258–267.

Falkenmark, Malin, and Johan Rockström. *Balancing Water for Humans and Nature: The New Approach in Ecohydrology.* London: Earthscan, 2004.

Fasseur, Cornelis. *The Politics of Colonial Exploitation: Java, the Dutch, and the Cultivation System.* Translated by R. E. Elson and Ary Kraal. Ithaca, NY: Southeast Asia Program, Cornell University, 1992.

Feldman, David. *Water Resources Management: In Search of an Environmental Ethic.* Baltimore: Johns Hopkins University Press, 1995.

Feldman, David. *Water Policy for Sustainable Development*. Baltimore: Johns Hopkins University Press, 2007.

Feminist Review. Special Issue, "Water." vol. 103, no. 1 (March 2013).

Ferguson, James. *The Anti-politics Machine: "Development," Depoliticization, and Bureaucratic Power in Lesotho*. Cambridge: Cambridge University Press, 1990.

Finer, Herman. *T.V.A.: Lessons for International Application*. Montreal: International Labor Office, 1944.

Finley, John, and James Seiber. "The Nexus of Food, Energy, and Water." *Journal of Agricultural and Food Chemistry* 62, no. 27 (2014): 6255–6262.

Fisher, Christopher. "The Illusion of Progress." *Pacific Historical Review* 75, no. 1 (2006): 25–51.

Fisher, Christopher. "'Moral Purpose Is the Important Thing': David Lilienthal, Iran, and the Meaning of Development in the US, 1956–63." *International History Review* 33, no. 3 (2011): 431–451.

Fisher, Irving. *Memorial relating to the Conservation of Human Life as Contemplated by Bill (S. 1) Providing for a United States Public-Health Service*. Washington, DC: Government Printing Office, 1912.

Fishman, Charles. *The Big Thirst: The Secret Life and Turbulent Future of Water*. New York: Free Press, 2011.

Fitzsimmons, Stephen, and Ovadia Salama. *Man and Water: A Social Report*. Boulder, CO: Westview Press, 1977.

Flader, Susan. "Building Conservation on the Land: Aldo Leopold and the Tensions of Professionalism and Citizenship." In *Reconstructing Conservation: Finding Common Ground*, edited by B. A. Minteer and R. A. Manning, 115–132. Washington, DC: Island Press, 2003.

Folke, Carl. "Freshwater for Resilience: A Shift in Thinking." *Philosophical Transactions of the Royal Society of London B* 358 (2003): 2027–2036.

Folke, Carl. "Resilience: The Emergence of a Perspective for Social-Ecological Systems Analyses." *Global Environmental Change* 16 (2006): 253–267.

Folke, Carl, S. Carpenter, B. Walker, et al. "Resilience Thinking: Integrating Resilience, Adaptability and Transformability." *Ecology and Society* 15, no. 4 (2010): art. 20.

Foltz, Richard. "Iran's Water Crisis: Cultural, Political, and Ethical Dimensions." *Journal of Agriculture and Environmental Ethics* 15 (2002): 357–380.

Fontana, Hazel, and Bernard Fontana, eds. *Trails to Tiburon: The 1894 and 1895 Field Diaries of W. J. McGee*. Tucson: University of Arizona Press, 2000.

Food and Agricultural Organization. *Coping with Water Scarcity: An Action Framework for Agriculture and Food Security*. Rome: Food and Agricultural Organization of the United Nations, 2012.

Frazer, James. *The Golden Bough: A Study in Magic and Religion*. London: Macmillian, 1980.

Freyfogle, Eric. "Water Rights and the Common Wealth." *Environmental Law* 26 (1996): 27–51.

Gaard, Greta. "Women, Water, Energy: An Ecofeminist Approach." *Organization and Environment* 14, no. 2 (2001): 157–172.

Gandy, Matthew. 2015. *The Fabric of Space: Water, Modernity, and the Urban Imagination.* Cambridge, MA: MIT Press.

Gardner, Lloyd. "From the Colorado to the Mekong." In *Vietnam: The Early Decisions,* edited by Lloyd Gardner and Ted Gittinger, 37–57. Austin: University of Texas Press, 1997.

Gary, Brett. *The Nervous Liberals: Propaganda Anxieties from World War I to the Cold War.* New York: Columbia University Press, 1999.

Gaston, Sean. *The Concept of World from Kant to Derrida.* New York: Rowman & Littlefield, 2013.

Gearey, Mary, and Paul Jeffrey. "Concepts of Legitimacy within the Context of Adaptive Management Strategies." *Ecological Economics* 60, no. 1 (2006): 129–137.

Gilb, Corinne. *Frederick Webb Hodge, Ethnologist: A Tape Recorded Interview, 8/7/69.* Berkeley: University of California Berkeley, 1969.

Gilbert, Grove Karl. "Inculcation of Scientific Method." *American Journal of Science* 31, no. 184 (1886): 284–299.

Gilbert, Grove Karl. "The Origin of Hypotheses." *Science* 3, no. 53 (1896): 1–13.

Gilman, Nils. *Mandarins of the Future: Modernization Theory in Cold War America.* Baltimore: Johns Hopkins University Press, 2004.

Giordano, Mark, and Tushaar Shah. "From IWRM back to Integrated Water Resources Management." *International Journal of Water Resources Development* 30, no. 3 (2014): 364–376.

Giordano, Meredith, and Aaron T. Wolf. "Sharing Waters: Post-Rio International Water Management." *Natural Resources Forum* 27 (2003): 163–171.

Glacken, Clarence. *Traces on the Rhodian Shore: Nature and Culture in Western Thought from Ancient Times to the End of the Eighteenth Century.* Berkeley: University of California Press, 1967.

Gleick, Peter. "Climate Change, Hydrology, and Water Resources." *Review of Geophysics* 27, no. 3 (1989): 329–344.

Gleick, Peter. "Environment, Resources, and International Security and Politics." In *Science and International Security: Responding to a Changing World,* edited by Eric Arnett, 501–523. Washington, DC: American Association for the Advancement of Science, 1990.

Gleick, Peter. "Water and Conflict: Fresh Water Resources and International Security." *International Security* 18, no. 1 (1993): 79–112.

Gleick, Peter., ed. *Water in Crisis: A Guide to the World's Fresh Water Resources.* New York: Oxford University Press, 1993.

Gleick, Peter. "Water and Energy." *Annual Review of Energy and Environment* 19 (1994): 267–299.

Gleick, Peter, and John Lane. "Large International Water Meetings: Time for a Reappraisal." *Water International* 30, no. 3 (2005): 410–414.

Gleick, Peter, and Meena Palaniappan. "Peak Water Limits to Freshwater Withdrawal and Use." *Proceedings of the National Academy of Sciences* 107, no. 25 (2010): 11155–11162.

Global Water Partnership. *Global Water Security: Submission by the Global Water Partnership to ICE/RAE/CIWEM Report to Professor John Beddington, Chief Scientific Adviser to HM Government.* Stockholm: Global Water Partnership, 2009.

Global Water Partnership Technical Advisory Committee. *Integrated Water Resources Management*, vol. 4, Technical Advisory Committee background papers. Stockholm: Global Water Partnership, 2000.

Global Water System Project. *Call to Action for Implementing the Water-Energy-Food Nexus.* Bonn: Global Water System Project, 2014.

Goldman, Michael. "How 'Water for All!' Policy Became Hegemonic: The Power of the World Bank and Its Transnational Policy Networks." *Geoforum* 38 (2007): 786–800.

Goldschmidt, Arthur. "The Development of the U.S. South." *Scientific American* 209, no. 3 (1963): 225–232.

Goldstein, Rebecca. *Plato at the Googleplex: Why Philosophy Won't Go Away.* New York: Vintage Books, 2014.

Goodman, Nelson. *Ways of Worldmaking.* Hassocks: Harvester Press, 1978.

Goodwin, Craufurd. "The Valley Authority Idea—The Fading of a National Vision," In *TVA: Fifty Years of Grass-Roots Democracy*, edited by Erwin Hargrove and Paul Conkin, 263–298. Urbana: University of Illinois Press, 1983.

Grafton, Quentin, Jamie Pittock, Maree Tait, and Chris White, eds. *Water: Security, Economics and Governance.* Prahran: Tilde University Press, 2013.

Gregory, Derek. "(Post)Colonialism and the Production of Nature." In *Social Nature: Theory, Practice and Politics*, edited by N. Castree, and B. Braun, 84–111. Malden, MA: Blackwell, 2001.

Grey, David, D. Garrick, D. Blackmore, J. Kelman, M. Muller, and C. Sadoff. "Water Security in One Blue Planet: Twenty-First Century Policy Challenges for Science." *Philosophical Transactions of the Royal Society A* 371 (2013): 1–10. doi: 10.1098/rsta.2012.0406.

Grey, David, and Caudia Sadoff. "Sink or Swim? Water Security for Growth and Development." *Water Policy* 9 (2007): 545–571.

Guha, Ramachandra. *Environmentalism: A Global History.* New York: Longman, 2000.

Gunderson, Lance, and C. S. Holling, eds. *Panarchy: Understanding Transformations in Human and Natural Systems.* Washington, DC: Island Press, 2002.

Gupta, Akhil. *Post-colonial Developments: Agriculture in the Making of Modern India.* Durham, NC: Duke University Press, 1998.

Gupta, Joyeeta, Claudia Pahl-Wostl, and Ruben Zondervan. "'Glocal' Water Governance: A Multi-level Challenge in the Anthropocene." *Current Opinion in Environmental Sustainability* 5, no. 6 (2013): 573–580.

Habermas, Jürgen. *Between Facts and Norms: Contributions to a Discourse Theory of Law and Democracy.* Cambridge, MA: MIT Press, 1996.

Hacking, Ian. *The Taming of Chance*. Cambridge: Cambridge University Press, 1990.

Hacking, Ian. *Historical Ontology*. Cambridge, MA: Harvard University Press, 2002.

The Hague. "Ministerial Declaration of The Hague on Water Security in the 21st Century" (Ministerial Declaration). March 22, 2000. Hosted at the World Water Council website. www.worldwatercouncil.org.

Haines, Daniel. "(Inter)Nationalist Rivers? Cooperative Development in David Lilienthal's Plan for the Indus Basin, 1951." *Water History* 6, no. 2 (2014): 133–151.

Hamblin, Jacob. *Arming Mother Nature: The Birth of Catastrophic Environmentalism.* Oxford: Oxford University Press, 2013.

Hamilton, Clive, François Gemenne, and Christophe Bonneuil, eds. *The Anthropocene and the Global Environmental Crisis: Rethinking Modernity in a New Epoch.* London: Routledge, 2015.

Hamilton, Clive, and Jacques Grinevald. "Was the Anthropocene Anticipated?" *Anthropocene Review* 2, no. 1 (2015): 59–72.

Hamlin, Christopher. "'Waters' or 'Water'?—Master Narratives in Water History and Their Implications for Contemporary Water Policy." *Water Policy* 2, nos. 4–5 (2000): 313–325.

Haraway, Donna. *When Species Meet*. Minneapolis: University of Minnesota Press, 2008.

Haraway, Donna. "Anthropocene, Capitalocene, Plantationocene, Chthulucene: Making Kin." *Environmental Humanities* 6 (2015): 159–165.

Harding, Sandra. *Objectivity and Diversity: Another Logic of Scientific Research*. Chicago: University of Chicago Press, 2015.

Hargrove, Erwin. "David Lilienthal and the Tennessee Valley Authority." In *Leadership and Innovation: Entrepreneurs in Government*, edited by Jameson W. Doig and Erwin C. Hargrove, 25–60. Baltimore: Johns Hopkins University Press, 1990.

Hargrove, Erwin. *Prisoners of Myth: The Leadership of the Tennessee Valley Authority, 1933–1990*. Princeton, NJ: Princeton University Press, 1994.

Harvey, David. "The Nature of Environment: The Dialectics of Social and Environmental Change." *Socialist Register* 1 (1993): 1–51.

Harvey, David. *A Brief History of Neoliberalism*. New York: Oxford University Press, 2005.

Hayek, Friedrich von. "A Commodity Reserve Currency." *Economic Journal* 53, nos. 210/211 (1943): 176–184.

Hayek, Friedrich von. *The Road to Serfdom*. Chicago: University of Chicago Press, 1944.

Hayek, Friedrich von. "The Use of Knowledge in Society." *American Economic Review* 35, no. 4 (1945): 519–530.

Hays, Samuel. "The Mythology of Conservation." In *Perspectives on Conservation*, edited by Henry Jarrett. Baltimore: Johns Hopkins University Press, 1958.

Hays, Samuel. *Conservation and the Gospel of Efficiency: The Progressive Conservation Movement, 1890–1920*. Cambridge, MA: Harvard University Press, 1959.

Healy, Richard, William Alley, Mark Engle, et al. *The Water-Energy Nexus: An Earth Science Perspective*. Reston, VA: U.S. Geological Survey, 2015.

Heathcote, Isobel. *Integrated Watershed Management: Principles and Practice*. New York: Wiley, 1998.

Hegel, Georg. *The Philosophy of History*. Translated by John Sibree. New York: Dover, 1956.

Hegel, Georg. *Phenomenology of Mind*. Translated by J. B. Baillie. New York: Humanities Press, 1964.

Heidegger, Martin. *Poetry, Language, Thought*. Translated by Albert Hofstadter. New York: Harper & Row, 1971.

Heise, Ursula. *Sense of Place and Sense of Planet: The Environmental Imagination of the Global*. New York: Oxford University Press, 2008.

Helmer, Richard. "Water Quality Monitoring: National and International Approaches." In *Hydrological, Chemical and Biological Processes of Transformation and Transport of Contaminants in Aquatic Environments*, edited by Norman E. Peters, Rod J. Allan, and Vladimir V. Tsirkunov, 1–20. Wallingford: International Association of Hydrological Sciences, 1994.

Helmreich, Stefan. *Alien Ocean: Anthropological Voyages in Microbial Seas*. Berkeley: University of California Press, 2009.

Hespanhol, Ivanildo. "Wastewater as a Resource." In *Water Pollution Control—A Guide to the Use of Water Quality Management Principles*, edited by Richard Helmer and Ivanildo Hespanhol, 91–124. London: E & F Spon, 1997.

Hibbard, K. A., P. Crutzen, E. Lambin, et al. "Decadal Interactions of Humans and the Environment." In *An Integrated History and Future of People on Earth*, edited by R. Costanza, L. Graumlich, and W. Steffen, 341–375. Cambridge, MA: MIT Press, 2006.

Hinshaw, Robert. *Living within Nature's Extremes: The Life of Gilbert Fowler White*. Boulder, CO: Johnson Books, 2006.

Hoag, Heather. *Developing the Rivers of East and West Africa: An Environmental History*. London: Bloomsbury, 2013.

Hobbs, Richard, Eric Higgs, and Carol Hall, eds. *Novel Ecosystems: Intervening in the New Ecological World Order*. Hoboken, NJ: Wiley-Blackwell, 2013.

Hoff, Holger. *Understanding the Nexus. Background Paper for the Bonn2011 Conference: The Water, Energy and Food Security Nexus*. Stockholm: Stockholm Environment Institute, 2011.

Hofstadter, Richard. *Social Darwinism in American Thought, 1860–1915*. Philadelphia: University of Pennsylvania Press, 1944.

Holdgate, Martin, Mohammed Kassas, and Gilbert White, eds. *The World Environment, 1972–1982: A Report by the United Nations Environmental Programme*. Dublin: Tycooly International, 1982.

Holling, C. S. "Resilience and Stability of Ecological Systems." *Annual Review of Ecology and Systematics* 4 (1973): 1–23.

Holling, C. S., ed. *Adaptive Environmental Assessment and Management*. New York: Wiley, 1978.

Holling, C. S. "The Resilience of Terrestrial Ecosystems: Local Surprise and Global Change." In *Sustainable Development of the Biosphere*, edited by William C. Clark and R. E. Munn, 292–316. Cambridge: Cambridge University Press, 1986.

Holling, C. S., and G. K. Meffe. "Command and Control and the Pathology of Natural Resource Management." *Conservation Biology* 10, no. 2 (1996): 328–337.

Howells, Mark, and Holger Rogner. "Water-Energy Nexus: Assessing Integrated Systems." *Nature Climate Change* 4, no. 4 (2014): 246–247.

Hubbard, Preston. *Origins of the TVA: The Muscle Shoals Controversy, 1920–1932.* Nashville, TN: Vanderbilt University Press, 1961.

Hulme, Mike, Suraje Dessai, Irene Lorenzoni, and Donald Nelson. "Unstable Climates: Exploring the Statistical and Social Constructions of 'Normal' Climate." *Geoforum* 40 (2009): 197–206.

Hussey, Karen, and Jamie Pittock. "The Energy-Water Nexus: Managing the Links between Energy and Water for a Sustainable Future." *Ecology and Society* 17, no. 1 (2012): 31.

Huxley, Julian. "Plans for Tomorrow: The Tennessee Valley Authority." *Listener* (November 1935): 897–900.

Huxley, Thomas. "Science and Pseudo-science." *Eclectic Magazine of Foreign Literature, Science and Art* 45, no. 6 (1887): 721–733.

Huxley, Thomas H. *Man's Place in Nature: And Other Anthropological Essays.* New York: D. Appleton & Co., 1897.

Illich, Ivan. *H₂O and the Waters of Forgetfulness.* London: Marion Boyars, 1986.

Ingold, Tim. "Toward an Ecology of Materials." *Annual Review of Anthropology* 41 (2012): 427–442.

Ingram, Helen. "The Political Economy of Regional Water Institutions." *American Journal of Agricultural Economics* 55, no. 1 (1973): 10–18.

Ingram, Helen. "Beyond Universal Remedies for Good Water Governance: A Political and Contextual Approach." In *Water for Food in a Changing World*, edited by Alberto Garrido and Helen Ingram, 241–261. Oxford: Oxford University Press, 2008.

Ingram, Helen, Dean Mann, Gary Weatherford, and Hanna Cortner. "Guidelines for Improved Institutional Analysis in Water Resources Planning." *Water Resources Research* 20, no. 3 (1984): 323–334.

Ingram, Helen, and C. Oggins. "The Public Trust Doctrine and Community Values in Water." *Natural Resources Journal* 32 (1992): 515–537.

Ingram, Helen, Lawrence Scaff, and Leslie Silko. "Replacing Confusion with Equity: Alternatives for Water Policy in the Colorado River Basin." In *New Courses for the Colorado River: Major Issues for the Next Century*, edited by Gary Weatherford, and F. Lee Brown, 177–200. Albuquerque: University of New Mexico Press, 1986.

Inland Waterways Commission. *Preliminary Report.* 60th Congress, 1st Session, Senate Document no. 325. Washington, DC: Government Printing Office, 1908.

Institution of Civil Engineers. *Engineering Hydrology Today.* London: Institution of Civil Engineers, 1975.

International Water Resources Association. "Sustainable Development and Water: Statement on the WCED Report *Our Common Future*." In *Water: The International Crisis*, edited by Robin Clarke, 182–185. London: Earthscan, 1991.

Ioris, Antonio. "The Political Nexus between Water and Economics in Brazil: A Critique of Recent Policy Reforms." *Review of Radical Political Economics* 24, no. 2 (2010): 231–250.

Irvine, Richard. "Deep Time: An Anthropological Problem." *Social Anthropology* 22, no. 2 (2014): 157–172.

James, William. "Remarks on Spencer's Definition of Mind as Correspondence." *Journal of Speculative Philosophy* 12, no. 1 (1878): 1–18.

James, William. "Great Men, Great Thoughts, and the Environment." *Atlantic Monthly* 46, no. 276 (October 1880): 441–459.

James, William. "Does Consciousness Exist?" *Journal of Philosophy, Psychology and Scientific Methods* 1, no. 18 (1904): 477–491.

James, William. *The Varieties of Religious Experience: A Study in Human Nature.* Amherst, NY: Prometheus Books, 2002.

Jaramillo, Fernando, and Georgia Destouni. "Local Flow Regulation and Irrigation Raise Global Water Consumption and Footprint." *Science* 350, no. 6265 (2015): 1248–1251.

Jasanoff, Sheila, ed. *States of Knowledge: The Co-production of Science and Social Order* London: Routledge, 2004.

Jeffrey, Paul, and Mary Gearey. "Integrated Water Resources Management: Lost on the Road from Ambition to Realisation?" *Water, Science and Technology* 53, no. 1 (2006): 1–8.

Jewish Telegraphic Agency. "TVA Head Says $150,000,000 Palestine Irrigation Plan Is 'Technically Feasible.'" June 20, 1944.

Johnson, Lyndon B. "Pattern for Peace in Southeast Asia: Address by President Johnson, Johns Hopkins University, April 17, 1965." In *Background Information relating to Southeast Asia and Vietnam, 90th Congress, 1st Session,* edited by Committee on Foreign Relations, U.S. Senate, 148–153. Washington, DC: Government Printing Office, 1967.

Kant, Immanuel. *Perpetual Peace.* Translated by Lewis White Beck. New York: Liberal Arts Press, 1957.

Kant, Immanuel. *Critique of Pure Reason.* Translated by N. K. Smith. New York: Palgrave Macmillan, 2003.

Kant, Immanuel. *Lectures on Anthropology.* Translated by Robert R. Clewis, Robert B. Louden, G. Felicitas Munzel, and Allen Wood. Cambridge: Cambridge University Press, 2012.

Kierkegaard, Søren. *The Concept of Irony, with Constant Reference to Socrates.* Translated by Lee M. Capel. New York: Harper & Row, 1966.

Kierkegaard, Søren. *Søren Kierkegaard's Journals and Papers,* vol. 2, F–K. Translated by H. V. Hong and E. H. Hong. Bloomington: Indiana University Press, 1970.

Kierkegaard, Søren. *Concluding Unscientific Postscript to Philosophical Fragments.* Translated by Howard V. Hong and Edna H. Hong. Princeton, NJ: Princeton University Press, 1992.

Kierkegaard, Søren. *Johannes Climacus: Or: A Life of Doubt.* Translated by T. H. Croxhall. London: Serpent's Tail, 2001.

Klingensmith, Daniel. *"One Valley and a Thousand": Dams, Nationalism, and Development*. Oxford: Oxford University Press, 2007.

Kneese, Allen, and Blair Bower. *Managing Water Quality: Economics, Technology, Institutions*. Baltimore: Johns Hopkins University Press, 1968.

Knighton, David. *Fluvial Forms and Processes: A New Perspective*. New York: Oxford University Press, 1998.

Kohn, Eduardo. *How Forests Think: Toward an Anthropology beyond the Human*. Berkeley: University of California Press, 2013.

Korzoun, V. I., A. A. Sokolov, M. I. Budyko, et al., eds. *Atlas of World Water Balance: Water Resources of the Earth*. Paris: UNESCO, 1978.

Kysar, Douglas. *Regulating from Nowhere: Environmental Law and the Search for Objectivity*. New Haven, CT: Yale University Press, 2010.

Lacey, Michael. "The Mysteries of Earth-Making Dissolve: A Study of Washington's Intellectual Community and the Origins of American Environmentalism in the Late Nineteenth Century." PhD diss., George Washington University, 1979.

Lacey, Michael. "The World of the Bureaus: Government and the Positivist Project in the Late Nineteenth Century." In *The State and Social Investigation in Britain and the United States*, edited by Michael Lacey and Mary Furner, 127–170. Cambridge: Cambridge University Press, 1993.

Lacey, Michael. "Federalism and National Planning: The Nineteenth-Century Legacy." In *The American Planning Tradition*, edited by R. Fishman, 89–146. Washington, DC: Woodrow Wilson Center Press, 2000.

Lamb, Daniel. "The Story of the Anthropological Society of Washington." *American Anthropologist* 8 (1906): 564–579.

Lankford, Bruce, Karen Bakker, Mark Zeitoun, and Declan Conway, eds. *Water Security: Principles, Perspectives and Practices*. London: Earthscan/Routledge, 2013.

Latour, Bruno. *We Have Never Been Modern*. Translated by C. Porter. Cambridge, MA: Harvard University Press, 1993.

Latour, Bruno. *Politics of Nature: How to Bring the Sciences into Democracy*. Cambridge, MA: Harvard University Press, 2004.

Latour, Bruno. "Why Has Critique Run out of Steam? From Matters of Fact to Matters of Concern." *Critical Inquiry* 30, no. 2 (2004): 225–248.

Latour, Bruno. "Politics of Nature: East and West Perspectives." *Ethics and Global Politics* 4, no. 1 (2011): 71–80.

Latour, Bruno. "Agency at the Time of the Anthropocene." *New Literary History* 45, no. 1 (2014): 1–18.

Latour, Bruno. "Telling Friends from Foes in the Time of the Anthropocene." In *The Anthropocene and the Global Environmental Crisis*, edited by Clive Hamilton, Christophe Bonneuil, and François Gemenne, 145–155. London: Routledge, 2015.

Latour, Bruno, and Peter Weibel, eds. *Making Things Public: Atmospheres of Democracy*. Cambridge, MA: MIT Press, 2005.

Lazarus, Richard. *The Making of Environmental Law*. Chicago: University of Chicago Press, 2004.

Lear, Jonathan. *A Case for Irony*. Cambridge, MA: Harvard University Press, 2011.

Lee, Kai. *Compass and Gyroscope: Integrating Science and Politics for the Environment*. Washington, DC: Island Press, 1993.

Leopold, Aldo. "Lakes in Relation to Terrestrial Life Patterns." In *A Symposium on Hydrobiology*, by James G. Needham, Paul B. Sears, Aldo Leopold, and the Wisconsin Alumni Research Foundation, 17–22. Madison: University of Wisconsin Press, 1941.

Leopold, Aldo. *A Sand County Almanac: With Essays on Conservation from Round River*. New York: Oxford University Press, 1966.

Leopold, Aldo. *The River of the Mother of God and Other Essays by Aldo Leopold*. Edited by Susan Flader and Baird Callicott. Madison: University of Wisconsin Press, 1991.

Leopold, Aldo. "Some Fundamentals of Conservation in the Southwest." In *The River of the Mother of God and Other Essays by Aldo Leopold*, edited by Susan Flader and Baird Callicott, 86–97. Madison: University of Wisconsin Press, 1991.

Leopold, Aldo. "Standards of Conservation." In *The River of the Mother of God and Other Essays by Aldo Leopold*, edited by Susan Flader and Baird Callicott, 82–85. Madison: University of Wisconsin Press, 1991.

Leopold, Aldo. "What Is a Weed?" In *The River of the Mother of God and Other Essays by Aldo Leopold*, edited by Susan Flader and Baird Callicott, 306–309. Madison: University of Wisconsin Press, 1991.

Leopold, Aldo. "The Wilderness and Its Place in Forest Reclamation." In *The River of the Mother of God and Other Essays by Aldo Leopold*, edited by Susan Flader and Baird Callicott, 78–81. Madison: University of Wisconsin Press, 1991.

Leopold, Aldo. *A Sand County Almanac and Other Writings on Ecology and Conservation*, edited by Curt Meine. New York: Library of America, 2013.

Leopold, Luna. "A Reverence for Rivers." *Geology* 5 (1977): 429–430.

Leopold, Luna. "Ethos, Equity, and the Water Resource." *Environment: Science and Policy for Sustainable Development* 32, no. 2 (1990): 16–42.

Leopold, Luna, and Thomas Maddock. *The Flood Control Controversy: Big Dams, Little Dams, and Land Management*. New York: Ronald Press Co., 1954.

LeRoy, Pamela. "Troubled Waters: Population and Water Scarcity." *Colorado Journal of International Environmental Law* 6 (1995): 299–326.

Lévi-Strauss, Claude. "Anthropology: Its Achievements and Future." In *Knowledge among Men: Eleven Essays on Science, Culture, and Society Commemorating the 200th Anniversary of the Birth of James Smithson*, edited by Paul H. Oehser, 109–122. New York: Simon & Schuster, 1966.

Lewis, Simon, and Mark Maslin. "Defining the Anthropocene." *Nature* 519 (2015): 171–180.

Li, Tania. *The Will to Improve: Governmentality, Development, and the Practice of Politics*. Durham, NC: Duke University Press, 2007.

Li, Tania Murray. *Land's End: Capitalist Relations on an Indigenous Frontier*. Durham, NC: Duke University Press, 2014.

Lilienthal, David. "Electricity: The People's Business." *Annals of the American Academy of Political and Social Science* 201 (1939): 58–63.

Lilienthal, David. *The TVA: An Experiment in the "Grass Roots" Administration of Federal Functions.* Knoxville, TN: n.p., 1939.

Lilienthal, David. "Another 'Korea' in the Making?" *Collier's* (August 4, 1951): 23, 56–58.

Lilienthal, David. *Big Business: A New Era.* New York: Harper, 1953.

Lilienthal, David. *TVA: Democracy on the March,* 2nd ed. New York: Harper & Bros., 1953.

Lilienthal, David. *The Journals of David E. Lilienthal: The TVA Years, 1939–1945.* New York: Harper & Row, 1964.

Lilienthal, David. *The Journals of David E. Lilienthal: The Venturesome Years, 1950–1955.* New York: Harper & Row, 1966.

Lindblom, Charles. "A Century of Planning." In *Planning Sustainability,* edited by K. M. Meadowcroft, 39–65. New York: Routledge, 1999.

Linton, Jamie. *What Is Water? The History of a Modern Abstraction.* Vancouver: UBC Press, 2010.

Locke, John. *Two Treatises of Government.* New York: Cambridge University Press, 1963.

Logan, J. D. Review of Powell's "Truth and Error; or, The Science of Intellection" [untitled]. *Philosophical Review* 8, no. 3 (1899): 313–318.

Loorbach, Derk. "Transition Management for Sustainable Development: A Prescriptive, Complexity-Based Governance Framework." *Governance* 23, no. 1 (2010): 161–183.

Losurdo, Domenico. *Liberalism: A Counter-history.* New York: Verso, 2011.

Lövbrand, Eva, Johannes Stripple, and Bo Wiman. "Earth System Governmentality: Reflections on Science in the Anthropocene." *Global Environmental Change* 19 (2010): 7–13.

Lovelock, James. *Gaia: A New Look at Life on Earth.* New York: Oxford University Press, 1987.

Lowdermilk, Walter C. *Palestine: Land of Promise.* New York: Harper & Bros., 1944.

Lundqvist, J., J. Grönwall, and A. Jägerskog. *Water, Food Security and Human Dignity: A Nutrition Perspective.* Stockholm: Ministry of Enterprise and Innovation, Swedish FAO Committee, 2015.

Lutz, Catherine. "Empire Is in the Details." *American Ethnologist* 33, no. 4 (2006): 593–611.

L'vovich, Mark I., and Gilbert F. White. "Use and Transformation of Terrestrial Water Systems." In *The Earth as Transformed by Human Action: Global and Regional Changes in the Biosphere over the Past 300 Years,* edited by B. L. Turner II, William Clark, Robert Kates, et al., 235–252. Cambridge: Cambridge University Press, 1990.

Lyell, Charles. *Principles of Geology.* Philadelphia: J. Kay, 1837.

Maass, Arthur. *Muddy Waters: The Army Engineers and the Nation's Rivers.* Cambridge, MA: Harvard University Press, 1951.

Maass, Arthur, and Raymond L. Anderson. . . . *And the Desert Shall Rejoice: Conflict, Growth, and Justice in Arid Environments.* Cambridge, MA: MIT Press, 1978.

Maass, Arthur, and Maynard M. Hufschmidt. "Report on the Harvard Program of Research in Water Resources Development." In *Resources Development: Frontiers for Research*, edited by Franklin S. Pollak, 133–179. Boulder: University of Colorado Press, 1960.

Mach, Ernst. *The Analysis of Sensations and the Relation of the Physical to the Psychical.* Translated by C. M. Williams. New York: Dover, 1886.

Malm, Andreas. *Fossil Capital: The Rise of Steam Power and the Roots of Global Warming.* London: Verso, 2016.

Mandler, Peter. *Return from the Natives: How Margaret Mead Won the Second World War and Lost the Cold War.* New Haven, CT: Yale University Press, 2013.

March, Hug, and Thomas Purcell. "The Muddy Waters of Financialisation and New Accumulation Strategies in the Global Water Industry: The Case of Agbar." *Geoforum* 53 (2014): 11–20

Margulis, Lynn, and Dorion Sagan. *What Is Life?* London: Weidenfeld & Nicolson, 1995.

Marsh, George P. *The Earth as Modified by Human Action; a Last Revision of "Man and Nature."* New York: Scribner's, 1898.

Mason, Edward S., and Robert E. Asher. *The World Bank since Bretton Woods.* Washington, DC: Brookings Institution, 1973.

Mason, Otis Tufton. "The Land Problem." In *Man and the State: Studies in Applied Sociology*, 111–145. New York: D. Appleton & Co., 1892.

Mason, Otis Tufton. "Technogeography; or, The Relation of the Earth to the Industries of Mankind." *American Anthropologist* 7, no. 2 (1894): 137–161.

Mason, Otis Tufton. "Influence of Environment upon Human Industries or Arts." In *Annual Report of the Board of Regents of the Smithsonian Institution*, 639–665. Washington, DC: Government Printing Office, 1896.

Matthews, Nate, and Jeremy J. Schmidt. "False Promises: The Contours, Contexts and Contestation of Good Water Governance in Lao PDR and Alberta, Canada." *International Journal of Water Governance* 2, nos. 2/3 (2014): 21–40.

Mauss, Marcel. *The Gift: The Form and Reason for Exchange in Archaic Societies.* Translated by W. D. Halls. London: Routledge, 1990.

McCraw, Thomas K. *Morgan vs. Lilienthal: The Feud within the TVA.* Chicago: Loyola University Press, 1970.

McDonald, Robert I., Katherine Weber, Julie Padowski, et al. "Water on an Urban Planet: Urbanization and the Reach of Urban Water Infrastructure." *Global Environmental Change* 27 (2014): 96–105.

McGee, Emma, ed. *The Life of W.J. McGee: Extracts from Addresses and Writings.* Farley, IA: privately printed, 1915.

McGee, WJ "On Local Subsidence Produced by an Ice-Sheet." *American Journal of Science* 22 (1881): 368–369.

McGee, WJ "Shale and Davis' 'Glaciers.'" *Science* 2 (1881): 581–584, 624–630.

McGee, WJ "On the Cause of the Glacial Period." *American Journal of Science* 26 (1883): 244.

McGee, WJ "What Is a Glacier?" *Philosophical Society Bulletin of Washington* 7 (1884): 38.

McGee, WJ "The Classification of Geographic Forms by Genesis." *National Geographic* 1, no. 1 (1888): 27–36.

McGee, WJ "The Field of Geology and Its Promise for the Future." *Bulletin of the Minnesota Academy of Natural Sciences* 3, no. 2 (1888): 191–206.

McGee, WJ "Geology for 1887 and 1888." In *Annual Report of the Board of Regents of the Smithsonian Institution Showing the Operations, Expenditures, and Condition of the Institution to July, 1888*, 217–260. Washington, DC: Government Printing Office, 1890.

McGee, WJ "The Flood Plains of Rivers." *Forum* 11 (April 1891): 221–234.

McGee, WJ "The Earth the Home of Man." Part of a course of lectures prepared under the auspices of the Anthropological Society of Washington [DC] and delivered in the United States National Museum. *Special Papers*, vol. 1, no. 2 (1894): 21–48.

McGee, WJ "Glacial Canyons." *Journal of Geology* 2 (1894): 350–364.

McGee, WJ *The Potable Waters of the Eastern United States.* Washington, DC: Government Printing Office, 1895.

McGee, WJ "The Relation of Institutions to Environment." In *Annual Report of the Board of Regents of the Smithsonian Institution*, 701–711. Washington, DC: Government Printing Office, 1896.

McGee, WJ "The Science of Humanity." *Science* 6, no. 142 (1897): 413–433.

McGee, WJ "Fifty Years of American Science." *Atlantic Monthly* 82, no. 491 (September 1898): 307–321.

McGee, WJ "The Growth of the United States." *National Geographic* 9, no. 9 (1898): 377–386.

McGee, WJ "The Beginnings of Mathematics." *American Anthropologist* 1 (1899): 646–674.

McGee, WJ "The Foundation of Science." *Forum* 27 (April 1899): 168–178.

McGee, WJ "National Growth and National Character." *National Geographic* 10, no. 6 (1899): 185–206.

McGee, WJ "The Trend of Human Progress." *American Anthropologist* 1, no. 3 (1899): 1–26.

McGee, WJ "Cardinal Principles of Science." *Proceedings of the Washington Academy of Sciences* 2 (1900): 1–12.

McGee, WJ "The Superstructure of Science." *Forum* April 29 (1900): 171–182.

McGee, WJ "Man's Place in Nature." *American Anthropologist* 3, no. 1 (1901): 1–13.

McGee, WJ "Our Great River, What It Is and May Be Made for Commerce, Agriculture, and Sanitation—The Largest Inland Project of Our Time." *World's Work* 13 (November 1907): 8576–8584.

McGee, WJ "Movement of Water in Semi-arid Regions." *Conservation* 14 (November 1908): 596–599.

McGee, WJ "Our Inland Waterways." *Popular Science Monthly* 72, (April 1908): 289–303.

McGee, WJ "Outlines of Hydrology." *Bulletin of the Geologic Society of America* 19 (1908): 193–220.

McGee, WJ "Water as a Resource." *Annals of the American Academy of Political and Social Science* 33, no. 3 (1909): 521–534.

McGee, WJ "The Five-Fold Functions of Government." *Popular Science Monthly* 77 (September 1910): 274–285.

McGee, WJ "Principles of Water-Power Development." *Science* 34, no. 885 (1911): 813–825.

McGee, WJ "The Conservation of Natural Resources." In *Life of WJ McGee*, edited by Emma McGee, 88–100. Farley, IA: privately printed, 1915.

McGee, WJ "The Cult of Conservation." In *The Life of WJ McGee*, edited by Emma McGee, 186–193. Farley, IA: privately printed, 1915.

McGee, WJ "Desert Thirst as Disease." *Journal of the Southwest* 30, no. 2 (1988): 228–253.

The McGee Memorial Meeting of the Washington Academy of Sciences: Held at the Carnegie Institution, Washington, D.C., December 5, 1913 (Baltimore: Williams & Wilkins, 1916).

McLeod, Ian. "TVA Tutors Foreign Utility Engineers." *Electrical World* (October 1983): 25–26.

McNay, Lois. *The Misguided Search for the Political: Social Weightlessness in Radical Democratic Theory*. Cambridge: Polity Press, 2014.

Mead, Margaret. *Cultural Patterns and Technical Change*. Paris: UNESCO, 1953.

Meehan, Katie M. "Tool-Power: Water Infrastructure as Wellsprings of State Power." *Geoforum* 57 (2014): 215–224.

Mehta, Lyla. *The Politics and Poetics of Water: Naturalising Scarcity in Western India*. New Delhi: Orient Longman, 2005.

Mehta, Lyla, ed. *The Limits to Scarcity: Contesting the Politics of Allocation*. London: Earthscan, 2010.

Mehta, Lyla, and Synne Movik. *Flows and Practices: Integrated Water Resources Management (IWRM) in African Contexts*. Brighton: Institute of Development Studies, 2014.

Meigs, Peveril. "Water Problems in the United States." *Geographical Review* 42, no. 3 (1952): 346–366.

Meine, Curt. *Aldo Leopold: His Life and Work*. Madison: University of Wisconsin Press, 1988.

Meinzen-Dick, Ruth. "Beyond Panaceas in Water Institutions." *Proceedings of the National Academy of Sciences* 104, no. 39 (2007): 15200–15205.

Meinzen-Dick, Ruth, and Leticia Nkonya. "Understanding Legal Pluralism in Water Rights: Lessons from Africa and Asia." Presented at the International Workshop on "African Water Laws: Plural Legislative Frameworks for Water Management in Africa," Johannesburg, January 26–28, 2005.

Melosi, Martin V. *The Sanitary City: Urban Infrastructure in America from Colonial Times to the Present*. Baltimore: Johns Hopkins University Press, 2000.

Menand, Louis. *The Metaphysical Club: A Story of Ideas in America*. New York: Farrar, Straus & Giroux, 2001.

Merchant, Carolyn. 1980. *The Death of Nature: Women, Ecology, and the Scientific Revolution*. San Francisco: Harper & Row.

Merchant, Carolyn. "Fish First! The Changing Ethics of Ecosystem Management." *Human Ecology Review* 4, no. 1 (1997): 25–30.

Merchant, Carolyn. *Reinventing Eden: The Fate of Nature in Western Culture*. New York: Routledge, 2004.

Meybeck, Michel. "Global Analysis of River Systems: From Earth System Controls to Anthropocene Syndromes." *Philosophical Transactions of the Royal Society B* 358 (2003): 1935–1955.

Mill, John Stuart. *A System of Logic, Ratiocinative and Inductive: Being a Connected View of the Principles of Evidence, and the Methods of Scientific Investigation*. London: Longmans, Green, Reader, & Dyer, 1878.

Mill, John Stuart. *Principles of Political Economy*. Toronto: Routledge & Kegan Paul, 1965.

Mill, John Stuart. *On Liberty*. Harmondsworth: Penguin, 1985.

Mill, John Stuart. *Three Essays on Religion: Nature, the Utility of Religion, and Theism*. Amherst, NY: Prometheus Books, 1998.

Millennium Ecosystem Assessment. *Ecosystems and Human Well-Being: Wetlands and Water Synthesis*. Washington, DC: World Resources Institute, 2005.

Milly, P. C. D., J. Betancourt, M. Falkenmark, et al. "Stationarity Is Dead: Whither Water Management?" *Science* 319 (2008): 573–574.

Mitchell, Timothy. *Rule of Experts: Egypt, Techno-politics, Modernity*. Berkeley: University of California Press, 2002.

Mitchell, Timothy. *Carbon Democracy: Political Power in the Age of Oil*. London: Verso, 2011.

Mitchell, Timothy. "Economentality: How the Future Entered Government." *Critical Inquiry* 40, no. 4 (2014): 479–507.

Monk, Ray. *Ludwig Wittgenstein: The Duty of Genius*. New York: Penguin Books, 1990.

Monk, Ray. *Robert Oppenheimer: A Life inside the Centre*. New York: Anchor Books, 2012.

Moore, Jason W. *Capitalism in the Web of Life: Ecology and the Accumulation of Capital*. London: Verso, 2015.

Morgan, Arthur. *The Making of the TVA*. Buffalo: Prometheus Books, 1974.

Morton, Timothy. *Ecology without Nature: Rethinking Environmental Aesthetics*. Cambridge, MA: Harvard University Press, 2007.

Morton, Timothy. *The Ecological Thought*. Cambridge, MA: Harvard University Press, 2010.

Morton, Timothy. *Hyperobjects: Philosophy and Ecology after the End of the World*. Minneapolis: University of Minnesota Press, 2013.

Moss, Frank E. *The Water Crisis*. New York: Praeger, 1967.

Moss, Marshall E. "Space, Time, and the Third Dimension (Model Error)." *Water Resources Research* 15, no. 6 (1979): 1797–1800.

Moss, Marshall, and Gary Tasker. "The Role of Stochastic Hydrology in Dealing with Climatic Variability." In *The Influence of Climate Change and Climatic Variability on the Hydrologic Regime and Water Resources*, edited by S. I Solomon, M. Beran, and W. Hogg. Proceedings of the Vancouver Symposium, 1987. IAHS publication no. 168. Wallingford: International Association of Hydrological Sciences, 1987.

Mukerji, Chandra. *Impossible Engineering: Technology and Territoriality on the Canal Du Midi*. Princeton, NJ: Princeton University Press, 2009.

Nace, Raymond L. "Water Resources: A Global Problem with Local Roots." *Environmental Science and Technology* 1, no. 7 (1967): 550–560.

Nace, Raymond L. *Water and Man: A World View*. Paris: UNESCO, 1969.

Nace, Raymond L. "The International Hydrological Decade." *Transactions, American Geophysical Union* 45, no. 3 (1964): 413–421.

Nace, Raymond L. "The Hydrological Cycle: Historical Evolution of the Concept." *Water International* 1, no. 1 (1975): 15–21.

Nace, Raymond L., and Panel on Hydrology (USA). "A Plan for International Cooperation in Hydrology." *International Association of Scientific Hydrology Bulletin* 6, no. 4 (1961): 10–26.

Natural Research Council. *Water Transfers in the West: Efficiency, Equity, and the Environment*. Washington, DC: National Academy Press, 1992.

Neuse, Steven M. *David E. Lilienthal: The Journey of an American Liberal*. Knoxville: University of Tennessee Press, 1996.

Newton, Julianne Lutz. *Aldo Leopold's Odyssey*. Washington, DC: Island Press, 2006.

New York Times. "David E. Lilienthal Is Dead at 81; Led US Effort in Atomic Power." January 16, 1981.

Nilsson, Anders, and Lars Petterson. "The Structural Origin of Anomalous Properties of Liquid Water." *Nature Communications* 6, no. 8998 (2015): 1–11.

Norton, Bryan G. *Sustainability: A Philosophy for Adaptive Ecosystem Management*. Chicago: University of Chicago Press, 2005.

Odum, Eugene P. *Fundamentals of Ecology*, 2nd ed. Philadelphia: Saunders, 1959.

Office of the Director of National Intelligence. *Global Water Security*. Washington, DC: Government Printing Office, 2012.

Ohlsson, Leif. "Water Conflicts and Social Resource Scarcity." *Physics and Chemistry of the Earth B* 25 (2000): 213–220.

Olivera, Oscar. *Cochamaba! Water War in Bolivia*. Cambridge, MA: South End Press, 2004.

Oravec, Christine. "Presidential Public Policy and Conservation: W. J. McGee and the People." In *Green Talk in the White House: The Rhetorical Presidency Encounters Ecology*, edited by Tarla Rai Peterson, 62–81. College Station: Texas A&M University Press, 2004.

Orlove, Ben, and Steven Caton. "Water Sustainability: Anthropological Approaches and Prospects." *Annual Review of Anthropology* 39 (2010): 401–415.

Ostrom, Elinor. *Governing the Commons: The Evolution of Institutions for Collective Action*. New York: Cambridge University Press, 1990.

Ostrom, Elinor. *Understanding Institutional Diversity.* Princeton, NJ: Princeton University Press, 2005.

Ostrom, Elinor. "A Diagnostic Approach for Going beyond Panaceas." *Proceedings of the National Academy of Sciences* 104, no. 39 (2007): 15181–15187.

Ostrom, Elinor. "Beyond Markets and States: Polycentric Governance of Complex Systems." *American Economic Review* 100, no. 3 (2010): 641–672.

Ouspensky, P. D. *Tertium Organum: A Key to the Enigmas of the World,* 2nd American ed. Translated by Nichola Bessaraboff and Claude Bragdon. New York: Knopf, 1922.

Pachova, Nevelina, Mikiyasu Nakayama, and Libor Jansky, eds. *International Water Security: Domestic Threats and Opportunities.* Tokyo: United Nations University Press, 2008.

Pahl-Wostl, Claudia. "Transitions towards Adaptive Management of Water Facing Climate and Global Change." *Water Resources Management* 21 (2007): 49–62.

Pahl-Wostl, Claudia, M. Craps, A. Dewulf, et al. "Social Learning and Water Resources Management." *Ecology and Society* 12, no. 2, article 5 (2007).

Pappas, Gregory F. *John Dewey's Ethics: Democracy as Experience.* Indianapolis: Indiana University Press, 2008.

Parekh, Bhikhu. "Superior People: The Narrowness of Liberalism from Mill to Rawls." *Times Literary Supplement,* February (1994): 11–13.

Pearce, Trevor. "From 'Circumstances' to 'Environment': Herbert Spencer and the Origins of the Idea of Organism-Environment Interaction." *Studies in History and Philosophy of Biological and Biomedical Sciences* 41 (2010): 241–252.

Peirce, Charles S. "Deduction, Induction, and Hypothesis." *Popular Science Monthly* 13 (1878): 470–482.

Peirce, Charles S. "The Order of Nature." *Popular Science Monthly* June (1878): 203–217.

Peirce, Charles S. "The Architecture of Theories." *The Monist* 1, no. 2 (1891): 161–176.

Peirce, Charles S. "The Law of Mind." *The Monist* 2 (1892): 533–559.

Peirce, Charles S. "Man's Glassy Essence." *The Monist* 3, no. 1 (1892): 1–22.

Peirce, Charles S. "The Century's Great Men in Science." In *Annual Report of the Smithsonian Institute for the Year Ending June 30, 1900,* 693–699. Washington, DC: Smithsonian Institute, 1901.

Peirce, Charles S. "Some Consequences of Four Incapacities." In *Philosophical Writings of Peirce,* edited by Justus Buchler, 228–250. New York: Dover, 1955.

Peirce, Charles S. "Synechism, Fallibilism, and Evolution." In *Philosophical Writings of Peirce,* edited by Justus Buchler, 354–360. New York: Dover, 1955.

Peirce, Charles S. "Uniformity." In *Philosophical Writings of Peirce,* edited by Justus Buchler, 218–227. New York: Dover, 1955.

Peirce, Charles S. "Pragmatism as the Logic of Abduction." In *The Essential Peirce: Selected Philosophical Writings, Volume 2 (1893–1913),* edited by Peirce Edition Project, 226–241. Bloomington: Indiana University Press, 1998.

Person, Harlow S. *Little Waters: A Study of Headwater Streams and Other Little Waters, Their Use and Relations to Land.* Washington, DC: Government Printing Office, 1936.

Phare, Merrell-Ann S. *Denying the Source: The Crisis of First Nations Water Rights.* Surrey, BC: Rocky Mountain Books, 2009.

Picha, Paul. "Joseph N. Nicollet and Great Plains Ethnohistory: Interfaces among Nineteenth-Century French Science, Enlightenment, and Revolution." *Plains Anthropologist* 54, no. 210 (2009): 155–162.

Pigman, Geoffrey A. *The World Economic Forum: A Multi-stakeholder Approach to Global Governance.* London: Routledge, 2007.

Pietz, David. *The Yellow River: The Problem of Water in Modern China.* Cambridge, MA: Harvard University Press, 2015.

Pinchot, Gifford. "Speech on March 5, 1913." In *The McGee Memorial Meeting of the Washington Academy of Sciences: Held at the Carnegie Institution, Washington, D.C., December 5, 1913,* 20–24. Baltimore: Williams & Wilkins, 1916.

Pinchot, Gifford. *Breaking New Ground.* Washington, DC: Island Press, 1998.

Pisani, Donald. "Water Planning in the Progressive Era: The Inland Waterways Commission Reconsidered." *Journal of Policy History* 18, no. 4 (2006): 389–418.

Plumwood, Val. *Feminism and the Mastery of Nature.* New York: Routledge, 1993.

Polanyi, Karl. *The Great Transformation: The Political and Economic Origins of Our Time.* Boston: Beacon Press, 2001.

Porter, Theodore, M. *Trust in Numbers: The Pursuit of Objectivity in Science and Public Life.* Princeton, NJ: Princeton University Press, 1995.

Postel, Sandra. *Last Oasis: Facing Water Scarcity.* New York: Norton, 1992.

Postel, Sandra, Gretchen Daily, and Paul Ehrlich. "Human Appropriation of Renewable Fresh Water." *Science* 271 (1996): 785–788.

Povinelli, Elizabeth. *Economies of Abandonment: Social Belonging and Endurance in Late Liberalism.* Durham, NC: Duke University Press, 2011.

Powell, John Wesley. *Exploration of the Colorado River of the West and Its Tributaries.* 43rd Congress, 1st Session, H.R. Document 300. Washington, DC: Government Printing Office, 1875.

Powell, John Wesley. *Lands of the Arid Region of the United States (with a More Detailed Account of the Lands of Utah).* Washington, DC: Government Printing Office, 1879.

Powell, John Wesley. *Introduction to the Study of Indian Languages with Words, Phrases and Sentences to be Collected.* Washington, DC: Government Printing Office, 1880.

Powell, John Wesley. "Darwin's Contributions to Philosophy." *Proceedings of the Biological Society of Washington,* 1:60–70. Washington, DC: Smithsonian Institution, 1882.

Powell, John Wesley. "Competition as a Factor in Human Evolution." *American Anthropologist* 1, no. 4 (1888): 297–323.

Powell, John Wesley. "The Course of Human Progress." *Science* 11 (1888): 220–222.

Powell, John Wesley. "Outlines of Sociology." *Transactions of the Anthropological Society of Washington* 1 (1888): 106–129.

Powell, John Wesley. "Sociology, or The Science of Institutions." *American Anthropologist* 1, no. 4 (1899): 695–745.

Powell, John Wesley. "The Lessons of Folklore." *American Anthropologist* 2, no. 1 (1900): 1–36.

Powell, John Wesley. *Truth and Error; or, The Science of Intellection.* Chicago: Open Court Publishing, 2009.

Priscoli, Jerome Delli. "The Development of Transnational Regimes for Water Resources Management." In *River Basin Planning and Management*, edited by M. A. Abu-Zeid, and A. K. Biswas, 19–38. Calcutta: Oxford University Press, 1996.

Priscoli, Jerome Delli. "Water and Civilization: Using History to Reframe Water Policy Debates and to Build a New Ecological Realism." *Water Policy* 1 (2000): 623–636.

Priscoli, Jerome Delli. "What Is Public Participation in Water Resources Management and Why Is It Important?" *Water International* 29, no. 2 (2004): 221–227.

Priscoli, Jerome Delli. "Evolution of Public Involvement in Water Planning." In *The Evolution of Water Resource Planning and Decision Making*, edited by Clifford S. Russell and Duane D. Baumann, 62–79. Cheltenham: Edward Elgar, 2009.

Priscoli, Jerome Delli, J. Dooge, and R. Llamas. *Water and Ethics: Overview.* Paris: UNESCO, 2004.

Pritchard, Sara. *Confluence: The Nature of Technology and the Remaking of the Rhône.* Cambridge, MA: Harvard University Press, 2011.

Pritchett, C. Herman. *The Tennessee Valley Authority: A Study in Public Administration.* Chapel Hill: University of North Carolina Press, 1943.

Purdy, Jedediah. *After Nature: A Politics for the Anthropocene.* Cambridge, MA: Harvard University Press, 2015.

Pyne, Stephen. "Methodologies for Geology: G. K. Gilbert and T. C. Chamberlin." *Isis* 69, no. 3 (1978): 413–424.

Pyne, Stephen. *Grove Karl Gilbert: A Great Engine of Research.* Austin: University of Texas Press, 1980.

Rademacher, Anne. *Reigning the River: Urban Ecologies and Political Transformation in Kathmandu.* Durham, NC: Duke University Press, 2011.

Rawls, John. *Justice as Fairness: A Restatement.* Cambridge, MA: Belknap Press of Harvard University Press, 2001.

Reed, David. *The Global Environmental Facility: Sharing Responsibility for the Biosphere.* [Washington, DC]: Multilateral Development Bank Program, WWF-International, 1991.

Reisch, George. *How the Cold War Transformed Philosophy of Science: To the Icy Slopes of Logic.* Cambridge: Cambridge University Press, 2005.

Reisner, Marc. *Cadillac Desert: The American West and Its Disappearing Water.* New York: Viking, 1986.

Reuss, Martin. "Coping with Uncertainty: Social Scientists, Engineers, and Federal Water Resources Planning." *Natural Resource Journal* 32, no. 1 (1992): 101–135.

Reuss, Martin. *Water Resources People and Issues: Interview with Gilbert F. White.* Fort Belvoir, VA: U.S. Army Corps of Engineers, 1993.

Reuss, Martin. "Seeing like an Engineer: Water Projects and the Mediation of the Incommensurable." *Technology and Culture* 49, no. 3 (2008): 531–546.

Rijsberman, Frank. "Water Scarcity: Fact or Fiction?" *Agricultural Water Management* 80 (2006): 5–22.

Ringler, Claudia, Anik Bhaduri, and Richard Lawford. "The Nexus across Water, Energy, Land and Food (WELF): Potential for Improved Resource Use Efficiency?" *Current Opinion in Environmental Sustainability* 5, no. 6 (2013): 617–624.

Ripl, Wilhelm. "Water: The Bloodstream of the Biosphere." *Philosophical Transactions of the Royal Society of London B* 358 (2003): 1921–1934.

Rockström, Johan, M. Falkenmark, J. A. [Tony] Allan, et al. "The Unfolding Water Drama in the Anthropocene: Towards a Resilience-Based Perspective on Water for Global Sustainability." *Ecohydrology* 7 (2014): 1249–1261.

Rockström, Johan, and Mattias Klum. *Big World, Small Planet: Abundance within Planetary Boundaries.* New Haven, CT: Yale University Press, 2015.

Rockström, Johan, W. Steffen, K. Noone, et al. "A Safe Operating Space for Humanity." *Nature* 461 (2009): 472–475.

Rodriguez, Sylvia. *Acequia: Water Sharing, Sanctity, and Place.* Sante Fe, NM: School for Advanced Research Press, 2007.

Rogers, Peter, Ramesh Bhatia, and Annette Huber. *Water as a Social and Economic Good: How to Put the Principle into Practice.* Technical Advisory Committee Background Papers. Stockholm: Global Water Partnership, 1998.

Rogers, Peter, and Alan Hall. *Effective Water Governance.* Global Water Partnership Technical Committee. TEC background paper no. 7. Sweden: Evander Novum, 2003.

Rorty, Richard. *Contingency, Irony, and Solidarity.* Cambridge: Cambridge University Press, 1989.

Rose, Carol. "Energy and Efficiency in the Realignment of Common-Law Water Rights." *Journal of Legal Studies* 19 (1990): 261–296.

Rose, Nikolas. "The Death of the Social? Re-figuring the Territory of Government." *Economy and Society* 25, no. 3 (1996): 327–356.

Ross, John. "Man over Nature: Origins of the Conservation Movement." *American Studies* 16, no. 1 (1975): 49–62.

Rostow, W. W. *The Stages of Economic Growth: A Non-Communist Manifesto.* Cambridge: Cambridge University Press, 1964.

Rousseau, Jean-Jacques. *Politics and the Arts: Letter to M. D'Alembert on the Theatre.* Translated by Allan Bloom. Ithaca, NY: Cornell University Press, 1960.

Ruddiman, William. "The Anthropocene." *Annual Review of Earth and Planetary Sciences* 41 (2013): 45–68.

Rudwick, Martin. *Bursting the Limits of Time: The Reconstruction of Geohistory in the Age of Revolution.* Chicago: University of Chicago Press, 2007.

Sabatier, Paul, Will Focht, Mark Lubell, et al., eds. *Swimming Upstream: Collaborative Approaches to Watershed Management.* Cambridge, MA: MIT Press, 2005.

Sabin, Paul. *The Bet: Paul Ehrlich, Julian Simon, and Our Gamble over Earth's Future.* New Haven, CT: Yale University Press, 2013.

Sachs, Jeffrey, and J. W. McArthur. "The Millennium Project: A Plan for Meeting the Millennium Development Goals." *Lancet* 365 (2005): 347–353.

Sachs, Wolfgang. *Planet Dialectics: Explorations in Environment and Development*. New York: Zed Books, 1999.

Sadoff, Claudia, J. Hall, D. Grey, et al. *Securing Water, Sustaining Growth: Report of the GWP/OECD Task Force on Water Security and Sustainable Growth*. Oxford: University of Oxford, 2015.

Sagoff, Mark. *Price, Principle, and the Environment*. New York: Cambridge University Press, 2004.

Salman, Salman M. A. *The World Bank Policy for Projects on International Waterways: An Historical and Legal Analysis*. Washington, DC: World Bank, 2009.

Sandel, Michael. *Democracy's Discontent: America in Search of a Public Philosophy*. Cambridge, MA: Belknap Press of Harvard University Press, 1996.

Sant, Girish, and Shantanu Dixit. "Beneficiaries of IPS Subsidy and Impact of Tariff Hike." *Economic and Political Weekly* 31, no. 51 (1996): 3315–3321.

Santayana, George. "Dewey's Naturalistic Metaphysics." *Journal of Philosophy* 22, no. 25 (1925): 673–688.

Satterthwaite, David. *Barbara Ward and the Origins of Sustainable Development*. London: International Institute for Environment and Development, 2006.

Sauer, Carl. "The Agency of Man on the Earth." In *Man's Role in Changing the Face of the Earth*, edited by William R. Thomas, 49–69. Chicago: University of Chicago Press, 1956.

Savenije, H. H. G. "Water Scarcity Indicators; the Deception of the Numbers." *Physics and Chemistry of the Earth B* 25, no. 3 (2000): 199–204.

Savenije, H. H. G., A. Y. Hoekstra, and P. van der Zaag. "Evolving Water Science in the Anthropocene." *Hydrology and Earth System Sciences* 18 (2014): 319–332.

Sax, Joseph. "The Public Trust Doctrine in Natural Resources Law: Effective Judicial Intervention." *Michigan Law Review* 68 (1969): 471–566.

Sax, Joseph. "Understanding Transfers: Community Rights and the Privatization of Water." *West-Northwest Journal of Environmental Law and Policy* 1 (1994): 13–16.

Sayre, Nathan. "Ecological and Geographical Scale: Parallels and Potential for Integration." *Progress in Human Geography* 29, no. 3 (2005): 276–290.

Schleifer, Ronald. *Modernism and Time: The Logic of Abundance in Literature, Science, and Culture, 1880–1930*. Cambridge: Cambridge University Press, 2000.

Schlesinger, Arthur. *The Vital Center: The Politics of Freedom*. Boston: Houghton Mifflin, 1949.

Schlesinger, Arthur. *The Coming of the New Deal, 1933–1935*. Boston: Houghton Mifflin, 2003.

Schmidt, Jeremy. "Integrating Water Management in the Anthropocene." *Society and Natural Resources* 26, no. 1 (2013): 105–112.

Schmidt, Jeremy. "Historicising the Hydrosocial Cycle." *Water Alternatives* 7, no. 1 (2014): 220–234.

Schmidt, Jeremy. "Water Management and the Procedural Turn: Norms and Transitions in Alberta." *Water Resources Management* 28, no. 4 (2014): 1127–1141.

Schmidt, Jeremy, and Kyle Mitchell. "Property and the Right to Water: Toward a Non-liberal Commons." *Review of Radical Political Economics* 46, no. 1 (2014): 54–69.

Schmidt, Jeremy, and Christiana Peppard. "Water Ethics on a Human Dominated Planet: Rationality, Context and Values in Global Governance." *WIREs Water* 1, no. 6 (2014): 533–547.

Schorr, David. *The Colorado Doctrine: Water Rights, Corporations, and Distributive Justice on the American Frontier.* New Haven, CT: Yale University Press, 2012.

Schubert, Susanne, and Joyeeta Gupta. "Comparing Global Coordination Mechanisms on Energy, Environment, and Water." *Ecology and Society* 18, no. 2, article 22 (2013).

Schweitzer, Albert. *The Philosophy of Civilization.* New York: Prometheus Books, 1987.

Scott, Christopher, Matthew Kurian, and James Wescoat. "The Water-Energy-Food Nexus: Enhancing Adaptive Capacity to Complex Global Challenges." In *Governing the Nexus: Water, Soil and Waste Resources considering Global Change,* edited by Matthew Kurian and Reza Ardakanian, 15–38. Dordrecht: Springer, 2015.

Scott, James. *Seeing like a State: How Certain Schemes to Improve the Human Condition Have Failed.* New Haven, CT: Yale University Press, 1998.

Scott, James. "High Modernist Social Engineering: The Case of the Tennessee Valley Authority." In *Experiencing the State,* edited by L. I. Rudolph and J. K. Jacobsen, 3–52. Oxford: Oxford University Press, 2006.

Selborne, Lord [John Roundell Palmer]. "The Ethics of Freshwater: A Survey." Paris: UNESCO, 2000.

Selznick, Philip. *TVA and the Grass Roots: A Study of Politics and Organization.* Berkeley: University of California Press, 1949.

Shaler, Nathaniel. *Man and the Earth.* New York: Fox, Duffield & Co., 1905.

Sherlock, Robert. *Man as a Geological Agent: An Account of His Action on Inanimate Nature.* London: H. F. & G. Witherby, 1922.

Simpson, Audra. *Mohawk Interruptus: Political Life across the Borders of Settler States.* Durham, NC: Duke University Press, 2014.

Singer, Joseph. *Entitlement: The Paradoxes of Property.* New Haven, CT: Yale University Press, 2000.

Singer, Joseph. "Original Acquisition of Property: From Conquest and Possession to Democracy and Equal Opportunity." *Indiana Law Journal* 86, no. 3 (2011): 763–778.

Skinner, Quentin. *The Foundations of Modern Political Thought,* vols. 1–2. Cambridge: Cambridge University Press, 1978.

Smith, Neil. *American Empire: Roosevelt's Geographer and the Prelude to Globalization.* Berkeley: University of California Press, 2003.

Smith, Norman. *Man and Water: A History of Hydro-technology.* London: Peter Davies, 1975.

Sneddon, Christopher. *Concrete Revolution: Large Dams, Cold War Geopolitics, and the U.S. Bureau of Reclamation.* Chicago: University of Chicago Press, 2015.

Solanes, Miguel, and Fernando Gonzalez-Villarreal. *The Dublin Principles for Water as Reflected in a Comparative Assessment of Institutional and Legal Arrangements for Integrated Water Resources Management*, vol. 3. Technical Advisory Committee background paper. Stockholm: Global Water Partnership, 1999.

Solomon, Steven. *Water: The Epic Struggle for Wealth, Power, and Civilization.* New York: HarperCollins, 2010.

Spencer, Herbert. *Social Statistics; the Conditions Essential to Human Happiness Specified, and the First of Them Developed.* New York: Chapman, 1851.

Spencer, Herbert. *The Principles of Psychology*, 3rd ed. New York: Appleton & Co., 1888.

Spencer, Herbert. *The Man versus the State: With Six Essays on Government, Society and Freedom.* Indianapolis: Liberty Classics, 1981.

Spivak, Gayati. "Can the Subaltern Speak?" In *Marxism and the Interpretation of Culture*, edited by Cary Nelson and Larry Grossberg, 271–313. Chicago: University of Illinois Press, 1988.

Srinivasan, R. "International World Water Day 2014, Focus: Water-Energy Nexus." *Current Science* 106, no. 7 (2014): 911–912.

Stamm, Gilbert. "Bureau of Reclamation International Technical Assistance in Development of Arid Lands." Presented at the International Conference on Arid Lands in a Changing World, Tucson, AZ, June 5, 1969.

Stegner, Wallace. *Beyond the Hundredth Meridian: John Wesley Powell and the Second Opening of the West.* Boston: Houghton Mifflin, 1954.

Steffen, Will, J. Grinevald, P. Crutzen, and J. McNeill. "The Anthropocene: Conceptual and Historical Perspectives." *Philosophical Transactions of the Royal Society of London A* 369 (2011): 842–867.

Steffen, Will, A. Persson, L. Deutsch, et al. "The Anthropocene: From Global Change to Planetary Stewardship." *Ambio* 40 (2011): 739–761.

Steffen, Will, K. Richardson, J. Rockström, et al. "Planetary Boundaries: Guiding Human Development on a Changing Planet." *Science* 347, no. 6223 (2015). doi: 10.1126/science.1259855.

Stein, Jane. *Water: Life or Death: A Report in Preparation for the United Nations Water Conference, Mar Del Plata, Argentina, March 1977.* Washington, DC: International Institute for Environmental and Development, 1977.

Stengers, Isabelle. "A Constructivist Reading of *Process and Reality.*" *Theory, Culture and Society* 25, no. 4 (2008): 91–110.

Stocking, George. *Victorian Anthropology.* New York: Free Press, 1987.

Stoll, Mark. *Inherit the Holy Mountain: Religion and the Rise of American Environmentalism.* New York: Oxford University Press, 2015.

Stone, Christopher D. *Should Trees Have Standing? Towards Legal Rights for Natural Objects.* New York: Avon, 1974.

Strang, Veronica. *The Meaning of Water.* New York: Berg, 2004.

Strang, Veronica. *Gardening the World: Agency, Identity, and the Ownership of Water.* Oxford: Berghahn Books, 2009.

Strang, Veronica. "The Taniwha and the Crown: Defending Water Rights in Aotearoa/New Zealand." *WIREs Water* 1 (2014): 121–131.

Swyngedouw, Erik. *Social Power and the Urbanization of Water*. New York: Oxford University Press, 2004.

Swyngedouw, Erik. *Liquid Power: Contested Hydro-modernities in Twentieth-Century Spain*. Cambridge, MA: MIT Press, 2015.

Szasz, Andrew. *Ecopopulism: Toxic Waste and the Movement for Environmental Justice*. Minneapolis: University of Minnesota Press, 1994.

Szerszynski, Bronislaw. "The End of the End of Nature: The Anthropocene and the Fate of the Human." *Oxford Literary Review* 34, no. 2 (2012): 165–184.

Taylor, Charles. *Modern Social Imaginaries*. Durham, NC: Duke University Press, 2004.

Teilhard de Chardin, Pierre. *The Phenomenon of Man*. New York: Harper, 1959.

Teisch, Jessica. *Engineering Nature: Water, Development, and the Global Spread of American Environmental Expertise*. Chapel Hill: University of North Carolina Press, 2011.

Tennessee Valley Authority. *TVA: Its Work and Accomplishments*. Washington, DC: Government Printing Office, 1940.

Tennessee Valley Authority. *Nature's Constant Gift: A Report on the Water Resource of the Tennessee Valley*. Knoxville: Tennessee Valley Authority, 1963.

Tennessee Valley Public Power Association. *National Defense and TVA*. Chatanooga: Tennessee Valley Public Power Association, [1958?].

Thacher, Peter. "Master Plan for the Watery Planet." *Uniterra* 6 (1981): 5–7.

Thobani, Mateen. "Formal Water Markets: Why, When, and How to Introduce Tradable Water Rights." *World Bank Research Observer* 12, no. 2 (1997): 161–179.

Thomas, William, ed. *Man's Role in Changing the Face of the Earth*. Chicago: University of Chicago Press, 1956.

Trottier, Julie. "Water Crises: Political Construction or Physical Reality?" *Contemporary Politics* 14, no. 2 (2008): 197–214.

Truman, Harry S. "Truman's Inaugural Address, January 20, 1949." Harry S. Truman Library and Museum. //www.trumanlibrary.org.

Tsing, Anna. "On Nonscalability." *Common Knowledge* 18, no. 3 (2012): 505–524.

Tsing, Anna. *The Mushroom at the End of the World: On the Possibility of Life in Capitalist Ruins*. Princeton, NJ: Princeton University Press, 2015.

Tuan, Yi-Fu. *The Hydrologic Cycle and the Wisdom of God: A Theme in Geoteleology*. Toronto: University of Toronto Press, 1968.

Tully, James. *Strange Multiplicity: Constitutionalism in an Age of Diversity*. Cambridge: Cambridge University Press, 1995.

Tully, James. *Public Philosophy in a New Key*, vols. 1–2. Cambridge: Cambridge University Press, 2008.

Turner, B. L., II, William Clark, Robert Kates, et al., eds. *The Earth as Transformed by Human Action: Global and Regional Changes in the Biosphere over the Past 300 Years*. Cambridge: Cambridge University Press, 1990.

Turner, Frederick. *The Significance of the Frontier in American History*. Washington, DC: Government Printing Office, 1893.

Tyler, Charles. "Impacts of Environmental Endocrine Disruptors and Other Emerging Contaminants on Fish and Fish Populations." Presented at "Cloudy with a Chance of Solutions: The Future of Water," the annual science symposium at the Radcliffe Institute for Advanced Study, Harvard University, Cambridge, MA, October 12, 2012. Video available at YouTube. www.youtube.com.

Tyrrell, Ian. *Crisis of the Wasteful Nation: Empire and Conservation in Theodore Roosevelt's America.* Chicago: University of Chicago Press, 2015.

UN Conference on Environment and Development. *Agenda 21: Programme of Action for Sustainable Development; Rio Declaration on Environment and Development; Statement of Forest Principles.* New York: United Nations, 1993.

UN Development Program. *Beyond Scarcity: Power, Poverty and the Global Water Crisis.* New York: UN Development Program, 2006.

UN Economic Commission for Asia and the Far East. *Development of Water Resources in the Lower Mekong Basin.* Bangkok: United Nations, 1957.

UN General Assembly. "3513 (XXX) United Nations Water Conference." *Resolutions Adopted on the Reports of the Second Committee* (1975): 69.

UN General Assembly. "Resolution A/RES/44/228." 85th Plenary Meeting, 22 December 1989.

UN General Assembly. *Transforming Our World: The 2030 Agenda for Sustainable Development.* A/70/L.1. New York: United Nations, 2015.

UNEP [UN Environment Program]. *The UN-Water Status Report on the Application of Integrated Approaches to Water Resources Management.* Nairobi: UN Environment Program, 2012.

UNESCO. *The Scientific Conference on Resource Conservation and Utilization.* Paris: UNESCO, 1948.

UNESCO. *Three Centuries of Scientific Hydrology: Key Papers Submitted on the Occasion of the Celebration of the Tercentenary of Scientific Hydrology, Paris, 9–12 September 1974: A Contribution to the International Hydrological Decade.* Paris: UNESCO, 1974.

United Nations. *Proceedings of the United Nations Conference on the Conservation and Utilization of Resources, 17 August–6 September, 1949, Lake Success, New York.* Lake Success, NY: United Nations, 1950.

United Nations. *Integrated River Basin Development: Report by a Panel of Experts.* New York: UN Department of Economic and Social Affairs, 1958.

United Nations. *Resolution 55/2: United Nations Millennium Declaration.* New York: United Nations, 2000.

United Nations. *Global Sustainable Development Report, 2015 Edition (Advanced Unedited Version).* New York: United Nations, 2015.

UN Water. *Water in a Changing World: The United Nations World Water Development Report 3.* Paris: UNESCO; London: Earthscan, 2009.

UN Water. *Water Security and the Global Water Agenda: A UN-Water Analytical Brief.* Hamilton, ON: United Nations University, 2013.

UN Water. *World Water Development Report, 2014: Water and Energy.* Paris: UNESCO, 2014.

UN Water Conference. *Report of the United Nations Water Conference, Mar Del Plata, 14–25 March, 1977.* E/conf.70/29. New York: United Nations, 1977.

U.S. Department of Energy. *Energy Demands on Water Resources: Report to Congress on the Interdependency of Energy and Water.* Washington, DC: U.S. Department of Energy, 2006.

U.S. Federal Council for Science and Technology Ad Hoc Panel on Hydrology. *Scientific Hydrology.* Washington, DC: Government Printing Office, 1962.

U.S. Government Accountability Office. *Energy-Water Nexus: A Better and Coordinated Understanding of Water Resources Could Help Mitigate the Impacts of Potential Oil Shale Development.* Washington, DC: U.S. Government Accountability Office, 2010.

U.S. Government Accountability Office. *Energy-Water Nexus: Coordinated Federal Approach Needed to Better Manage Energy and Water Tradeoffs.* Washington, DC: U.S. Government Accountability Office, 2012.

U.S. Government Accountability Office. *Energy-Water Nexus: Information on the Quantity, Quality, and Management of Water Produced during Oil and Gas Production.* Washington, DC: U.S. Government Accountability Office, 2012.

U.S. President's Water Resources Policy Commission. *A Water Policy for the American People: Summary of Recommendations.* Washington, DC: Government Printing Office, 1950.

U.S. Senate Committee on Appropriations. *Financing of Aswan High Dam in Egypt.* Washington, DC: Government Printing Office, 1956.

VandeWall, Holly. "Why Water Is Not H₂O, and Other Critiques of Essentialist Ontology from the Philosophy of Chemistry." *Philosophy of Science* 74, no. 5 (2007): 906–919.

Vernadsky, Vladimir. "The Biosphere and the Noösphere." *American Scientist* 33, no. 1 (1945): 1–12.

Vernadsky, Vladimir. *The Biosphere.* Translated by David B. Langmuir. New York: Copernicus, 1998.

Vörösmarty, Charles J., D. Lettenmaier, C. Lévêque, et al. "Humans Transforming the Global Water System." *EOS* 85 (2004): 513–516.

Vörösmarty, Charles J., P. B. McIntyre, M. O. Gessner, et al. "Global Threats to Human Water Security and River Biodiversity." *Nature* 467 (2010): 555–561.

Walker, Brian, C. S. Holling, S. Carpenter, and J. Kinzig. "Resilience, Adaptability and Transformability in Social-Ecological Systems." *Ecology and Society* 9, no. 2 (2004): 5.

Ward, Barbara. *The Home of Man.* New York: Norton, 1976.

Ward, Barbara. *Progress for a Small Planet.* London: Earthscan, 1988.

Ward, Lester. "Mind as a Social Factor." *Mind* 36 (1884): 563–573.

Ward, Lester. "Status of the Mind Problem." Anthropological Society of Washington, Special Papers, vol. 1. Washington, DC: [Anthropological Society of Washington], 1894.

Ward, Lester. "Truth and Error." *Science* 9, no. 213 (1899): 126–137.

Ward, Lester. "Contemporary Sociology." *American Journal of Sociology* 7, no. 4 (1902): 475–500.

Ward, Lester. *Glimpses of the Cosmos,* vols. 1–5. New York: Putnam's, 1913.

Warford, J.J. "Pricing as a Means of Controlling the Use of Water Resources." In *Water Development and Management: Proceedings of the United Nations Water Conference*, vol. 2, edited by Asit K. Biswas, 659–684. New York: Pergamon, 1978.

Wark, McKenzie. *Molecular Red: Theory for the Anthropocene*. London: Verso, 2015.

Warren, Karen. "The Power and Promise of Ecological Feminism." *Environmental Ethics* 12 (1990): 125–146.

Waters, Colin, Jan Zalasiewicz, Colin Summerhayes, et al. "The Anthropocene Is Functionally and Stratigraphically Distinct from the Holocene." *Science* 351, no. 6269 (2016): 137.

Weber, Max. "Politics as a Vocation." In *From Max Weber: Essays in Sociology*, edited by H. H. Gerth and C. Wright Mills, 77–128. New York: Oxford University Press, 1946.

Wengert, Norman. "Antecedents of TVA: The Legislative History of Muscle Shoals." *Agricultural History* 26, no. 4 (1952): 141–147.

Wengert, Norman. "The Ideological Basis of Conservation and Natural-Resources Policies and Programs." *Annals of the American Academy of Political and Social Science* 344 (1962): 65–75.

Wescoat, James, Jr. "The 'Practical Range of Choice' in Water Resources Geography." *Progress in Human Geography* 11, no. 1 (1987): 41–59.

Wescoat, James, Jr. "Common Themes in the Work of Gilbert White and John Dewey: A Pragmatic Appraisal." *Annals of the Association of American Geographers* 82, no. 4 (1992): 587–607.

Wescoat, James, Jr. "'Watersheds' in Regional Planning." In *The American Planning Tradition: Culture and Policy*, edited by Robert Fishman, 147–172. Washington, DC: Wilson Center Press, 2000.

Wescoat, James, Jr., and Gilbert White. *Water for Life: Water Management and Environmental Policy*. Cambridge: Cambridge University Press, 2003.

Whatmore, Sarah, and Catharina Landström. "Flood Apprentices: An Exercise in Making Things Public." *Economy and Society* 40, no. 4 (2011): 582–610.

Wheeler, Virginia. "Co-operation for Development in the Lower Mekong Basin." *American Journal of International Law* 64, no. 3 (1970): 594–609.

White, Gilbert. "Human Adjustment to Floods: A Geographical Approach to the Flood Problem in the United States." PhD diss. University of Chicago Department of Geography Research Paper no. 29. Chicago: University of Chicago, 1945.

White, Gilbert. "Broader Bases for Choice: The Next Key Move." In *Perspectives on Conservation*, edited by Henry Jarrett, 205–226. Baltimore: Johns Hopkins University Press, 1958.

White, Gilbert. "Contributions of Geographical Analysis to River Basin Development." *Geographical Journal* 129, no. 4 (1963): 412–432.

White, Gilbert. "Vietnam: The Fourth Course: International Cooperation in Science." *Bulletin of the Atomic Scientists* 20, no. 10 (1964): 6–10.

White, Gilbert. *Strategies of American Water Management*. Ann Arbor: University of Michigan Press, 1969.

White, Gilbert. "Role of Geography in Water Resources Management." In *Man and Water: The Social Sciences in Management of Water Resources*, edited by L. Douglas James, 102–121. Lexington: University Press of Kentucky, 1974.

White, Gilbert. *Water for All: Statement of the International Institute for Environment and Development, in Preparation for the United Nations Water Conference, Mar Del Plata, Argentina, March 14–25, 1977*. Washington, DC: International Institute for Environment and Development, 1976.

White, Gilbert. "Comparative Analysis of Complex River Development." In *Environmental Effects of Complex River Development*, edited by Gilbert F. White, 1–22. Boulder, CO: Westview Press, 1977.

White, Gilbert. "Resources and Needs: Assessment of the World Water Situation." In *Water Development and Management: Proceedings of the United Nations Water Conference*, vol. 1, edited by A. K. Biswas, 1–46. New York: Pergamon, 1978.

White, Gilbert. "Paths to Risk Analysis." *Risk Analysis* 8, no. 2 (1988): 171–175.

White, Gilbert. "Reflections on the 50-Year International Search for Integrated Water Management." *Water Policy* 1 (1998): 21–27.

White, Gilbert, David Bradley, and Anne White. *Drawers of Water: Domestic Water Use in East Africa*. Chicago: University of Chicago Press, 1972.

White, Richard. *The Organic Machine*. New York: Hill & Wang, 1995.

Whitehead, Alfred. *The Concept of Nature*. Ann Arbor: University of Michigan Press, 1957.

Whitehead, Alfred. *Process and Reality*. New York: Harper & Row, 1957.

Whiteley, John, Helen Ingram, and Richard Perry, eds. *Water, Place and Equity*. Cambridge, MA: MIT Press, 2008.

Wiener, Philip, ed. *Charles S. Peirce: Selected Writings (Values in a Universe of Chance)*. New York: Dover, 1958.

Wilkinson, Charles. "Aldo Leopold and Western Water Law: Thinking Perpendicular to the Prior Appropriation Doctrine." *Land and Water Law Review* 24 (1989): 1–38.

Wilkinson, Charles. "The Headwaters of the Public Trust: Some Thought on the Source and Scope of the Traditional Doctrine." *Environmental Law* 19 (1989): 425–472.

Wilkinson, Charles. "Indian Water Rights in Conflict with State Water Rights: The Case of the Pyramid Lake Paiute Tribe in Nevada, US," In *Out of the Mainstream: Water Rights, Politics and Identity*, edited by R. Boelens, D. Getches, and A. Guerva-Gill, 213–222. London: Earthscan, 2010.

Willkie, Wendell. *One World*. New York: Limited Editions Club, 1944.

Wittfogel, Karl. *Oriental Despotism: A Comparative Study of Total Power*. New Haven, CT: Yale University Press, 1957.

Wittgenstein, Ludwig. *The Blue and the Brown Books*. Oxford: Basil Blackwell, 1964.

Wittgenstein, Ludwig. *On Certainty*. Translated by G. E. M. Anscombe. New York: Harper & Row, 1972.

Wittgenstein, Ludwig. *Philosophical Investigations*. Translated by G. E. M. Anscombe. Malden, MA: Blackwell Publishing, 2001.

Witzel, Michael. "Water in Mythology." *Daedalus* 144, no. 3 (2015): 18–26.

Wolf, Aaron. "Conflict and Cooperation along International Waterways." *Water Policy* 1, no. 2 (1998): 251–265.

World Bank. *Funding for the Global Environment: The Global Environment Facility.* Washington, DC: World Bank, 1990.

World Bank. *Water Resources Management: A World Bank Policy Paper.* Washington, DC: World Bank, 1993.

World Bank. *From Scarcity to Security: Averting a Water Crisis in the Middle East and North Africa.* Washington, DC: World Bank, 1995.

World Bank. *Public Communication Programs for Private Projects: A Toolkit for World Bank Task Team Leaders and Clients.* Washington, DC: World Bank, 2003.

World Bank. *Water Resources Sector Strategy: Strategic Directions for World Bank Engagement.* Washington, DC: World Bank, 2004.

World Commission on Environment and Development. *Our Common Future.* Oxford: Oxford University Press, 1987.

World Economic Forum. *Global Risks to the Business Environment.* Geneva: World Economic Forum, 2005.

World Economic Forum. *Global Risks, 2006.* Geneva: World Economic Forum, 2006.

World Economic Forum. *Thirsty Energy: Water and Energy in the 21st Century.* Geneva: World Economic Forum, 2008.

World Economic Forum. *Global Risks, 2008.* Geneva: World Economic Forum, 2008.

World Economic Forum. *Realizing the Potential of Public-Private Partnership Projects in Water.* Geneva: World Economic Forum, 2008.

World Economic Forum. *The Bubble Is Close to Bursting: A Forecast of the Main Economic and Geopolitical Water Issues Likely to Arise in the World during the Next Two Decades.* Geneva: World Economic Forum, 2009.

World Economic Forum. *Global Risks, 2009.* Geneva: World Economic Forum, 2009.

World Economic Forum. *Global Risks, 2010.* Geneva: World Economic Forum, 2010.

World Economic Forum. *Global Risks, 2011.* Geneva: World Economic Forum, 2011.

World Economic Forum. *Water Security: The Water-Food-Energy-Climate Nexus.* Washington, DC: Island Press, 2011.

World Economic Forum. *Global Risks, 2014.* Geneva: World Economic Forum, 2014.

World Economic Forum. *Global Risks, 2015.* Geneva: World Economic Forum, 2015.

World Water Council. *A Water Secure World: Vision for Water, Life and the Environment.* Paris: World Water Council, 2000.

Worster, Donald. *Nature's Economy: A History of Ecological Ideas.* Cambridge: Cambridge University Press, 1994.

Worster, Donald. *A River Running West: The Life of John Wesley Powell.* Oxford: Oxford University Press, 2001.

Worster, Donald. "Watershed Democracy: Recovering the Lost Vision of John Wesley Powell." *Journal of Land Resources and Environmental Law* 23 (2003): 57–66.

Wright, Jim. *The Coming Water Famine.* New York: Coward-McCann, 1966.

Wu, Peili, Nikolaos Christidis, and Peter Stott. "Anthropogenic Impact on Earth's Hydrological Cycle." *Nature Climate Change* 3 (2013): 807–810.

Wulf, Andrea. *The Invention of Nature: Alexander von Humboldt's New World.* New York: Knopf, 2015.

Yusoff, Kathryn. "Anthropogenesis: Origins and Endings in the Anthropocene." *Theory, Culture and Society,* published online before print (April 29, 2015). doi: 10.1177/0263276415581021.

Zalasiewicz, Jan, Colin Waters, Mark Williams, et al. "When Did the Anthropocene Begin? A Mid-Twentieth Century Boundary Level Is Stratigraphically Optimal." *Quaternary International,* online advance, 383 (2015): 196–203. doi:10.1016/j. quaint.2014.11.045.

INDEX

American Anthropological Society, 44
American Sociological Association, 45
Anderson, Raymond, 151, 274
Anthropocene: Chakrabarty, Dipesh, 195–
196; Committee on Problems of the
Environment, 12; conceptual history of,
10; Crutzen, Paul, 8, 167; defined, 8–9;
Earth as Modified by Human Action,
9, 275; Earth system, tipping points to,
170; Earth system and, 11, 169, 170, 182;
Earth-making *vs.*, 167, 179, 186, 190;
Earth's life support systems, 170; Earth's
new geological moment, 8; Earth's
water systems and climate change, 170;
Earth/world distinction, 198–199; ecofeminist, indigenous, and post-colonial
scholars, 10; environmental politics,
197; geological force of humans, 3, 209;
Glacken, Clarence, 117; Grinevald,
Jacques, 10, 11, 268; Hamilton, Clive,
10, 11, 190, 268; historical implications,
194–195; human agents and processes,
190; human and geologic histories, 191;
human appropriation of freshwater,
156; human impact on Earth's water
systems, 196; human impacts on Earth
systems, 10–12, 183; human impacts on
global water systems, 167; human privilege, 200–201, 207; human transformation of biosphere, 9; humanity's "water
drama," 196; humans and environmental degradation, 195; hydrology, risks
to planetary, 179; indigenous peoples,
229; key influences linking water to resilience, 169; Kierkegaard, Søren, 204;
Latour, Bruno, 194, 224–225; Lovelock,

James, 11; "making things public," 190,
192–196, 207; Marsh, George Perkins, 10–11; Morton, Timothy, 10, 195;
naturalization of process and, 189–207;
non-human agents, 194; normal water
and, 156, 200, 210; philosophies of
"becoming," 206; planetary stewardship, 9, 189; political task of, 201;
post-humanism, 201; Purdy, Jedediah,
201; Scientific Committee on Problems
of the Environment by the International Council of Scientific Unions, 11;
Shaler, Nathaniel, 12; Sherlock, Robert,
12; social and ecological systems, 182;
social sciences and, 16, 190; society/
nature dualism, 10, 190, 191, 224, 228;
Stoermer, Eugene, 8, 167; water, energy,
food, and climate relationships, 144;
water, ethics, and, 222–225; water connects multiple social worlds to Earth,
182; water in, 36, 39, 227–230; *Water
in Crisis*, 156, 266; water in the, 3, 13,
32, 39, 186, 190, 196, 200, 202, 223–
224, 227–230; water management, 3,
13–14, 166, 169, 170, 191–192, 230; water
management and conservation, 16;
water management and development,
186; water management and governance, 32; water resources, 167, 191, 223,
229; water resources as monuments to
world past, 191, 196; water security, 144,
167, 170, 182, 183; water system, global,
170; water-energy-food-climate nexus,
166; water's relationships to economies,
societies, and ecological communities,
181; White, Gilbert, 156

ABOUT THE AUTHOR

Jeremy J. Schmidt is Lecturer in Human Geography at Durham University. He is the co-editor of *Water Ethics: Foundational Readings for Students and Professionals.*